The Van R

GW01159374

J. C. Snaith

Alpha Editions

This edition published in 2024

ISBN : 9789362924407

Design and Setting By
Alpha Editions
www.alphaedis.com
Email - info@alphaedis.com

Contents

I

NORTH of the Strand, east of the National Gallery, a narrow street winds a devious course towards Long Acre. To the casual eye it is no more than a mean and dingy thoroughfare without charm or interest, but for the connoisseur it has its legend. Here Swinburne came upon his famous copy of "The Faerie Queene"; here more than one collection has been enriched by a Crome, a Morland, a choice miniature, a first proof or some rare unsuspected article of bigotry and virtue.

On the right, going from Charing Cross, halfway up the street, a shop, outwardly inconspicuous, bears on its front in plain gilt letters the name S. Gedge, Antiques.

A regard for the *mot juste* could omit the final letter. S. Gedge Antique was nearer the fact. To look at, the proprietor of the business was an antique of the most genuine kind, whose age, before he was dressed for the day, might have been anything. When, however, he had "tidied himself up" to sit at the receipt of a custom, a process involving a shave, the putting on of collar and dickey, prehistoric frock coat, new perhaps for the Prince Consort's funeral, and a pair of jemimas that also were "of the period," his years, in spite of a yellow parchment countenance of an incredible cunning, could at conservative estimate be reckoned as seventy.

On a certain morning of September, the years of the proprietor of S. Gedge Antiques, whatever they might be, sat heavily upon him. Tall, sombre, gaunt, a cross between a hop-pole and a moulting vulture, his tattered dressing gown and chessboard slippers lent a touch of fantasy to his look of eld, while the collar and dickey of commerce still adorned the back kitchen dresser.

Philosophers say that to find a reason for everything is only a question of looking. The reason for the undress of S. Gedge Antiques so late as eleven o'clock in the morning was not far to seek. His right hand man and sole assistant, who answered to the name of William, and who was never known or called by any other, had been away for an annual holiday of one week, which this year he had spent in Suffolk. He was due back in the course of that day and his master would raise a pæan on his return. In the absence of William the indispensable S. Gedge Antiques was like a windjammer on a lee shore.

There was a further reason for his lost air. He was "at outs" with Mrs. Runciman, his charwoman, a state of affairs which had long threatened to become chronic. An old, and in her own opinion, an undervalued retainer, the suspension of diplomatic relations between Mrs. Runciman and her employer could always be traced to one cause. S. Gedge attributed it to the phases of the moon and their effect on the human female, but the real root of the mischief was Mrs. Runciman's demand for "a raise in her celery." For many years past the lady had held that her services were worth more than "half a crown a day and her grub." The invariable reply of her master was that he had never paid more to a char all the time he had been in trade and that if she wanted more she could keep away. This Thursday morning, according to precedent when matters came to a head, Mrs. Runciman had taken him at his word. The old man knew, however, that her absence would only be temporary. A single day off would vindicate the rights of woman. As sure as the sun rose on the morrow Mrs. R. would return impenitent but in better fettle for charring. But as he made a point of telling her, she would play the trick once too often.

Char-less for the time being, assistant-less also, this morning S. Gedge was not only looking his age, he was feeling it; but he had already begun to examine the contents of a large packing case from Ipswich which Messrs. Carter Paterson had delivered half an hour ago at the back of the premises by the side entry. Handicapped as S. Gedge Antiques at the moment was, he could well have deferred these labours until later in the day. Human curiosity, however, had claimed him as a victim.

By a side wind he had heard of a sale at a small and rather inaccessible house in the country where a few things might be going cheap. As this was to take place in the course of William's holiday, the young man had been given a few pounds to invest, provided that in his opinion "the goods were full value." By trusting William to carry out an operation of such delicacy, his master whose name in trade circles was that of "a very keen buyer" was really paying him the highest compliment in his power. For the god of S. Gedge Antiques was money. In the art of "picking things up," however, William had a lucky touch. His master could depend as a rule on turning over a few shillings on each of the young man's purchases; indeed there were occasions when the few shillings had been many. The truth was that William's flair for a good thing was almost uncanny.

Adroit use of a screwdriver prised the lid off the packing case. A top layer of shavings was removed. With the air of a *dévot* the old man dug out William's first purchase and held it up to the light of New Cross Street, or to as much of that dubious commodity as could filter down the side entry.

Purchase the first proved to be a copy of an engraving by P. Bartolozzi: the *Mrs. Lumley and Her Children* of Sir Joshua Reynolds. An expert eye priced it at once a safe thirty shillings in the window of the front shop, although William had been told not to exceed a third of that sum at Loseby Grange, Saxmundham. So far so good. With a feeling of satisfaction S. Gedge laid the engraving upon a chair of ornate appearance but doubtful authenticity, and proceeded to remove more straw from the packing case. Before, however, he could deal with William's second purchase, whatever it might be, he was interrupted.

A voice came from the front shop.

"Uncle Si! Uncle Si! Where are you?"

The voice was feminine. S. Gedge Antiques, crusted bachelor and confirmed hater of women, felt a sudden pang of dismay.

"Where are you, Uncle Si?"

"Com-ming!" A low roar boomed from the interior of the packing case. It failed, however, to get beyond the door of the lumber room.

"That girl of Abe's" ruminated the old man deep in straw. In the stress of affairs, he had almost forgotten that the only child of a half brother many years his junior, was coming to London by the morning train.

"Uncle Si!"

With a hiss of disgust worthy of an elderly cobra he writhed his head free of the straw. "Confound her, turning up like this. Why couldn't she come this afternoon when the boy'd be home? But that's a woman. They're born as cross as Christmas."

A third time his name was called.

S. Gedge Antiques, unshaven, beslippered, bespectacled, slowly emerged from the decent obscurity of the back premises into the fierce publicity of the front shop. He was greeted by a sight of which his every instinct profoundly disapproved.

The sight was youthful, smiling, fresh complexioned. In a weak moment, for which mentally he had been kicking himself round the shop ever since, he had been so unwise as to offer to adopt this girl who had lost her father some years ago and had lately buried her mother. Carter Paterson had delivered her trunk along with the packing case from Ipswich, a fact he now recalled.

Had S. Gedge had an eye for anything but antiques, he must have seen at once that his niece was by way of being a decidedly attractive young woman. She was nineteen, and she wore a neat well-fitting black dress and a plain black hat in which cunning and good taste were mingled. Inclined to be tall she was slender and straight and carried herself well. Her eyes were clear, shrewd and smiling. In fact they appeared to smile quite considerably at the slow emergence from the back premises of S. Gedge Antiques.

In the girl's hand was a pilgrim basket, which she put carefully on a gate-legged table, marked "£4.19.6, a great bargain" and then very fearlessly embraced its owner.

"How are you, niece?" gasped the old man who felt that an affront had been offered to the dignity of the human male.

"Thank you, Uncle Si, I'm first rate," said the girl trying for the sake of good manners not to smile too broadly.

"Had a comfortable journey?"

"Oh, yes, thank you."

"Didn't expect you so soon. However, your box has come. By the way, what's your name? I've forgotten it."

"June."

"June, eh? One of these new fangled affairs," S. Gedge spoke aggrievedly. "Why not call yourself December and have done with it?"

"I will if you like," said June obligingly. "But it seems rather long. Do you care for De, Cem, or Ber for short?"

"It don't matter. What's in a name? I only thought it sounded a bit sloppy and new fangled."

The eyes of June continued to regard S. Gedge Antiques with a demure smile. He did not see the smile. He only saw her and she was a matter for grave reflection.

II

S. GEDGE ANTIQUES peered dubiously at his niece. He had a dislike of women and more than any other kind he disliked young women. But one fact was already clear; he had let himself in for it. Frowning at this bitter thought he cast his mind back in search of a reason. Knowing himself so well he was sure that a reason there must be and a good one for so grave an indiscretion. Suddenly he remembered the charwoman and his brow cleared a little.

"Let me have a look at you, niece." As a hawk might gaze at a wren he gazed at June through his spectacles. "Tall and strong seemingly. I hope you're not afraid of hard work."

"I'm not afraid of anything, Uncle Si," said June with calm precision.

"No answers," said S. Gedge curtly. "If you intend to stay here you've got to mind your p's and q's and you've got to earn your keep." He sighed and impatiently plucked the spectacles from his nose. "Thought so," he snarled. "I'm looking at you with my selling spectacles. For this job I'll need my buying ones."

Delving into the capacious pockets of his dressing gown, the old man was able to produce a second pair of glasses. He adjusted them grimly. "Now I can begin to see you. Favour your father seemingly. And he was never a mucher—wasn't your father."

"Dad is dead, Uncle Si." There was reproof in June's strong voice. "And he was a very good man. There was never a better father than Dad."

"Must have been a good man. He hardly left you and your mother the price of his funeral."

"It wasn't Dad's fault that he was unlucky in business."

"Unlucky." S. Gedge Antiques gave a sharp tilt to his "buying" spectacles. "I don't believe in luck myself."

"Don't you?" said June, with a touch of defiance.

"No answers." Uncle Si held up a finger of warning. "Your luck is you're not afraid of work. If you stop here you'll have to stir yourself."

June confessed a modest willingness to do her best.

S. Gedge continued to gaze at her. It was clear that he had undertaken an immense responsibility. A live sharp girl, nineteen years of age, one of these modern hussies, with opinions of her own, was going to alter things. It was no use burking the fact, but a wise man would have looked it in the face a little sooner.

"The char is taking a day off," he said, breaking this reverie. "So I'd better give you a hand with your box. You can then change your frock and come and tidy up. If you give your mind to your job I daresay I'll be able to do without the char altogether. The woman's a nuisance, as all women are. But she's the worst kind of a nuisance, and I've been trying to be quit of her any time this ten years."

In silence June followed Uncle Si kitchenwards, slowly removing a pair of black kid gloves as she did so. He helped her to carry a trunk containing all her worldly possessions up a steep, narrow, twisty flight of uncarpeted stairs to a tiny attic, divided by a wooden partition from a larger one, and lit by a grimy window in the roof. It was provided with a bedstead, a mattress, a chest of drawers, a washing stand and a crazy looking-glass.

"When the boy comes, he'll find you a couple o' blankets, I daresay. Meantime you can fall to as soon as you like."

June lost no time in unpacking. She then exchanged her new mourning for an old dress in which to begin work. As she did so her depression was terrible. The death of her mother, a month ago, had meant the loss of everything she valued in the world. There was no one else, no other thing that mattered. But she had promised that she would be a brave girl and face life with a stout heart, and she was going to be as good as her word.

For that reason she did not allow herself to spend much time over the changing of her dress. She would have liked to sit on the edge of the small bed in that dismal room and weep. The future was an abyss. Her prospects were nil. She had ambition, but she lacked the kind of education and training that could get her out of the rut; and all the money she had in the world, something less than twenty pounds, was in her purse in a roll of notes, together with a few odd shillings and coppers. Nothing more remained of the sum that had been realized by the sale of her home, which her mother and she had striven so hard to keep together. And when this was gone she would have to live on the charity of her Uncle Si, who was said to be a very hard man and for whom she had already conceived an odd dislike, or go out and find something to do.

Such an outlook was grim. But as June put on an old house frock she shut her lips tight and determined not to think about to-morrow. Uncle Si had told her to clean out the grate in the back kitchen. She flattered herself that she could clean out a grate with anybody. Merely to stop the cruel ache at the back of her brain she would just think of her task, and nothing else.

In about ten minutes June came down the attic stairs, fully equipped even to an overall which she had been undecided whether to pack in her box but had prudently done so.

"Where are the brushes and dust pan, Uncle Si?"

"In the cupboard under the scullery sink." A growl emerged from the packing case, followed by a gargoyle head. "And when you are through with the kitchen grate you can come and clear up this litter, and then you can cook a few potatoes for dinner—that's if you know how."

"Of course I know how," said June.

"Your mother seems to have brought you up properly. If you give your mind to your job and you're not above soiling your hands I quite expect we'll be able to do without the char."

June, her large eyes fixed on Uncle Si, did not flinch from the prospect. She went boldly, head high, in the direction of the scullery sink while S. Gedge Antiques proceeded to burrow deeper and deeper into the packing case.

Presently he dug out a bowl of Lowestoft china, which he tapped with a finger nail and held up to the light.

"It's a good piece," he reflected. "There's one thing to be said for that boy— he don't often make mistakes. I wonder what he paid for this. However, I shall know presently," and S. Gedge placed the bowl on a chair opposite the engraving "after" P. Bartolozzi.

His researches continued, but there was not much to follow. Still, that was to be expected. William had only been given twenty pounds and the bowl alone was a safe fiver. The old man was rather sorry that William had not been given more to invest. However, there was a copper coal-scuttle that might be polished up to fetch three pounds, and a set of fire irons and other odds and ends, not of much account in themselves, but all going to show that good use had been made of the money.

"Niece," called Uncle Si when at last the packing case was empty, "come and give a hand here."

With bright and prompt efficiency June helped to clear up the débris and to haul the packing case into the backyard.

The old man said at the successful conclusion of these operations:

"Now see what you can do with those potatoes. Boil 'em in their skins. There's less waste that way and there's more flavour."

"What time is dinner, Uncle Si?"

"One o'clock sharp."

S. Gedge Antiques, having put on his collar, and discarded his dressing gown for the frock coat of commerce, shambled forward into the front shop with the air of a man who has no time to waste upon trivialities. So far things were all right. The girl seemed willing and capable and he hoped she would continue to be respectful. The times were against it, certainly. In the present era of short skirts, open-work stockings, fancy shoes and bare necks, it was hard, even for experts like himself, to say what the world was coming to. Girls of the new generation were terribly independent. They would sauce you as soon as look at you, and there was no doubt they knew far more than their grandmothers. In taking under his roof the only child of a half-brother who had died worth precious little, S. Gedge Antiques was simply asking for trouble. At the same time there was no need to deny that June had begun well, and if at eight o'clock the next morning he was in a position to say, "Mrs. R. you can take another day off and get yourself a better billet," he would feel a happier man.

A voice with a ring in it came from the shop threshold. "Uncle Si, how many potatoes shall I cook?"

"Three middling size. One for me, one for you, one for William if he comes. And if he don't come, he can have it cold for his supper."

"Or I can fry it," said the voice from the threshold.

"You can fry it?" S. Gedge peered towards the voice over the top of his "buying" spectacles. "Before we go in for fancy work let us see what sort of a job you make of a plain bilin'. Pigs mustn't begin to fly too early—not in the West Central postal district."

"I don't know much about pigs," said June, calmly, "but I'll boil a potato with anyone."

"And eat one too I expect," said S. Gedge severely closuring the incident.

The axiom he had just laid down applied to young female pigs particularly.

***

III

S. GEDGE ANTIQUES, feather duster in hand, began to flick pensively a number of articles of bigotry and virtue. The occupation amused him. It was not that he had any great regard for the things he sold, but each was registered in his mind as having been bought for so much at So-and-So's sale. A thoroughly competent man he understood his trade. He had first set up in business in the year 1879. That was a long time ago, but it was his proud boast that he had yet to make his first serious mistake. Like everyone else, he had made mistakes, but it pleased him to think that he had never been badly "let in." His simple rule was not to pay a high price for anything. Sometimes he missed a bargain by not taking chances, but banking on certainties brought peace of mind and a steady growth of capital.

Perhaps the worst shot he had ever made was the queer article to which he now applied the duster. A huge black jar, about six feet high and so fantastically hideous in design as to suggest the familiar of a Caribbean witch doctor or the joss of a barbarous king, held a position of sufficient prominence on the shop floor for his folly to be ever before him. Years ago he had taken this grinning, wide-mouthed monster, shaped and featured like Moloch, in exchange for a bad debt, hoping that in the course of time he would be able to trade it away. As yet he had not succeeded. Few people apparently had a use for such an evil-looking thing which took up so much house room. S. Gedge Antiques was loth to write it off a dead loss, but he had now come to regard it as "a hoodoo." He was not a superstitious man but he declared it brought bad luck. On several occasions when a chance seemed to arise of parting with it to advantage, something had happened to the intending purchaser; indeed it would have called for no great effort of the imagination to believe that a curse was upon it.

By an association of ideas, as the feathers flicked that surface of black lacquer, the mind of S. Gedge reverted to his niece. She, too, was a speculation, a leap in the dark. You never knew where you were with women. Now that the fools in Parliament had given females a vote the whole sex was demoralised. He had been terribly rash; and he could tell by the look of the girl that she had a large appetite. Still if he could do without "that woman" it would be something.

The picture, however, was not all dark. A flick of the feathers emphasised its brighter side as William recurred suddenly to his mind. Taking all things into account, he was ready to own that the able youth was the best bargain he had ever made. Some years ago, William, a needy lad of unknown origin, had been engaged at a very small wage to run errands and to make himself of general use. Finding him extremely intelligent and possessed of real aptitude, his master with an eye to the future, had taught him the trade. And he had now become so knowledgeable that for some little time past he had been promoted to an active part in the business.

If William had a fault it was that in his master's opinion he was almost too honest. Had it been humanly possible for S. Gedge Antiques to trust any man with a thousand pounds, William undoubtedly would have been that man. Besides, he had grown so expert that his employer was learning to rely more and more upon his judgment. The time had come when S. Gedge Antiques had need of young eyes in the most delicate art of choosing the right thing to buy; and this absolutely dependable young man had now taken rank in his master's mind, perhaps in a higher degree than that master recognised, as an asset of priceless value. Sooner or later, if William went on in his present way, the long-deferred rise in his wages would have to enter the region of practical politics. For example, there was this packing case from Ipswich. Without indulgence in flagrant optimism—and the old man was seldom guilty of that—there was a clear profit already in sight. The bowl of Lowestoft might fetch anything up to ten pounds and even then it would be "a great bargain at clearance sale prices." Then there was the engraving. William had a nose for such things; indeed his master often wondered how a young chap with no education to speak of could have come by it.

At this point there was heard a quiet and respectful: "Good morning, sir."

S. Gedge, standing with his back to the shop door, the china bowl again in hand, was taken by surprise. William was not expected before the afternoon.

That young man was rather tall and rather slight; he was decidedly brown from the sun of East Anglia; and some people might have considered him handsome. In his left hand he carried a small gladstone bag. And beneath his right arm was an article wrapped in brown paper.

"Ah, that's the bowl," said William eagerly. "A nice piece, sir, isn't it?"

"I may be able to tell you more about that," the cautious answer, "when I know what you gave for it."

William had given thirty shillings.

S. Gedge Antiques tapped the bowl appraisingly. "Thirty shillings! But that's money."

"I'm sure it's a good piece, sir."

"Well, you may be right," said S. Gedge grudgingly. "Lowestoft is fetching fair prices just now. What's that under your arm?"

"It's something I've bought for myself, sir."

"Out of the money I gave you?" said the old man as keen as a goshawk.

"No, sir," said William with great simplicity. "Your money was all in the packing case. I'll give you an account of every penny."

"Well, what's the thing you've bought for yourself," said the master sternly.

"It's a small picture I happened to come across in an old shop at Crowdham Market."

"Picture, eh?" S. Gedge Antiques dubiously scratched a scrub of whisker with the nail of his forefinger. "Don't fancy pictures myself. Chancey things are pictures. Never brought *me* much luck. However, I'll have a look at it. Take off the paper."

William took off the paper and handed to his master the article it had contained. With a frown of petulant disgust the old man held an ancient and dilapidated daub up to the light. So black it was with grime and age that to his failing eyes not so much as a hint of the subject was visible.

"Nothing to write home about anyhow," was the sour comment. "Worth nothing beyond the price of the frame. And I should put that"—S. Gedge pursed a mouth of professional knowledge—"at five shillings."

"Five shillings, sir, is what I paid for it."

"Not worth bringing home." S. Gedge shook a dour head. Somehow he resented his assistant making a private purchase, but that may have been because there was nothing in the purchase when made. "Why buy a thing like that?"

William took the picture gravely from his master and held it near the window.

"I have an idea, sir, there may be a subject underneath."

"Don't believe in ideas myself," snapped S. Gedge, taking a microscope from the counter. After a brief use of it he added, "There may be a bit o' badly painted still life, but what's the good o' that."

"I've a feeling, sir, there's something below it."

"Rubbish anyhow. It'll be a fortnight's job to get the top off and then like as not you'll have wasted your time. Why buy a pig in a poke when you might have invested your five shillings in a bit more china? However, it's no affair of mine."

"There's something there, sir, under those flowers, I feel sure," said the young man taking up the microscope and gazing earnestly at the picture. "But what it is I can't say."

"Nor can anyone else. However, as I say, it's your funeral. In our trade there's such a thing as being too speculative, and don't forget it, boy."

"I might find a thing worth having, sir," William ventured to say.

"Pigs might fly," snapped S. Gedge Antiques, his favourite formula for clinching an argument.

The mention of pigs, no doubt again by an association of ideas, enabled S. Gedge to notice, which he might have done any time for two minutes past, that his niece had emerged from the back premises, and that she was regarding William and the picture with frank curiosity.

"Well, niece," said the old man sharply. "What do you want now?"

"Is the cold mutton in the larder for dinner, Uncle Si?" said June with a slight but becoming blush at being called upon to speak in the presence of such a very nice looking young man.

"What else do you think we are going to have? Truffles in aspic or patty de four grass?"

"No, Uncle Si," said June gravely.

"Very well then," growled S. Gedge Antiques.

IV

I⊤ was not until the evening, after tea, when S. Gedge Antiques had gone by bus to Clerkenwell in order to buy a Queen Anne sofa from a dealer in difficulties that William and June really became known to one another. Before then, however, their respective presences had already charged the atmosphere of No. 46 New Cross Street with a rare and subtle quality.

William, even at a first glance, had been intrigued more than a little by the appearance of the niece. To begin with she was a great contrast to Mrs. Runciman. She looked as clean and bright as a new pin, she had beautiful teeth, her hair was of the kind that artists want to paint and her way of doing it was cunning. Moreover, she was as straight as a willow, her movements had charm and grace, and her eyes were grey. And beyond all else her smile was full of friendship.

As for June, her first thought had been, when she had unexpectedly come upon William holding up to the light the picture he had bought at Crowdham Market, that the young man had an air at once very gentle and very nice. And in the first talk they had together in the course of that evening, during the providential absence of Uncle Si, this view of William was fully confirmed.

He was very gentle and he was very nice.

The conversation began shortly after seven o'clock when William had put up the shutters and locked the door of the shop. It was he who opened the ball.

"You've come to stay, Miss Gedge, haven't you?"

"Yes," said June, "if I can make myself useful to Uncle Si."

"But aren't you adopted? The master said a fortnight ago he was going to adopt you."

"Uncle Si says I'm half and half at present," said June demurely. "I'm a month on trial. If I suit his ways he says I can stay, but if I don't I must get after a job."

"I hope you will stay," said William with obvious sincerity.

There was enough Woman in the heart of the niece of S. Gedge Antiques to cause her to smile to herself. This was a perfect Simple Simon of a fellow, yet she could not deny that there was something about him which gave her quite a thrill.

"Why do you hope so?" asked Woman, with seeming innocence.

"I don't know why I do, unless it is that you are so perfectly nice to talk to." And the Simpleton grew suddenly red at his own immoderation.

Woman in her cardinal aspect might have said "Really" in a tone of ice; she might even have been tempted to ridicule such a statement made by such a young man; but Woman in the shrewdly perceptive person of June was now aware that this air of quaint sincerity was a thing with which no girl truly wise would dare to trifle. William was William and must be treated accordingly.

"Aren't you very clever?"

She knew he was clever, but for a reason she couldn't divine she was anxious to let him know that she knew it.

"I don't think I am at all."

"But you are," said June. "You must be very clever indeed to go about the country buying rare things cheap for Uncle Si to sell."

"Oh, anybody can pick up a few odds and ends now and again if one has been given the money to buy them."

"Anybody couldn't. I couldn't for one."

"Isn't that because you've not been brought up to the business?"

"It's more than that," said June shrewdly. "You must have a special gift for picking up things of value."

"I may have," the young man modestly allowed. "The master trusts me as a rule to tell whether a thing is genuine."

June pinned him with her eyes. "Then tell me this." Her suddenness took him completely by surprise. "Is *he* genuine?"

"Who? The master!"

"Yes—Uncle Si."

The answer came without an instant's hesitation. "Yes, Miss June, he is. The master is a genuine piece."

"I am very glad to hear it," said June with a slight frown.

"Yes, the master is genuine." Depth and conviction were in the young man's tone. "In fact," he added slowly, "you might say he is a museum piece."

At this solemnity June smiled.

"He's a very good man." A warmth of affection fused the simple words. "Why he took me from down there as you might say." William pointed to the ground. "And now I'm his assistant."

"At how much a week," said the practical June, "if the question isn't rude?"

"I get fifteen shillings."

"A week?"

"Yes. And board and lodging."

She looked the young man steadily in the eyes. "You are worth more."

"If the master thinks I'm worth more, he'll give it to me."

June pursed her lips and shook a dubious head. Evidently she was not convinced.

"Oh, yes, I'm sure he will. In fact, he's promised to raise my wages half a crown from the first of the new year."

"I should just think so!" said June looking him still in the eyes.

"Of course I always get everything found."

"What about your clothes?"

With an air of apology he had to own that clothes were not included; yet to offset this reluctant admission he laid stress on the fact that his master had taught him all that he knew.

June could not resist a frown. Nice as he was, she would not have minded shaking him a little. No Simon had a right to be quite so simple as this one.

A pause followed. And then the young man suddenly said: "Miss June would you care to see something I bought the other day at Crowdham Market?"

"I'd love to," said the gracious Miss June. She had seen 'the something' already but just now she was by no means averse from having another look at it.

"Perhaps you wouldn't mind coming up to the studio." William laughed shyly. "I call it that, although of course it isn't a studio really. And I only call it that to myself you know," he added naïvely.

"Then why did you call it 'the studio' to me?" archly demanded Woman in the person of the niece of S. Gedge Antiques.

"I don't know why, I'm sure. It was silly."

"No, it wasn't," said Woman. "Rather nice of you, I think."

The simpleton flushed to the roots of his thick and waving chestnut hair which was brushed back from a high forehead in a most becoming manner; and then with rare presence of mind, in order to give his confusion a chance, he showed the way up the two flights of stairs which led direct to June's attic. Next to it, with only a thin wall dividing them, was a kind of extension of her own private cubicle, a fairly large and well lit room, which its occupant had immodestly called "a studio." A bed, a washing stand, and a chest of drawers were tucked away in a far corner, as if they didn't belong.

"The master lets me have this all to myself for the sake of the light," said the young man in a happy voice as he threw open the door. "One needs a good light to work by."

With the air of a Leonardo receiving a lady of the Colonnas he ushered her in.

A feminine eye embraced all at a glance. The walls of bare whitewash bathed in the glories of an autumn sunset, the clean skylight, the two easels with rather dilapidated objects upon them, a litter of tools and canvases and frames, a pervading odour of turpentine, and a look of rapture upon the young man's face.

"But it *is* a studio," said June. Somehow she felt greatly impressed by it. "I've never seen one before, but it's just like what one reads about in books."

"Oh, no, a studio is where pictures are painted. Here they are only cleaned and restored."

"One day perhaps you'll paint them."

"Perhaps I will; I don't know." He sighed a little, too shy to confess his dream. "But that day's a long way off."

"It mayn't be, you know."

He had begun already to try, but as yet it was a secret from the world. "*Ars est celare artem*," he said.

"What do you mean by that?"

"Life is short, art eternal. It is the motto of the old man who teaches me how to clean and renovate these things. He says it keeps him up to his work."

"You go to an art school?"

"I should hardly call it that. But the master wants me to learn as much as I can of the practical side of the trade, so he's having me taught. And the more I can pick up about pictures, the better it will be for the business. You see, the master doesn't pretend to know much about pictures himself. His line is furniture."

"Didn't I say you were clever?" June could not help feeling a little proud of her own perception.

"You wouldn't say that"—the young man's tone was sad—"if you really knew how little I know. But allow me to show you what I bought at Crowdham Market. There it is." He pointed to the old picture on the smaller easel, which now divorced from its frame seemed to June a mere daub, black, dilapidated, old and worthless.

She could not conceal her disappointment. "I don't call that anything."

"No!" He could not conceal his disappointment either. "Take this glass." A microscope was handed to her. "Please look at it ve-ry ve-ry closely while I hold it for you in the light."

June gave the canvas a most rigorous scrutiny, but she had to own at last that the only thing she could see was dirt.

"Can't you see water?"

"Where?"

With his finger nail the young man found water.

"No," said June stoutly. "I don't see a single drop. And that's a pity, because in my opinion, it would be none the worse for a good wash."

This was a facer but he met it valiantly.

"Don't you see trees?"

"Where are the trees?"

The young man disclosed trees with his finger nail.

"I can't see a twig."

"But you can see a cloud." With his finger nail he traced a cloud.

"I only see dirt and smudge," said June the downright. "To my mind this isn't a picture at all."

"Surely, you can see a windmill?"

"A windmill! Why there's not a sign of one."

"Wait till it's really clean," said William with the optimism of genius. He took up a knife and began delicately to scrape that dark surface from which already he had half removed a top layer of paint that some inferior artist had placed there.

June shook her head. There was a lovely fall in the young man's voice but it would take more than that to convince her. She believed her eyes to be as good as most people's, but even with a microscope and William's finger to help them they could see never a sign of a cloud or so much as a hint of water. As for a tree!... and a windmill!... either this handsome young man ... he really was handsome ... had a sense that ordinary people had not ... or ... or...!

V

JUNE suddenly remembered that she must go and lay the supper.

William modestly asked to be allowed to help.

"Can you lay supper?" Polite the tone, but June was inclined to think that here was the limit to William's cleverness.

"Oh, yes, Miss June, I lay it nearly always. It's part of my work."

"Glad of your help, of course." The tone was gracious. "But I daresay you'd like to go on looking for a windmill."

"Yes, I think perhaps I would." It was not quite the answer of diplomacy, but behind it was a weight of sincerity that took away the sting.

"Thought so," said June, with a dark smile. It would have been pleasant to have had the help of this accomplished young man, but above all things she was practical and so understood that the time of such a one must be of great value.

"But I'm thinking you'll have to look some while for that windmill," she said, trying not to be satirical.

"The windmill I'll not swear to, but I'm sure there's water and trees; although, of course, it may take some time to find them." William took up a piece of cotton wool. "But we'll see."

He moistened the wool with a solvent, which he kept in a bottle, a mysterious compound of vegetable oils and mineral water; and then, not too hard, he began to rub the surface of the picture.

"I hope we shall," said June, doubtfully. And she went downstairs with an air of scepticism she was unable to hide.

Supper, in the main, was an affair of bread and cheese and a jug of beer, drawn from the barrel in the larder. It was not taken until a quarter past nine when S. Gedge Antiques had returned from Clerkenwell. The old man was in quite a good humour; in fact, it might be said, to verge upon the expansive. He had managed to buy the Queen Anne sofa for four pounds.

"You've got a bargain, sir," said William. It was William who had discovered the sofa, and had strongly advised its purchase.

"That remains to be seen," said his master, who would have been vastly disappointed had there been reason to think that he had not got a bargain.

After supper, when the old man had put on his slippers and an ancient smoking cap that made him look like a Turkish pasha, he took from the chimneypiece a pipe and a jar of tobacco, drew the easy chair to the fire, and began to read the evening paper.

"By the way, boy," he remarked, quizzingly, "have you started yet on that marvellous thing you were clever enough to buy at Ipswich?"

"Crowdham Market, sir."

"Crowdham Market, was it? Well, my father used to say that fools and money soon part company."

June, who was clearing the table, could not forbear from darting at the young man a gleam of triumph. It was clear that Uncle Si believed no more in the windmill, not to mention the trees and the water than did she.

A start had been made, but William confessed to a fear that it might be a long job to get it clean.

"And when you get it clean," said his master, "what do you expect to find, eh?—that's if you're lucky enough to find anything."

"I don't quite know," said William frankly.

"Neither do I," S. Gedge Antiques scratched a cheek of rather humorous cynicism. And then in sheer expansion of mood, he went to the length of winking at his niece. "Perhaps, boy," he said, "you'll find that Van Roon that was cut out of its frame at the Louvre in the Nineties, and has never been seen or heard of since."

"Was there one, sir?" asked William, interested and alert.

The old man took up the evening paper, and began to read. "Canvas sixteen inches by twelve—just about your size, eh? One of the world's masterpieces. Large reward for recovery been on offer for more than twenty-five years by French Government—but not claimed yet seemingly. Said to be finest Van Roon in existence. Now's your chance, boy." A second time S. Gedge Antiques winked at his niece; and then folding back the page of the *Evening News*, he handed it to William, with the air of a very sly dog indeed. "See for yourself. Special article. Mystery of Famous Missing Picture. When you find the signature of Mynheer Van Roon in the corner of this masterpiece of yours, I shouldn't wonder if you're able to set up in business for yourself."

Allowing Fancy a loose rein in this benign hour, the old man, for the third time honoured his niece with a solemn wink.

VI

THE next morning saw the beginning of a chain of epoch-making events in the history of S. Gedge Antiques.

Shortly before eight o'clock Mrs. Runciman turned up as usual after her day off. With a most businesslike promptitude, however, she was given her quietus. In dispensing with her services, from now on, Uncle Si took a real pleasure in what he called "telling her off." Many times had he warned her that she would play the trick once too often. And now that his prophecy had come true, he was able to say just what he thought of her, of her ancestry, and of her sex in general. She would greatly oblige him by not letting him see her face again.

Mrs. Runciman, for her part, professed a cheerful willingness to take her late employer at his word. There was plenty of work to be had; and she departed on a note of dignity which she sustained by informing him in a voice loud enough for the neighbours to hear that "he was a miser, and a screw, and that he would skin a flea for its feathers."

On the top of this ukase to the char, the old man held a short private conversation with his niece. June had begun very well; and if she continued to behave herself, got up in the morning without being called, was not afraid of hard work, and had the breakfast ready by a quarter to eight she would receive, in addition to board and lodging, two shillings a week pocket money, and perhaps a small present at Christmas.

As far as it went this was very well. "But," said June, "there's my clothes, Uncle Si."

"Clothes!" The old man scratched his cheek. "You've money of your own, haven't you?"

"Only twenty pounds."

"We'll think about clothes when the time comes to buy some."

S. Gedge, however, admitted to William privately that he had hopes of the niece. "But let me tell you this, boy: it's asking for trouble to have a young female sleeping in the house. Old ones are bad enough, even when they sleep out; young ones sleeping in may be the very mischief."

In fact, the old man deemed it wise to reinforce these observations with a solemn warning. "Understand, boy, there must be no carrying on between you and her."

"Carrying on, sir!" Such innocence might have touched the heart of King Herod.

"That's what I said. I can trust you; in some ways you hardly know you're born; but with a woman, and a young one at that, it's another pair o' shoes. Women are simply the devil."

William's blank face showed a fleck of scarlet; yet the true inwardness of these Menander-like words were lost upon him; and he was rebuked for being a perfect fool in things that mattered. However, the arrangement was merely temporary. If the girl behaved herself, well and good; if she didn't behave herself, niece or no niece, she would have to go. But—touching wood!—there was nothing to complain of so far.

William quite agreed, yet he dare not say as much to his master. In his opinion, there was no ground for comparison between the dethroned goddess of whom he had always been a little in awe, and the creature of grace and charm, of fine perception and feminine amenity who slept the other side the "studio" wall. For all that, in the sight of this young man, one aspect of the case was now a matter of concern.

"Miss June," he said on the evening of the second day, "do you mind if I get up early to-morrow and do a few odd jobs about the house?"

"What sort of jobs?" Miss June's air of suspicion was tinged with sternness. Now that she reigned in Mrs. Runciman's stead she could not help feeling rather important.

"If you'll show me where the brushes are kept, I'll blacklead the kitchen grate."

"Please don't come interfering." In June's manner was a touch of hauteur.

Beneath the tan of East Anglia, the young man coloured. "But you'll spoil your hands," he ventured.

"My hands are no affair of yours," said June, a little touched, and trying not to show it.

"Let me take over the kitchen grate for the future. And if you don't mind, I'll scrub the shop floor."

"Is there anything else you'd like to do?" said June, with amused scorn.

"I'd like to do all the really rough jobs if I may."

"For why?"

The Sawney had given his reason already, and, in spite of a growing embarrassment, he stuck to his guns.

Said June sternly: "You mustn't come interfering." Yet the light in her eyes was not anger. "You've got your department and I've got mine. Windmills are your department. Blackleading kitchen grates and cleaning floors won't help you to find windmills. Besides, you have the shop to look after, and you have to go out and find things for Uncle Si, and study art, and talk to customers, and goodness knows what you haven't got to do."

"Well, if you don't mind," said William tenaciously, "I'll get in the coal, anyway."

June shook her head. "No interference," was her last word.

Nevertheless, the following morning saw a division of labour within the precincts of No. 46, New Cross Street. When June came downstairs at a quarter to seven, she found a young man on his knees vigorously polishing the kitchen grate. He was sans coat, waistcoat and collar; there was a smudge on the side of his nose, and as the temper of a lady is apt to be short at so early an hour, it was no wonder that he was rebuked crushingly.

"Didn't I say I wouldn't have interference? I don't come into your studio and look for windmills, do I?"

William, still on his knees, had penitently to own that she didn't.

"It's—it's a great liberty," said June, hotly.

He looked up at her with an air to disarm the Furies. "Oh—please—no!"

"What is it then?" Secretly she was annoyed with herself for not being as much annoyed as the case demanded. "What is it then? Coming into my kitchen with your interference."

"I'm ever so sorry, but——"

"But what?"

"I simply can't bear to think of your spoiling your beautiful hands."

June's eyes were fire; her cheek flamed like a peony. "Go and look for your beautiful windmills, and leave my hands alone."

But the owner of the beautiful hands was now fettered by the knowledge that she was beginning to blush horribly.

VII

IN the evening of the next day, about half an hour before supper, June climbed the attic stairs and knocked boldly upon the studio door.

"Come in," a gentle voice invited her.

William, a lump of cotton wool in one hand, the mysterious bottle in the other, was absorbed in the task of looking for a windmill. He had to own, the queer fellow, that so far success had not crowned his search.

"I should think not," said June, uncompromisingly.

"But there are the trees." William took up a knife and laid the point to a canvas that was already several tones lighter than of yore.

There was a pause while June screwed up her eyes like an expert; and in consequence she had reluctantly to admit that they were unmistakable trees.

"And now we are coming to the water, don't you see?" said the young man in a tone of quiet ecstasy.

"Where's the water?"

With a lover's delicacy, William ran the point of the knife along the canvas.

"Don't you see it, Miss June?" There was a thrill in the low voice.

"Why, yes," said June. "It's water, right enough." No use trying now not to be impressed. "Now I call that rather clever!"

"I knew it was there. And if you know a thing's there, sooner or later you are bound to find it. Do you know what my opinion is?" Of a sudden, the exalted voice sank mysteriously.

June had no idea what William's opinion was, but she was quite willing to hear it, whatever it might be, for he had just had a considerable rise in her estimation.

"It wouldn't surprise me at all if this turns out to be a——" He broke off with a perplexing smile.

"Turns out to be a what?"

"Perhaps I'd better not say." The words, in their caution and their gravity intrigued a shrewd daughter of the midlands. June, in spite of herself, was beginning to respect this odd young man.

"You think it might be something very good?"

"It might be something almost *too* good." William's tone had a deep vibration. "If it keeps on coming out like this, it'll be wonderful. Do you see that cloud?"

June peered hard, but she could not see a suspicion of a cloud.

"Take the microscope."

Even with the microscope no cloud was visible to June.

"I'm as sure of it as I ever was of anything," said William. "There's a cloud— oh, yes!" The note of faith was music. "And there's a sky—oh, yes!" A stray beam of the September sunset made an effect so remarkable, as it slanted across the upturned eyes, that June paid them rather more attention at the moment than she gave to the canvas.

"Has Uncle Si seen those trees?" she asked suddenly.

"Yes, the master came up to look at them a few minutes ago."

"What did he say?"

"He just scratched his cheek and changed his spectacles."

"Did you tell him what you've just told me?"

The young man nodded.

"Did Uncle Si believe you?"

"He said he'd wait till he saw it."

"Well, he can't deny the trees, anyway."

"No, he can't deny the trees. But, of course the real picture is only just beginning to come out, as you might say. All the same, he's made me an offer for it, even as it stands."

With a swift, sudden intuition, June cried: "I hope you haven't taken it!"

"As a matter of fact, I haven't," said William, casually. "I feel I'd like to keep the picture until I find out what it really is."

"Well, mind you do. And, if the question isn't a rude one, what did Uncle Si offer?"

"Seven and sixpence. But that's for the frame mainly."

June grew magisterial. "You mustn't think of parting with it."

With an innocence hard to credit in one so clever, William asked why.

"Why!" June almost snorted. "Because if Uncle Si offers you seven and sixpence for a thing which he knows you bought for five shillings, you can be sure that he considers it may be valuable."

"The master has always been very good to me," said the young man with extreme simplicity.

At these words June felt a stab of pain, so great was the contrast between the two men. One saw the wares in which they dealt only in terms of beauty, the other in terms of money.

"You are too modest. And, although you are so clever, if you don't mind my saying so, you are also rather foolish in some ways—at least that's my opinion."

William frankly admitted the impeachment.

"Well, now," said June, a cool and steady eye upon him, "suppose you tell me where you think your foolishness lies?"

"Why, I was foolish enough to think that patch"—the Simpleton pressed the finger of an artist upon the patch—"was really and truly a windmill. But, of course, it's nothing of the kind."

"I'm not speaking of windmills now," said June severely. "I'm speaking of things much more important."

"Oh, but a windmill can be very important. Have you ever really seen a windmill?"

"Yes, of course, I have."

The Sawney asked where.

June had seen a windmill in Lincolnshire.

"Lincolnshire! Oh, but you should see the one in the National Gallery."

"The one in the where?" said June, with a frown.

Of a sudden his voice took its delicious fall. The rare smile, which lit his face, was for June an enchantment: "It's a Hobbema."

"A what!—emma!"

"A Hobbema. On Saturdays the shop closes at one, so that I could take you to see it, if you'd care to. I should like you so much to see it—that's if it interests you at all. It will give you an idea of what a windmill can be."

"But I meant a real windmill. I'm only interested in real things, anyway."

"A Hobbema is better than real."

"Better than real," said June, opening wide eyes.

"When you see it, you'll understand what I mean. I do hope you'll come and look at it."

June was such a practical person that her first instinct was to refuse to do anything of the kind. But that instinct was overborne by the complexity of her feelings. In some ways he was the simplest Simon of them all; a longing to shake him was growing upon her, but the disconcerting fact remained that after a fashion he was decidedly clever. And leaving his mental qualities out of the case, when you got his face at an angle and you caught the light in his eyes, he was by far the handsomest young man she had ever seen. Therefore her promise was reluctantly given that on Saturday afternoon she would go with him to the National Gallery to see what a windmill was really like.

VIII

JUNE'S promise was made on the evening of Monday. Before it could be fulfilled, however, much had to happen. Saturday itself was put out of the case by the departure of William early that morning to attend a sale in Essex, where several things might be going cheap. And on the following Thursday he had to go to Tunbridge Wells. During his absence on that day, moreover, June's interest in the picture he had bought at Crowdham Market was roused suddenly to a very high pitch.

Even before this significant event occurred, her mind had been full of this much-discussed purchase. Day by day William wrought upon it with growing enthusiasm. There was now no more doubt in regard to the clouds and the sky than there was as to the trees and the water. S. Gedge Antiques had been up to the attic several times to see for himself, and although in his opinion, the best that could be said for the picture was that it might turn out to be a copy of a fair example of the Dutch School, he went to the length of doubling his offer of seven and sixpence. In other words, which he issued with point at the supper table on the evening prior to William's trip to Tunbridge Wells, there was "a full week's extra wages sticking out," if only the young man cared to take it in exchange for a dubious work of little or no value.

William needed, among other things, a new pair of boots; he was short of the materials of his craft, and the sum of fifteen shillings meant a great deal to him at any time, facts with which his employer was well acquainted. The temptation was great. While the offer was under consideration, June held her breath. She had a frantic desire to signal across the table to William not to part with his treasure. Much to her relief, however, the young man resisted the lure. His master told him roundly that only a fool would refuse such an offer. William allowed that it was princely, but he had quite an affection for the picture now, besides, much had to be done to get it really clean.

At present, moreover, he had not even begun to look for the signature.

"Signature!" S. Gedge Antiques took up the word sarcastically. And there were times, as June knew already, when the old man could be terribly sarcastic. "You'll be looking, I suppose, for the signature of Hobbema. Seems to me, boy, you're cracked on that subject."

"I don't think, sir," said William, in his gentle voice, "that this picture is a Hobbema."

"Don't you indeed?" To conceal a rising impatience Uncle Si made a face at his niece. "You're cracked, my boy." He gave his own forehead a symbolical tap. "Why waste your time looking for a signature to a thing you bought for five shillings at an old serendipity shop at Crowdham Market! You'd far better turn over a snug little profit of two hundred per cent and forget all about it."

The next day, however, when William set out for Tunbridge Wells, he was still the owner of the picture. And in the light of what was to follow it was a fact of considerable importance.

In the course of that morning, while June was helping Uncle Si to dress the front window, there sauntered into the shop a funny, oldish, foxy little man, who wore a brown billycock hat at the back of his head, and had a pair of legs as crooked as a Louis Quinze chair. She set him down at once as a character out of Dickens.

"Mornin' to you, Mr. Gedge," said this quaint visitor.

"Mornin' to you, Mr. Thornton!" said S. Gedge Antiques returning the salutation with deference.

June cocked her ears. The note in Uncle Si's rasping voice, which always seemed to need a file, told her at once that the visitor was no common man.

As a preliminary to business, whatever that business might be, Mr. Thornton fixed an eye like a small bright bead on the Hoodoo, whose sinister bulk seemed to dominate half the shop. It was fixed, moreover, with an air of whimsical appreciation as he murmured: "The British Museum is the place for that."

"There I'm with you, Mr. Thornton." S. Gedge Antiques looked his visitor steadily in the eye. "Wonderful example of early Polynesian craftsmanship."

"Early Polynesian craftsmanship." The little man stroked the belly of the Hoodoo with a kind of rapt delicacy which other men reserve for the fetlock of a horse.

"Only one of its kind."

"I should say so," murmured Louis Quinze-legs, screwing up his eyes; and then, by way of after-thought: "I've just dropped in, Mr. Gedge, to have a look at that picture you mentioned to me yesterday."

"Oh, *that*, Mr. Thornton." The voice of S. Gedge Antiques suggested that the matter was of such little consequence that it had almost passed from his mind. "S'pose I'd better get it for you." And then with an odd burst of agility, which in one of his years was quite surprising, the old man left the shop, while June, her heart beating high, went on dressing the window.

In three minutes or less, William's picture appeared under the arm of William's master. "Here you are, Mr. Thornton!" The voice was oil.

June made herself small between a Chinese cabinet and a tallboys in the window's deepest gorge. From this point of vantage, the privilege of seeing and hearing all that passed in the shop was still hers.

Foxy Face received the picture in silence from Uncle Si, held it to his eyes, pursed his lips, took a glass from his pocket, and examined it minutely back and front, turning it over and tapping it several times in the process. The slow care he gave to this ritual began to get on June's nerves.

"There's good work in it," said Louis Quinze-legs, at last.

"Good work in it!" said S. Gedge Antiques in what June called his "selling" voice. "I should just think there was."

"But there's one thing it lacks." The little man, looking more than ever like a fox, chose each word with delicacy. "It's a pity—a very great pity—there's no signature."

"Signature!" The old man's tone had lost the drawling sneer of the previous evening. "Tell me, Mr. Thornton,——" He must have forgotten that June was so near—"if we happened to come upon the signature of Hobbema down there in that left hand corner—in that black splotch—what do you suppose it might be worth?"

Mr. Thornton did not answer the question at once. And when answer he did, his voice was so low that June could hardly hear it. "I wouldn't like to say offhand, Mr. Gedge. Mosby sent a Hobbema to New York last year, but what he got for it I don't know."

"I heard twenty-eight thousand dollars."

"So did I, but I doubt it. Still, the Americans are paying big money just now. Did you see that thing of Mosby's, by the way?"

"Yes; it was a bit larger than this chap, but it hadn't the work in it."

"Well, get it a bit cleaner; and then, if you can show me Hobbema's signature with the date, about the place where I've got my finger, I dare say we can come to business, Mr. Gedge."

"I quite expect we'll be able to do that," said the old man with an air of robust optimism which surprised June considerably.

Foxy Face ventured to hope that such might be the case, whereupon the voice of Uncle Si fell to a pitch which his niece had to strain a keen ear to catch.

"Suppose, Mr. Thornton, we omit the question of the signature? Do you feel inclined to make an offer for the picture as it stands?"

The pause which followed was long and tense, and then June was just able to hear the cautious voice of Foxy Face. "Possibly, Mr. Gedge—I dare say I might. But before I could think of doing that, I should like a friend of mine to vet it. He's wise in these things, and knows what can be done with them."

"Right you are, Mr. Thornton," said S. Gedge Antiques brisk and businesslike. "If you can tell me when your friend is likely to call, I'll be here to meet him."

"Shall we say to-morrow morning at ten?"

"Very well, Mr. Gedge. And if my friend can't come, I'll telephone."

Foxy Face was bowed out of the shop with a politeness that fairly astonished June. She could hardly believe that this mirror of courtesy was Uncle Si. In fact, it was as if the old man had had a change of heart. With the light step of a boy, he took back the picture to the attic, while June, thinking hard, retired to the back premises to cook two middling-sized potatoes for dinner.

IX

IT was not until the evening that William returned from Tunbridge Wells. He had been to look at a picture which his master had seen already, but S. Gedge Antiques was wise enough to recognise that his assistant had an instinct for pictures far beyond his own. In the matter of bric-à-brac he would always trust his own judgment, but when it came to an oil painting he was very glad to have it fortified by the special and peculiar knowledge that William had now acquired. There was no doubt that in this sphere, which for his master was comparatively new and full of pitfalls, the young man had a remarkable gift. It was a gift, moreover, of which he had yet to learn the true value.

In "summer-time" September the days are long; and as supper was not until nine o'clock, there was light enough for William, on getting home, to spend a rare hour in the studio, delving for further beauties in that derelict canvas which already had far exceeded his hopes.

"I know where you are going," whispered June, in the young man's ear as he left the little sitting-room behind the shop, where sat Uncle Si, spectacles on nose, poring over the pages of Crowe and Cavalcaselle.

The young man glowed at this friendly interest on the part of Miss June; in fact, he was touched by it. She was the master's niece; therefore she was on a plane of being superior to his own. And he had learned already that those who are above you in the world, are apt to turn their advantage to your detriment; but Miss June, for all that she was the master's niece and had been one term at the Blackhampton High School, and was therefore a person of social weight, had been careful so far not to assert her status. And so his heart was open to her; besides this present keen interest in his labours was most encouraging.

"I'm coming up to look at it again, if I may," whispered June, as she followed him out of the room.

"Please, please do," he said, delightedly.

As she climbed the steep stairs, William in the seventh heaven, followed close upon her heels. What a pleasure to expound the merits of such a work to one so sympathetic! As for June, her quick mind was at work. Even before the coming of Foxy Face she had guessed, or some instinct had told her, that this picture was no ordinary one, and now that she had overheard that gentleman's recent talk with Uncle Si she had been given furiously to think. To understand all its implications needed far more knowledge of a deep, not to say "tricky," subject than she possessed, but one fact was clear: her opinion as to the picture's value was fully confirmed. Here was a treasure whose real worth even William himself might not be able to guess.

Now was the moment, June shrewdly saw, for prompt and decisive action. Uncle Si had set his heart upon this rare thing; but if flesh and blood was equal to the task, she must take immediate steps to baulk him. Alas, she knew only too well that it was likely to prove an immensely difficult matter.

June stood in front of the easel, and set her head to one side quite in the manner of an expert.

"It seems to grow finer and finer," she said, in a soft voice.

"Yes, it does," said William, touching it here and there with loverly fingers. "If I can but manage to get the top off without hurting the fabric, I'm sure it'll be a non-such."

June fervently said that she hoped it would be.

"There's the cloud I spoke to you about the other day."

"Why, yes," said June, screwing up her eyes, in unconscious imitation of Foxy Face. "I see it now. And it's very beautiful indeed."

"And the touch of sunlight in it. I hope you notice that!" As William spoke, it almost seemed to June that she could see the reflection of the sunlight in the eyes of this enthusiast.

"Yes, I do," said June stoutly.

"A real painter has done that!" The young man's voice took that dying fall she had learnt already to listen for. "This is a lovely thing, Miss June!" Pure cadence touched her heart with fire. "Do you know, I am beginning to think this little picture is the most perfect thing I have ever seen?"

"Very valuable, I dare say," said June, bringing him to earth.

"I only know it's good."

"But surely if it's good it's valuable? What do you think it might be worth?"

"Miss June,"—the queer little tremble in his voice sounded divine—"don't let us think of it as money."

But at those hushed words, at the far-off look in the deep eyes, she felt once more a touch of pain.

"Uncle Si would call that sentiment. He believes that money is the most important thing there is; he believes it is the only thing that matters."

She meant it as a facer for this Sawney, who had declared to her that Uncle Si could neither think wrong nor ensue it. A hit, shrewd and fair, but the Sawney was still in business.

"In a manner of speaking, it may be so. But I am sure the master will tell you there are things money can't buy."

"What are they?" June's frown was the fiercer for the effort to repress it.

"Take this glint of sun striking through that wonderful cloud. All the money in the world couldn't buy that."

"Of course it could. And I don't suppose it would take much to buy it either."

He solemnly dissented. She asked why not.

"Because," said he, "that bit of sunlight only exists in the eye that sees it."

"That's sentiment," said June severely. "You might say the same of anything."

"You might, of course. Nothing is, but thinking makes it so."

Again June heard the queer little tremble in his voice, again she saw that strange look steal across his face.

"What you say sounds very deep, but if you talk in that way I'm quite sure you'll never get on in the world."

"I'll be quite happy to live as I am, if only I'm allowed to see the wonderful things that are in it."

June had a fierce desire to shake him, but he beamed upon her, and she became a lamb.

"On Saturday," he said, "when we go to our little treasure house, you will see what I mean."

"If you talk in this way," said June once more severe, "I shall not go with you on Saturday to your little treasure house. Or on Sunday either. Or on any day of the week. If you were a millionaire, you could afford to be fanciful. Being what you are, and your salary less than half what it should be, I really think you ought to be ashamed of yourself."

She was a little astonished at her own vehemence. He seemed a little astonished at it also.

"Nothing is, but thinking makes it so," said June, with fine scorn. "That's what Mr. Boultby, the druggist at the bottom of our street at home, would call poppycock. It means you'll be very lucky if some fine morning you don't wake up and find yourself in the workhouse."

One smile more he gave her out of his deep eyes.

"That sort of talk," said June, with growing fierceness, "is just *potty*. It won't find you tools and a place to work in, or three meals a day, and a bed at night."

"But don't you see what I mean?"

"No, I don't. As I say, to my mind it's potty. But now tell me, what do you think this picture's worth if you were buying it for Uncle Si to sell again?"

"That is a very difficult question to answer. The master is so clever at selling things that he might get a big price for it in the market."

"Even without the signature?" And June fixed the eye of a hawk on the young man's face.

"I don't say that. The signature might make a lot of difference to a dealer. But don't let us talk of the price. There are things in this picture that money ought not to buy."

An impatient "Poppycock!" all but escaped Mr. Boultby's disciple. Yet of a sudden, in a fashion so unexpected as to verge upon drama, her own voice took that soft quick fall he had taught her the trick of.

"I can't tell you how much I love it," she said, dreamily. "I would give almost anything if it were mine."

William's limpid glance betrayed that he was only too happy to believe her.

"It is quite as beautiful to me as it is to you." June plunged on, but she did not dare to look at him. "And I think it would be a terrible pity if it ever came to be sold by Uncle Si. I simply love it. Suppose you sell it to me?"

"To you, Miss June!"

"Yes—to me." There was swift decision and the fixing of the will. "I like it so much that I'll give you nineteen pounds for it, and that's all I have in the world."

William was astonished.

"I hadn't realised," he said, in charmed surprise, "that you admire it so much as all that."

"Yes, I do admire it." Her heart beat fast and high. "And I want it. I can't tell you just what that picture means to me. But nineteen pounds is all I can pay."

He shook his head in slow finality.

She did not try to conceal her disappointment.

"I couldn't think of taking a penny of your money," he said, shyly. "But as you love it so much, I hope you will allow me to give it you."

She gave a little gasp. An act of such pure generosity was rather staggering.

"I hope you will, Miss June." He spoke with a delicious embarrassment. "Loving it so much really makes it yours. To love a thing is to possess it. And I shall always have the happiness of feeling that it has made you happy."

She turned away a face glowing with shame. She could never hope to feel about it in the way that he did, and it seemed almost wicked to deceive him. But a young man so poor as he could not afford to be so simple; and she soothed her conscience by telling herself what she was now doing was for his future good.

Conscience, however, was not to be put out of action that way. The part she was playing hurt like a scald on the hand. Both their tongues were tied by the pause which followed, and then she said in a weak, halting manner that was not like her: "You must have something in exchange for it, of course—not that I shall ever be able to offer anything near its true value."

"I ask no more than what you have given me already."

"What have I given you?"

"You have given me the wonderful look I see sometimes in your face, and the light that springs from your eyes and the glow of your hair. When you came to this house, you brought something with you that was never in it before."

"How funny you are!" June's cheek was a flame. But he spoke so impersonally, delicately weighing each word before a passion of sincerity gave it birth, that any effective form of rebuke was out of the question.

"Miss June," this amazing fellow went on, speaking for all the world as if she were a picture whose signature he was looking for, "when you came here, you brought the sun of beauty. Colour and harmony and grace, you brought those too. If only I knew how to paint,"—he sighed gently,—"I could never rest until I had put you on canvas just as you stand at this moment."

It was clear that he had forgotten completely that this was the niece of his employer. She also forgot that no young man had ventured yet to speak to her like that. This was William the wonderful who was addressing her, and his voice was music, his eyes slow fire, his whole being a golden web of poetry and romance.

"You oughtn't to give away such a thing," she persisted, but with none of her usual force. "It's valuable; and I oughtn't to take it." The sound of her voice, she knew only too well, was thin and strange.

"Please, please take it, Miss June," he quaintly entreated her. "It will give me more pleasure to know that you are caring for it, and that its beauty speaks to you than if I kept it all to myself. I love it, but you love it, too. If you'll share the happiness it brings me, then I shall love it even more."

Shadows of the evening were now in the room. His face was half hidden, and the wildness of her heart scarcely allowed his voice to be heard. She thought no longer of the worth of the gift, nor was she now concerned with the propriety of its acceptance. Her mind was in the grip of other things. Was it to herself he was speaking? Or was he speaking merely to a fellow worshipper of beauty? To such questions there could be no answer; she trembled at the daring which gave them birth.

His mere presence was a lure. She longed to touch his hand very gently, and would perhaps have done so, had she not been cruelly aware that even the hem of her sleeve would defile it. She was cheating him, she was cheating him outrageously. The only excuse she had was that it was all for his own good; such, at least, must now be her prayer, her hope, her faith.

X

THE next morning Foxy Face, true to the appointment he had made with S. Gedge Antiques, came at ten o'clock with a friend. A quarter before that hour William had been sent to the King's Road, Chelsea, in quest of a Jacobean carving-table for which his master had a customer.

June, in anticipation of the event, took care to be busy in a distant corner of the shop when these gentlemen arrived. As on the occasion of Louis Quinze-legs' previous visit, Uncle Si lost no time in going himself to fetch the picture, but his prompt return was fraught for June with bitter disappointment. By sheer ill luck, as it seemed, his stern eye fell on her at the very moment he gave the picture to Mr. Thornton's friend, a morose-looking man in a seedy frock coat and a furry topper.

"Niece," sharply called S. Gedge Antiques, "go and do your dusting somewhere else."

There was no help for it. June could almost have shed tears of vexation, but she had to obey. The most she dared venture in the way of appeasing a curiosity that had grown terrific was to steal back on tiptoe a few minutes later, to retrieve a pot of furniture polish she had been clever enough to leave behind. Like a mouse she crept back for it, but Uncle Si flashed upon her such a truculent eye that, without trying to catch a word that was passing, she simply fled.

Fear seized her. She felt sure that she had seen the last of the picture. Her distrust of S. Gedge Antiques had become so great that she was now convinced that money would tempt him to anything. Twenty miserable minutes she spent wondering what she must do if the picture was disposed of there and then. She tried to steel her heart against the fact, now looming inevitable, that she would never see it again.

At last the visitors left the shop. June then discovered that her fears had carried her rather too far, and that for the time being, at any rate, Uncle Si had been done an injustice.

He shambled slowly into the kitchen and to June's intense relief the picture was in his hand.

"Niece," he said, threatfully; "understand once for all that I won't have you hanging about the shop when I am doing business with important customers."

The sight of the picture was so much more important than the words which came out of his mouth that June felt inclined to treat them lightly.

"I'm telling you," said the old man fiercely. "Mark what I say. I won't have females listening with their mouths open when I'm doing business. And don't laugh at me, else you'll have to pack your box. Here!" Uncle Si handed her the picture with a scowl. "Take this back to where it came from; and just remember what's been said to you, or you'll find yourself short of a week's pocket money."

Adjured thus, June was a model of discretion for the rest of that day; and yet she was the prey of a devouring curiosity. She would have given much to know what had taken place in the course of the morning's traffic with Louis Quinze-legs and his friend. It was not until supper-time that she was able to gather a clue, when Uncle Si mentioned the matter to William. He was careful to do so, however, in the most casual way.

"By the way, boy," said the old man gravely balancing a piece of cheese on the end of his knife, and fixing June with his eye as he did so; "that daub of yours—I've had Mr. Thornton here to look at it."

"I hope he liked it, sir," said William, with his eager smile.

Uncle Si pursed his mouth. Then he went through the rest of his performance, which on this occasion ended in a noise through closed lips like a hornet's drone, which might have meant anything.

June felt an insane desire to give the old wretch a punch on his long and wicked nose.

"What did he think of the cloud?" asked William. "And the light of the sun striking through on to the water?"

"He says it's very rough and dirty, and in bad condition, but if I could buy it for two pounds he might be able to show me a small profit."

"I should think so," murmured June, holding a glass of water in suspense.

Uncle Si laid down his knife and looked at her.

"You *think* so, niece," he snarled. "Have the goodness to mind your own affairs, or you and I will quarrel. That's twice to-day I've had to speak to you."

June covered a retreat from the impossible position strong feelings had led her into by emptying her glass in one fierce draught.

"You see, boy," said Uncle Si, turning to William with a confidential air, "this—this *picture*."—It seemed a great concession on his part to allow that the thing was a picture at all—"is without a signature. That makes it almost valueless."

William smiled and gently shook his head.

"Beg your pardon, sir, but it is signed in every line."

"Rubbish. No theorising—this is a business proposition. And I tell you that without the signature, this bit of pretty-pretty just amounts to nix." The old man gave his fingers a contemptuous snap. "That's what it amounts to. But as you've taken the trouble to bring it all the way from Suffolk and you've spent a certain amount of your master's time in trying to get it clean, as I say, I'll spring a couple of pounds to encourage you. But why I should I really don't know."

June was hard-set to refrain from breaking the peace which followed, with the laugh of derision. Happily, by a triumph of will power, she bridled her tongue and kept her eyes modestly upon her plate.

"Now, boy!" Uncle Si made a series of conjuror's passes with his spectacles. "Two pounds! Take it or leave it! What do you say?"

William did not say anything, yet one of his shy smiles was winged to June across the table. She promptly sent back a scowl quite feral in its truculence, which yet was softened by a world of eloquence and humour behind it. There was no other way of intimating that Uncle Si must not learn too soon that the picture was now hers.

William, no fool, if he chose to use his wits, was able to interpret this wireless. Thus he began to temporise; and he did so in a way delightfully his own.

"What difference, sir, do you think the signature would make to our little masterpiece?"

The old man gave his assistant a look almost superhuman in its caution.

"Heh?" said he.

The question was repeated.

"Depends whose it is," was the testy answer. "You know that as well as I do. If it's Hobbema's, it might be worth money."

"It isn't Hobbema's."

"Ah!" said S. Gedge Antiques. "Interesting to know that." Had he been on winking terms with his niece, he would have winked at her; as it was, he had to be content with a sarcastic glance at the tablecloth. "But how do you know?" he added, idly careless.

"Anyone can see it isn't."

Anyone could not see it wasn't a Hobbema, and that was the snag in the mind of the old man at this moment. Neither Mr. Thornton nor his friend,

Mr. Finch, was quite certain it was not a Hobbema; they were even inclined to think that it was one, but in the absence of proof they were not disposed to gamble upon it.

"How do you mean, boy, that anyone can see it isn't?"

"That gleam of sunlight, sir." The voice of William was music and poetry in the ear of June. "I doubt whether even Hobbema could have painted that."

"You tell that to the Marines," said S. Gedge Antiques impatiently. All the same he knew better than to discourage William in the process of unbosoming himself. The young man was continually betraying such a knowledge of a difficult and abstruse subject that it was becoming a source of wonder to his master. "Maybe you've found somebody else's signature?" The tone was half a sneer.

"Yes, sir, I rather think I have," said William quite calmly and simply.

"You have!" A sudden excitement fused the cold voice. "When did you find it?"

"It would be about half an hour ago."

"Oh, indeed!" said the old man.

This queer fellow's casual tone was extremely puzzling. Why should he be inclined to apologise for having discovered the name of the artist, when it was of such vital importance? The only possible explanation of the mystery at once presented itself to the astute mind which asked the question.

"Then I expect you've been a fool. If you couldn't find Hobbema's signature you had no right to find the signature of anyone else."

William was out of his depth. He could only regard his master with eyes of bewilderment. But June was not out of hers; she was careful, all the same, not to regard Uncle Si with eyes of any kind. She merely regarded her plate. And as she did so, a little shiver that was almost pain ran through her. Uncle Si was such a deep one that she felt ashamed of knowing how deep he was.

"I don't understand, sir," said William, in the way that only he could have spoken.

"Boy," said his master, "you make me tired. In some ways you are clever, but in others you are just the biggest idiot that ever happened. I should have thought a child would have known that this has either got to be a Hobbema or it has got to be nothing. The best thing you can do is to go upstairs right now and take out that signature."

"But I understood you to say, sir, that the picture has no market value without a signature."

"No more it has, you fool. But there may be those who think it's a Hobbema. And if there are, it is up to us to help them to keep on thinking."

June hung breathlessly on every word that passed. She watched William shake his head in slow and grave perplexity.

"But anybody can see that it isn't a Hobbema."

"Anybody can't," said the old man. "Mr. Thornton can't for one, and he's a pretty good judge, as a rule. Mr. Finch is more doubtful, but even he wouldn't like to swear to it."

William shook his head.

"Boy, you are a fool. You are getting too clever; you are getting above your trade. Go at once and take out that signature, whatever it may be, provided it isn't Hobbema's, and I'll give you two pounds for the thing as it stands. And let me tell you two pounds is money."

William shook his head a little more decisively.

"I'd have to paint out the trees," he said, "and the water, and that cloud, and that gleam of sunlight before I could begin to touch the signature."

"What do you mean?"

"It's a Van Roon," said William, in a voice so gentle that he might have been speaking to himself.

S. Gedge Antiques laid his knife on his plate with a clatter. He gave an excited snort. "Van Fiddlestick!"

William's smile grew so intense that June could hardly bear to look at him.

"Every inch of it," said William, "and there are not so many, is Van Roon."

"Why, there are only about a dozen Van Roons in existence," said the old man, a queer little shake coming into his voice.

"There's one more now, sir." William's own voice was curiously soft.

- 42 -

XI

"IF you go on like this," said S. Gedge Antiques, after a pause, full of drama, "you will have to have a cold compress put on your head. Do you mean to tell me you have actually found the signature?"

"Yes, sir," said William, "right down in the corner about half an hour ago."

"Then why didn't you say so instead of keeping it all to yourself?"

"Because it doesn't seem half so important as the other things I've found."

"What other things?"

"The trees and the water and that——"

"We've heard more than enough about those. Here have you been rubbing for that signature for the best part of a fortnight, and you pretend to have found a Van Roon, and you keep it as close as the tomb."

"I had found Van Roon, sir, long before I came upon his name."

"Rubbish! What do you know of Van Roon?"

"There is a Van Roon in the treasure house in the Square," said William with his inward smile.

"There's only one," snapped S. Gedge Antiques, "in the treasure house in the Square, as you call it, and it's a very small one, too."

"Ours is very small, sir. All Van Roons are small. And they are very scarce."

"They are so scarce, my friend, that you'll never convince anybody that ours is genuine."

"There's no need, sir, provided you know it is yourself."

"But that's just what I don't know," said the old man. "Anyhow you had better go upstairs and fetch it. I'll have a look at the signature of Mynheer Van Roon." And then Uncle Si scowled at his niece who, in a state of growing excitement, had already begun to remove the bread and cheese from the supper table.

While the young man went up to the attic, his master ruminated.

"Fellow's cracked," he declared, a hostile eye still fixed upon June. "That's his trouble. I'll never be able to make anything of him. This comes of Hobbemaising. Van Fiddlestick!"

"Uncle Si," said June, in the voice of a dove, "if it is a Van Roon, what is the value of it?"

"Heh?" growled Uncle Si, and his eye became that of a kite. "Never you mind. Get on with the clearing of that table, and don't interfere. I never knew such creatures as women for minding other people's business. But I can tell you this, only a born fool would talk of Van Roon."

A born fool came down the stairs at that moment, the picture in one hand, a microscope in the other.

"It's not a very good light, sir—" William's voice trembled a little—"but I think if you hold it up to the gas, you will be able to see the signature right down in the corner. Just there, sir, along by my thumb."

The old man, glass in hand, brought a close scrutiny to bear upon the spot along by William's thumb. Then he shook his head.

"No, it is just as I thought. There doesn't begin to be the sign of a signature."

"Don't you see the upstroke of the R?"

"Don't I see the leg of my grandmother!"

"Just there, sir. Round by the edge of my finger nail."

S. Gedge Antiques solemnly exchanged his "selling" spectacles for his "buying" ones, screwed up his eyes and grunted: "Why, that's the tail of a Q, you fool." Again he took up the microscope and made prodigious play with it. "That's if it's anything. Which I take leave to doubt."

William, however, was not to be moved. And then Uncle Si's manner had a bad relapse. He began to bully. William, all the same, stuck to his guns with a gentle persistence that June could only admire. This odd but charming fellow would have Van Roon, or he would have none.

At last the old man laid the microscope on the supper table, and there came into his cunning, greedy eyes what June called the "old crocodile" look. "If you'll take my advice, boy, you'll turn that R into an A, and you'll make that upstroke a bit longer, so that it can stand for an H, and you'll touch up those blurs in the middle, so that ordinary common people will really be able to see that it *is* a Hobbema. Now what do you say?"

William shook a silent, rather mournful, head.

"If you'll do that, you shall have five pounds for it. That's big money for a daub for which you paid five shillings, but Mr. Thornton says American buyers are in the market, and with Hobbemas in short supply, they might fall for a thing like this. But of course the job must be done well."

William was still silent.

"Now what do you say, boy?" The Old Crocodile was unable to conceal his eagerness. "Shall we say five pounds as it stands? We'll leave out the question of the signature. Mr. Thornton shall deal with that. Now what do you say? Five pounds for it now?"

William did not speak. It was at the tip of June's tongue to relieve his embarrassment by claiming the picture as her own; but, luckily, she remembered that to do so just now might have an effect opposite to the one intended. Even as it was, she could not refrain from making a "mouth" at William to tell him to stand firm.

He saw the "mouth," but unfortunately so did Uncle Si. There were few things escaped the old man when he happened to be wearing his "buying" spectacles.

"Niece, you cut off to bed," he said sternly. "And you must learn not to butt in, or one of these days you'll bite granite."

June showed no desire to obey, but Uncle Si, with a look set and dour, shuffled as far as the parlour door and opened it. "No more of it, my girl." The voice was full of menace.

One further instant June hesitated. The picture had been given to her, and the right and proper course was to claim it. But this daughter of the midlands was afraid of a false move. The revelation sprang to the tip of her tongue, yet a mysterious power seemed to hold it back. She may have expected help from William, but he, alas, seemed too much occupied in proving his case to be able to give a moment's thought to the picture's ownership.

"Off to bed with you." The old man's voice was now savage. "Or—!" There was a world of meaning in the strangled threat.

June climbed up to her attic with the best grace she could, her thunderbolt unlaunched. As slowly she undressed by the uncertain light of one poor candle, she felt very unhappy. Not only was there something unpleasant, one might almost say wicked, about Uncle Si, but his manner held a power of menace which fed her growing fear.

What *was* there to be afraid of? As she blew out the candle and leapt into the meagre, rickety bed which had lumps in the middle, that was the question she put to a rather stricken conscience. To ask the question was not to answer it; a fact she learnt after she had said her prayers in which Uncle Si was dutifully included. Perhaps the root of the mischief was that the old man was so horridly deceitful. While he held the picture up to the light, and he gazed at it through the microscope, she fancied that she had seen the devil peeping out of him. In a vivid flash she had caught the living image of the Hoodoo. And June was as certain as that her pillow was hard, that cost what it might he had made up his mind to get possession of the treasure.

At the same time, she lacked the knowledge to enter fully into the niceties of the case. The picture might be a thing of great value; on the other hand it might not. She was not in a position to know; yet she was quite sure that William in spite of his cleverness was in some ways a perfect gaby, and that his master was out to take advantage of the fact.

As she sought in vain for a soft place in her comfortless bed, she was inclined to admire her own astuteness in persuading William to bestow the picture upon herself. It was for the Sawney's own sake, that at least was how she chose to view the transaction now. But a sense of vague triumph was dashed by the thought lurking at the back of her mind. Uncle Si was bound to get the picture from the feckless William somehow; indeed the young man, being as clay in the hands of his master, she was soon besieged with a fear that he had parted with it already.

The slow passing of the tardy minutes gave form and pressure to this spectre. With an excitement that grew and grew she listened intently for William ascending to the room next door. Soon or late she would hear his feet on the carpetless stairs; but to one burning with impatience it seemed that an age had to pass.

At last came the sounds for which she was so expectantly listening. The door of the next room was softly closed. What had happened? Was the picture still in his keeping? To lie all night with that question unanswered was more than she could bear. Suddenly she jumped out of bed, flung a macintosh over her white nightdress, so that the proprieties might be observed, thrust her feet into slippers and then knocked upon William's door.

It was opened at once.

"Why, Miss June!" Astonishment was in the tone. "Are you ill?"

"The picture?" said June, in quick whisper, so that Uncle Si should not hear. "You haven't left it downstairs, I hope?"

Laughing gently, William half turned from the threshold and pointed to a small table in the middle of the room, on which lay the treasure with a bit of candle burning beside it.

A deep sigh expressed June's relief. "Please give it to me. I will lock it up in my box for safety."

He smiled at her eagerness, and declared that it was quite all right where it was. Besides, another week's work was needed to give the last touches to the delicate process of cleaning. June, whose careful bringing-up would not allow her to enter the room in such circumstances, tried from its threshold to make clear that the picture was already clean enough for her. But William was not to be moved. Many exquisite details yet called for the labours of a true lover.

"Well, you must promise," whispered June finally, "to take *enormous* care of it. You must promise not to let it out of your sight for a single moment."

William hesitated to give this pledge. It appeared that his master wanted to show the picture to a friend; a fact which did but serve to confirm June in her suspicions. But she had the wisdom not to put them into words. She was content to affirm once more that the picture was now hers and that she would not trust *anyone* with a thing of such value.

"But I'd trust the master with my life," said William softly.

June felt that she would like to beat him for his innocence, as her manner plainly showed. In some things he was almost too simple to live.

Suddenly she gave him a stern good-night, and abruptly closed the door. But it was long after Saint Martin's Church had struck the hour of two that sleep visited her pillow.

XII

THE next day was Saturday; and as the shop closed at one, June prepared to keep her promise of accompanying William to his "treasure house." Strategy was needed, all the same. After she had washed up, she put on her "going out" dress. But when she came downstairs in it, Uncle Si, who took a most unwelcome interest in all her movements, inquired what was in the wind.

"I'm going to look at a hat," was the answer, bland and cool.

"Going to look *at* a hat!" To the mind of Uncle Si it was an unheard-of proceeding. "Next thing you'll be wanting to buy a hat."

June confessed that it might be so.

"You've got one already, haven't you? Besides, the shops won't be open."

The good shops might not be open, June allowed. But she was not seeking a good hat. The article to which her fancy turned was for every-day use; yet when all was said it was a mere blind. She did not really intend to buy a hat, but she certainly meant if possible, to throw dust in the eyes of the Old Crocodile. Had he been able to guess that she was going with William to the National Gallery he would have banned the expedition.

In order to stand well with her conscience and not be a story teller in the eyes of the world, June walked as far as the Strand, and carefully inspected the window of a cheap milliner's. And then, as arranged, she met William as the clocks were striking three at the Charing Cross corner of Trafalgar Square.

It was a glorious September afternoon. And for June it was an exquisite if brief escape from servitude. She had yet to see William apart from the shop, yet now, as she came upon him standing by the post office, she was quite struck by his appearance. Tall and slight of form, he carried himself well, his neat suit of blue serge, old though it was in the revealing light of the sun, was brushed with scrupulous care, and his large flowing tie which he had the art of tying in a way of his own, made him look so interesting that June secretly was rather proud of being seen in his company. For undeniably he was handsome. In fact, standing there straight, alert and smiling upon the world, he had a look of mysterious charm which in the eye of one beholder raised him above the run of men.

At the sight of June, he lifted his old straw hat with a little air of homage, and also with a slight blush that became him adorably. And in his mood there was a poetry that delighted her, although she was careful not to let him know it.

"How wonderful it all is!" He waved his hand gaily to the sky. "And to think that every bit of it belongs to you and me!"

June, as matter-of-fact a young woman as the city of Blackhampton had ever produced, felt bound to ask what William meant by this extravagant remark. Charmed she was, and yet she was a little scandalised too.

"Beauty, beauty everywhere," said the young man, letting his voice take its delicious fall. "There was an old Frenchman who said, that to see Beauty is to possess it. Look, Miss June, at that marvellous blue, and those wonderful, wonderful clouds that even Van Roon himself could hardly have painted. It is all ours, you know, all for our enjoyment, all for you and me."

"But you are speaking of the world, aren't you?" There was a slight note of protest in June's solemn tone.

"If you fall in love with beauty, all the world is yours. There's no escape from beauty so long as the sky is above us. No matter where we walk we are face to face with beauty."

June was afraid that a girl who looked so smart in a lilac silk dress and a picture hat that she had the air of a fashion plate must have caught William's injudicious observation. At any rate, she smiled at him as they passed. But then arose the question, had he not first smiled at her? Certainly, to be up against that intriguing frock, to say nothing of the hat, must have meant rare provocation for such an out-and-out lover of the ornamental.

Miss Grandeur, no doubt, had caught the look in his eyes which a minute ago June herself had surprised there. He simply could not help paying tribute to such radiance.

But was the girl beautiful? There was no doubt that William thought so. Still, the worst of it was that in his eyes everything under the sun was beautiful.

"She'd be nothing at all if it were not for the money she spends on herself," June remarked, with more severity than relevance.

All the same it was a rare experience to walk abroad with William. He had an eye for all things and in all things he found the thing he sought.

On the steps of the National Gallery was a majestic policeman. To June he was but an ordinary symbol of the law, but for William he had a different message.

"Good morning, sir!"

At the compliment of this unwonted style of address, Constable X drew himself up, and returned the greeting with a proud smile.

"I can't tell you how grateful we are to you," said William, "for taking such care of our treasures."

The policeman seemed rather amused. "It's my job," he said, training, at the same time, upon June an eye of quizzical intelligence. It was odd, yet all in a moment Constable X had ceased to be a stern-looking fellow.

As soon as William crossed the threshold of his treasure house, a kind of rapture came upon him. His voice grew hushed. And to June it seemed doubtful whether he would ever get beyond the Hermes on the main staircase. Once within this palace of many enchantments, he began to lose all sense of time and place; and, in spite of the fact that he was the soul of chivalry, he even seemed in danger of forgetting that he was accompanied by a lady.

Troubled at last by the silence of her escort, June gently observed: "This place seems nearly as big as the Blackhampton Art Museum."

To William's fine perception it was a delicate reminder that art is eternal, and that in the month of September the National Gallery closes at six.

The young man sighed deeply and turned away from the Hermes. Up the main staircase they walked side by side.

"Keep straight on, Miss June. If we glance to the right or the left, we may not get to the Van Roon before next Saturday."

"We!" was June's thought. "Better speak for yourself. In the Blackhampton Art Museum we have things far nicer than a few old chipped statues." Happily, for the time being at least, it remained a thought without words.

They went through a room on the right, and then into an inner room. June was led to its farthest corner, and proudly marshalled into the presence of an object so small, and so insignificant, that she felt it was really surprising that even William should attach the least importance to it.

However, a mere glance proved that it was not so surprising after all. The picture contained a cloud, a tree, some water and a windmill. And these objects in themselves so trivial, yet sufficed, as June had learned already, to raise William at any time to the seventh heaven of bliss.

A moment's inspection of the picture was enough for June. To her mind the work was quite commonplace. Yet William stood in front of it in an attitude of silent adoration, his head a little to one side, and apparently holding his breath for such a long period that June began to wonder how the trick was done. She was bound in honour to share this silent ecstasy, but having varied the proceedings a little by standing first on her right foot, and then on her left, she decided at last to throw up her part.

Very gently she put an end to William's reverie.

"I think I will sit down," said June.

"Please, please do!" The queer fellow came back with a start to the world of reality. "Let us sit over there on the corner of that sofa. Perhaps we may be able to see it even better then than we do now."

To the sofa they went accordingly and to June's discomfiture her mentor was at pains to dispose them both in a way that should enable them to keep the picture in their eye. June had no wish to keep the picture in her eye. She had had more than enough of it already. Besides, the large room was full of things vastly more imposing, much better worth looking at. But William, even seated on the sofa by her side, was still in thrall to this remarkable work.

There is no saying how long June's trial would have lasted, but after it had gone on for a length of time that began to seem interminable, it came to an end in the most abrupt and dramatic way. Without any kind of warning, a strange appearance swam into their ken. Uncle Si, looking spruce and businesslike, and much better dressed than usual, entered the room through the door behind them.

XIII

JUNE held her breath, while S. Gedge Antiques with thought for nothing save the object that had brought him there, made a bee-line for the picture at which William was still solemnly staring. The old man put on his spectacles. Whether they were his "buying" or his "selling" ones, June was unable to decide, but whichever they might be they had an important function to perform. Uncle Si's long and foxlike nose bent so close to the paint that it might have been smelling it.

June's instinct was to flee before they were discovered. And perhaps she would have urged this course upon William had not pride said no. She was in mortal fear of the old man, yet she despised herself for that emotion. After all, they were doing no wrong in spending Saturday afternoon in such a very elevated form of amusement. Surely it devolved upon her to stand up to this tyrant.

William, for his part, was without misgiving. Thinking evil of none, least of all his master, he was a little awed by that odd arrival, and yet he was unfeignedly glad of his presence. The simpleton regarded it as a compliment to himself that S. Gedge Antiques should take the trouble to come in his own person to look at the Van Roon.

At last S. Gedge Antiques turned away from the Van Roon, and little suspecting who were so near to him, came full upon William and June seated together upon the adjacent sofa. For a moment it was as if a feather would have knocked him down. He could trust his eyes so little that he hastily changed his spectacles.

"What!" His brow was thunder. "You! Here!"

June, ready to carry the war into the country of the enemy, was prepared to offer a cool "Why not?" Happily, a second and wiser thought led her to await developments. Secretly, Uncle Si was in a pretty rage as June could tell by the look of him. But he was not one to let his feelings override his judgment. Whatever they were, they could keep. He had come there for a particular purpose; this afternoon he was bent on business only.

In the rasping voice which made June think of a file and sandpaper, S. Gedge Antiques remarked: "Still Hobbemaising, eh?"

William modestly admitted that he hoped Miss June would have a look at The Avenue.

"Let's hope she'll be the better for it." The old man did his best to be polite. "It will improve her mind, no doubt."

"But we have come to see the Van Roon, sir," said William impulsively.

"Oh, you have." There was a sudden narrowing of foxy eyes. "Seems to me, boy, you've got Van Roon on the brain."

William could not help laughing at his master's tone of playfulness, but June did not laugh. She knew but too well that as far as Uncle Si was concerned, Van Roon was an exceedingly serious matter.

"You are wise, boy"—the old man tried very hard to keep the sneer out of his voice—"to come and find out what a Van Roon really looks like."

William modestly said that he thought he knew that already.

His master shook the head of wisdom. "Judging by the way you've been going on lately I take leave to doubt it. If you can trace the slightest resemblance to that thing of ours"—as Uncle Si half turned to point to the picture, June noticed that he was careful to say "ours"—"I'm afraid, boy, you're qualifying for Colney Hatch."

William laughed gaily at his master's humour. He felt bound in honour to do so, since the jokes from that quarter were thin and few. But June did not laugh. Something cold, subtle, deadly, was creeping into her heart.

The old fox struck an attitude before the Van Roon. "How a man who has his wits can compare that daub of ours with this acknowledged masterpiece passes me altogether."

As a fact, William had not exactly compared his Crowdham Market purchase with Number 2020 in the official catalogue. He had merely affirmed that it was by the same hand.

June was privileged to hear great argument. And as at her birth a kind fairy had bestowed the gift of penetration upon her, she listened to all that passed with a fixity of mind that was almost painful. Carefully weighing the pros and the cons as they were advanced, she was fully determined to get a real insight into the merits of a most singular and perplexing matter.

Who was in the right? It was the opinion of William against the opinion of Uncle Si. From the first she had had horrid doubts of the old man's sincerity, yet she must not prejudge so grave an issue. Account must be taken, moreover, of the entire range of William's fantastic ideas. The thought was not pleasant, but on the face of it, Uncle Si was likely to be far the safer guide of the two.

As June listened, however, to the wheedling sneers of the one and the forthright tone of the other, almost too transparent in its honesty, she could only conclude that Uncle Si was deliberately cheapening William's discovery for purposes of his own.

Looking at the masterpiece on the opposite wall, with what June was only too keenly aware were the eyes of ignorance, it was impossible to deny an extraordinary similarity of subject and treatment. And this, as she perceived at once, was where Uncle Si overdid it. He would not allow that to the vision of a technical expert, the possession of which he did not scruple now to claim for himself, there was the slightest resemblance. Such similarities as might exist on the surface to delude the untutored eye he explained away in a flood of words whose force was intended to convince them both. But he convinced neither. June, pinning her wits to a plain argument, smiled secretly as more than once he contradicted himself. William on the other hand, was not permitted by the love and reverence he bore his master, to submit his speeches to the scale. He took his stand upon the divine instinct that was his by right of birth. Such being the case he could but gently dissent from the old man. It was one of his peculiarities that the surer he was, the more gentle he grew. And therein, as June perceived, he differed strangely from Uncle Si who could only render conviction in terms of vehemence.

Finally, as a clincher, S. Gedge Antiques growled: "Boy, you talk like a fool!" and head in air, marched with the aid of his knobby walking stick out of William's treasure house.

William and June having stood to talk with the old man, now sat down again.

"Thank goodness he's gone!" said June.

William confessed that the master had puzzled him considerably.

"'Tisn't like him to close his eyes to the facts of a case. I can't think what has happened to the master. He hardly ever makes a mistake."

Said June sagaciously: "Uncle Si being so wise about most things, isn't it likely that the mistake is yours?"

"It may be so," William allowed. But at once he added, with a divine simplicity: "I will stake my life, all the same, Miss June, that our picture is a Van Roon."

"Or a clever forgery, perhaps."

"No, no. As sure as you and I sit here, only one hand painted that little thing of ours."

"Then why should Uncle Si declare that it doesn't in the least resemble a Van Roon?"

"Ah, that I don't know. It is very strange that he should be so blind to the truth. As I say, it is the first time I have known it to happen."

"It may be," said June, "that this is the first time there has been so much money in the case."

William dissented gravely. "The master would never let money influence him in a matter of this kind."

"Uncle Si lets money influence him in matters of every kind."

William shook his head. "I am afraid you don't quite understand the master," he said, with a wonderful look in his deep eyes.

June was too wise to contest the point. He might know more about pictures than did she, but when it came to human nature it was another pair of shoes. It made her quite hot with anger to feel how easily he could be taken in.

Sitting by William's side on the edge of the sofa she made a vow. From now on it should be her aim in life to see that Uncle Si did not get the better of this young man. She had made a good and wise beginning by inducing him to bestow the picture upon herself, instead of giving it, as so easily might have happened, to the Old Crocodile. She knew that some bad quarters of an hour lay ahead, in the course of which she and her box might easily find themselves in the street; but come what might, let her cherish that picture as if it were life itself. For she saw with a startling clearness that William's future, and perhaps her own, was bound up in its fortunes.

This surmise as to trouble ahead was borne out very exactly by events. When accompanied by William she returned to tea in a state as near positive happiness as she had ever known, Uncle Si's aspect was so hostile that it would not have been surprising had she been sent packing there and then. The presence of William helped to restrain the anger of S. Gedge Antiques, since there was more to lose than to gain just now by fixing a quarrel upon him; but it was clear that the old man did not intend to pass over the incident lightly.

"Niece," he began the moment his cup had been handed to him, "kindly tell me what you mean by gallivanting about London."

A hot flame of resentment ran in June's cheek. But she was too proud to express it otherwise than by rather elaborately holding her peace. She continued to pour out tea just as if not a word had been said on the subject.

"It's my fault, sir," said William, stepping into the breach chivalrously, but with an absence of tact. "Miss June very kindly consented to come and look at the Van Roon."

"There must be no more of it." Miss June received the full benefit of a north eye. "I will not have you going about with a young man, least of all a young man earning fifteen shillings a week in my employ."

It was now the turn of William's cheek to feel the flame, but it was not in his nature to fight over a thing of that kind, even had he been in a position to do so. Besides, it hardly needed his master to tell him that he had been guilty of presumption.

Indeed, the circumstances of the case made it almost impossible for either of the culprits to defend such conduct in the other's presence. Yet June, to the intense astonishment of Uncle Si, and no doubt to her own, contrived to give battle in hostile territory.

"I can only say," she remarked, with a fearlessness so amazing that Uncle Si scalded his mouth by drinking out of his cup instead of out of his saucer, "that if fifteen shillings a week is all that William gets, it is just about time he had a rise in his wages."

For a moment Uncle Si could only splutter. Then he took off his spectacles and wiped them fiercely.

"Gracious goodness me! God bless my body and my soul!" June would not have been at all surprised had the old slave-driver "thrown a fit."

"William is very clever," she said undaunted.

"Niece, hold your tongue." The words came through clenched teeth. "And understand, once for all, that I'll have no more carryings-on. If you don't look out, you'll find your box in the street."

Having put June out of action, the old man turned his attention to William. But with him he walked more delicately. There must be no more Van Rooning, but the ukase was given in a tone so oily that June just had to smile.

In spite of his own edict, however, it was clear that Van Roon continued much in the mind of William's master. The next day, Sunday, instead of taking the air of the west central postal district, his custom as a rule, when the forenoon was fine, he spent most of the morning with the young man in the studio. June felt this boded so ill that she went about her household chores in a fever of anxiety. She was sure that Uncle Si had fully made up his mind to have the picture; he meant, also, to have it at his own price. However, she had fully made up hers that this tragedy simply must not occur.

XIV

JUNE, preparing for dinner a Yorkshire pudding, brought an acute mind to bear on the still graver problem before it. What would happen when Uncle Si found out that William had been persuaded to give her the picture? It was a question she was bound to ask, yet she dare not foretell the answer. William and she were completely in his power. Wholly dependent upon the food and lodging the old man provided and the few shillings a week with which he grudgingly supplemented them, they could not afford to come to an open breach with him; at the same time to June's practical mind, it would be an act of sheer madness to give up the rare thing that fortune had put into their hands.

Her need just then was the advice of some able and disinterested friend. There was only her power of putting two and two together to tell her that the picture might be worth a large sum. And even that did not allow her to know for certain; she must find a means of making sure. Unhappily, there was not one person in the world to whom she could turn for advice, unless it was William himself; and in plain matters of business he seemed so hopelessly at sea—if they involved dealings with his master at all events— that June was convinced he would be no use at all.

Beating up an egg for the Yorkshire pudding, she felt a deep concern for what was now taking place up that second pair of stairs in the garret next the tiles. Vainly she wished that she had had the sense to ask William to keep back as long as possible the fact that he had given the picture to her. But the mere request would have opened the door to another anxiety. If the picture was what he thought it was, could such a gift, made in such circumstances, be regarded as irrevocable? That must be left to the giver himself to decide: assuming the simpleton had enough strength of mind to prevent Uncle Si deciding it for him.

The pudding was just ready for the oven when she heard Uncle Si come downstairs. He went into the parlour, where every Sunday morning, with the help of the *Exchange and Mart* and half an ounce of shag, he spent an hour in meditation. As soon as the door closed upon the old man, June ran attic-wards to confer with William.

There was no beating about the bush. Bursting in upon him breathlessly, she cried: "I hope you have not told Uncle Si the picture is mine. I had meant to warn you not to do so on any account—not for the present, at least."

William looked up from the treasure with his absorbed air; but it appeared that as yet he had not let the cat out of the bag.

"I am very glad." June breathed freely again.

"I thought," said William sadly, "it would be best not to tell the master until after his dinner. But I fear that whenever he knows it will upset him terribly."

"Why should it?"

"It's like this, Miss June—the master is fairly setting his heart upon this picture."

"Then he'd better unset it," said June harshly.

Trouble came unmistakably into the expressive face of the picture's late owner.

"I am afraid it will be quite a blow to him if he doesn't get this beautiful thing," he said, gazing affectionately at what he held in his hand.

"And yet he thinks so little of it?"

"Oh no! Not now. This morning after a careful examination he's changed his mind."

June was not impressed by this face-about on the part of S. Gedge Antiques. "If you ask me," she declared scornfully, "he changed his mind some time ago. But he's a bit too artful to let you know that."

"But why?" said William perplexedly.

"Don't you see that he thinks the more he cheapens it the easier it will be to get it from you?"

William could not bring himself to take so harsh a view.

"What does he offer for it now?" the new owner of the Van Roon sternly inquired.

"You are not fair to the dear old master, believe me, Miss June." The young man spoke with charming earnestness. "He has such a reverence for beauty that he cannot reckon it in terms of money. This morning I have brought him to see with my eyes." Pride and affection deepened in the voice of the simpleton. "He has now such a regard for this lovely thing that he will not be happy until he possesses it, and I shall not be happy until you have given it to him."

June was simply aghast.

"But—but it was given to me!"

"I know—I know." The giver was pink with confusion. "But you see, Miss June, your uncle has quite set his heart on it. And I am wondering if you will return it to me, so that I may offer it to him, as a token of my love. No one could have had a better or kinder master. I owe everything to him." Suddenly, however, the young man was aware of her dismay. "I do hope you will not mind too much," he said, anxiously. "If you will allow me, I will give you something else."

June averted her eyes. "You gave me this. And you can't believe how much it means to me."

"Yes, I know you have a great feeling for it. To part with it will hurt you, I can see that. But please think of the dear old master's disappointment if he doesn't get it."

"He merely wants it to sell again."

"You are unjust to yourself, Miss June, in thinking so. Money does not enter into your feeling about this beautiful thing; it doesn't enter into mine. Why should it enter into the master's, whose love of art is so intense?"

"Because his love of money is intenser. It's his ruling passion. Where are your eyes that they can't see a thing as plain as that?"

She must be as gentle as she could with this absurd fellow, yet she feared that such words must cause a wound. And the wound was wilfully dealt. It was so important that he should be made to see the whole thing as really and truly it was. But her hope was slight that he would ever be brought to do so.

"I beg you," he said, almost with passion, "to let me have it back, so that I may give it to the dear old master."

"It is madness," said June bitterly. "He has no true feeling for the picture at all."

She saw that her words were unwise. They made her own position worse. But faced by such an appeal she had to do her best on the spur of the moment.

"I know how much it means to you." Pain was clouding the eyes of this dreamer. "I know your love for it is equal to mine, but that will make our joy in giving it to your uncle so much the greater."

"But why to Uncle Si—of all people?"

"He wants it." William's voice was low and solemn. "At this moment, I believe he wants it more than anything else in the world."

June said with scorn: "He wants it as much as he wants a thousand pounds. And he doesn't want it more. I believe money is his god. Think of the fifteen shilling he pays you a week. It makes my blood boil."

A quick flush sprang to the young man's cheek. "Money has nothing to do with this, Miss June."

"It has to do with everything."

Delicately he ventured to contradict. "Where love is, money doesn't come in. I simply want to offer this priceless thing to the old master out of a full heart, as you might say."

"Then you shouldn't have parted with it." She hated herself for her words, but she was not in a mood to soften them. "You have already had the pleasure of giving it to me, therefore it is only right that you should now deny yourself the pleasure of giving it to Uncle Si. It is like eating your cake and having it."

William was not apt in argument, and this was cogent reasoning. He lacked the wit to meet it, yet he stuck tenaciously to his guns. "When you realize what this rare treasure means to the old man, I'm sure you'll change your mind."

June shook her head. Secretly, however, she felt like weakening a bit. In the wistful voice was a note that hurt. But she could not afford to yield; there was far too much at stake. "I shall have to think the matter over very carefully," she temporised. "And, in the meantime, not a word to Uncle Si that the picture's mine."

She mustered the force of will to exact a promise. Bewildered, sad, a little incredulous, he gave it.

"*I hope he doesn't hate me half as much as I hate myself,*" was the swift and sickening thought that annihilated June, as she ran from the studio, having recollected with a pang of dismay that she had not put in the pudding for dinner.

XV

DINNER was a miserable meal. The Yorkshire pudding was light, the roast sirloin was done to a turn, the potatoes were white and floury, the kidney beans were tender, but June could find nothing in the way of appetite. The mere presence of William at the other side of the table was almost more than she could bear. So keen was her sense of a terribly false position that she dare not look at him. What did he think of her? How must she appear to one all high-minded goodness and generosity?

Surely he must know, after what had just passed, that her love of the picture was mere base deceit. Surely he must hold such an opinion of her now that he would never believe or trust her again. And the tragedy of it was that she could not hope to make him see the real motive which lay behind it all.

Seated at the table, making only a pretence of eating, but listening with growing anger and disgust to the artful change she now detected in the tone of Uncle Si, it was as if the chair in which she sat was poised on the edge of an abyss. William must despise her quite as much as she despised the Old Crocodile, was the thought which turned her heart to stone.

S. Gedge Antiques having had the wit to discover the set of the wind, had begun most successfully to trim his sails. An hour's careful examination of the picture that morning had convinced him that he had underrated its merits. There was very good work in it, and as a lifelong lover of art—with a devout glance at William—good work always appealed to him. But whether the thing, as a whole, was to be rated as highly as William put it, was decidedly an open question. Still the picture had merit, and personally he should treasure it as much for William's sake as for its own.

June realized that it was now the turn of this cunning old fox to make love to the Van Roon's owner. But was he cunninger than she? Yet what concerned her more than anything just now was the plain fact that he had already managed to persuade himself that the treasure was his property.

This was not the hour to disabuse his mind. And no matter when that hour came she foresaw a dire quarrel. She was now involved in a business to strain all the resources of her diplomacy. But William needed help. Cost what it might the task devolved upon her of looking after his affairs.

William, meanwhile, in his own peculiar way, seemed not averse from looking after hers. After dinner her first duty was to clear the table and wash up; and he simply insisted upon bearing a hand. He carried the tray into the back kitchen, and then, almost with defiance, presided at the washing of the crockery, while she had to be content with the humbler office of drying it.

"It's your hands I'm thinking of, Miss June."

"My hands are no affair of yours," was the terse reply.

The lover of beauty shyly declared that such hands were not meant for such a task.

"Nothing to write home about—my hands aren't."

Politely sceptical, William drew from his pocket a bit of pumice stone.

"It is to take the soils out of your fingers," he said, offering this talisman shyly.

June's face was now a tawny scarlet. She did not know whether to laugh or to be angry. Yet how was it possible to be angry with a creature who was so charmingly absurd?

"May I take them out for you?"

The answer was "no."

But somehow her face must have said "yes." For without more ado, the amazing fellow took one of her hands and with nice discretion began to apply the pumice stone.

"There, now," he said finally.

A stern rebuke trembled upon her lips, yet with the best will in the world it could not find a form of words whereby to get itself uttered.

XVI

A LITTLE later in the day Uncle Si came into the back kitchen where June was at work. It seemed that he had an announcement to make.

"Niece, there's a piece of news for you. I've decided to take Mrs. Runciman back."

June saw no reason why Mrs. Runciman should not be taken back. Indeed, she would welcome the return of the charwoman. It would certainly reduce the burden of her own labours which was by no means light.

"You and I are not going to hit it off, I can see that. Already there's been too much of your interference. Next thing you'll upset that boy. And I wouldn't have that happen—not for a thousand pounds. So I think the best thing I can do is to take Mrs. Runciman back, and get her to find you a job."

"For me!" said June slowly. "Mrs. Runciman find a job for me!"

"If she comes you'll have to go. I can't afford to keep a couple o' women eating their heads off. The times don't run to it."

"What sort of a job do you expect a charwoman to find for me?" June asked, biting her lip.

"She may know of somebody who wants a domestic help. As far as I can see, you are not fitted for anything else."

That was true enough, as June felt with a sharp pang. She was a girl without any sort of training except in the tedium of housework. No other career was open to her and she was going to be turned adrift. There came a hot flame to her cheeks, a sting of quick tears to her eyes. She was a proud and ambitious girl; never had she felt so keenly humiliated.

"If you stay here," said Uncle Si, "you're sure to upset that boy. And, as I say, rather than that should happen I'd pay a thousand pounds to a hospital."

June didn't reply. But in a surge of feeling she went up to her attic, and with rage in her heart flung herself full length on the bed.

The blow was fully expected, yet that hardly made the weight of it less. Soon or late this miser was bound to turn her out of doors; yet coming at such a time "the sack" was in the nature of a calamity.

Well, she must face it! Domestic service was the only thing to which she could turn her hand, and that, she foresaw, was likely to prove a form of slavery. A future, hard, confined and miserable, lay in front of her.

Bitterly she regretted now that she had not been able to fit herself for some other way of life. She had had a reasonably good education, as far as it went, in her native town of Blackhampton, where her father at one time had been in a moderately good position. But he had died when she was fourteen. And her mother, with health completely broken several years before her death had been left so badly off that June, perforce, had to give up all thoughts of a wider field. Stifling vague ambitions, she had bravely submitted to the yoke but, in spite of a sense of duty honestly, even nobly done, the sequel was a grim distaste of household drudgery. And this had not been made less by a month under the roof of S. Gedge Antiques.

With a gnawing sense of misery that was like a toothache, June slid off the bed and looked at herself in the cracked mirror which adorned the crazy dressing-table. Her only assets were comprised in her personal appearance. Instinctively she took stock of them. Alas, as she beheld them now, they were pretty much a "washout."

First to strike her was the tell-tale redness of her eyelids, and that disgusted her to begin with. But, apart from that, she felt in her own mind that her personality was not really attractive. Her education was small, her life had been restricted and narrow; and now there seemed no way out.

Honestly she was not pretty, she was not clever, and she knew next to nothing of the world. Even at Blackhampton, where the supply of smart girls was strictly limited, she had never passed for anything out of the common. She had felt sometimes that her nature was too serious. In a girl a serious nature was a handicap, she had once heard Mr. Boultby, the druggist at the corner of Curzon Street, remark. One "asset," however, she certainly had. The mop of golden-brown hair had always been her stand-by, and Mr. Boultby, that man of the world, had paid her compliments upon it. An artist would revel in it, he had said. Certainly there was a lot of it, and the colour having aroused comment even in her early days at the High School among her form-mates, it was no doubt rather striking. She was also inclined to be tall and long in the leg, she knew that her shoulders and chest were good, she prided herself upon the neatness of her ankles, yet at the back of her shrewd mind lurked the fear that the general effect must be plainness, not beauty. She had heard Mr. Boultby, always a friend, describe her as "unusual," but she had felt that it was his polite way of saying she was not so good-looking as she might be.

No, wherever her fortune might lie, it was not in her face. Once or twice, in her romantic Blackhampton phases, which at best were very brief and few, she had thought of the stage. But one month of London had convinced her that it was not her line. Considering her inexperience of life her fund of horse sense was rather remarkable. She was a great believer in the doctrine of "looking facts in the face." And the fact she had to meet now was that she was not in any way pretty or talented. Unless you were one or the other, and

London teemed with girls who were both, the doors of the theatre were locked and barred.

Back on the edge of the bed, she began to consider the question of learning shorthand and typing, so that she might become a clerk in an office. But her means were so scant that the plan was hardly feasible. Really it seemed that no career was open to her, other than the one she loathed. And then the thought of William came. At once, by a strange magic, it eased the pressure. Heart, brain and will were merged in an immediate task; she must stand between this child of nature and the avarice of his master.

The sudden thought of William brought courage, tenacity, fighting power. She knew that at this moment he was the other side the wall. An impelling need urged her to go to him. Forgetful of red and swollen lids she got up at once and went and knocked on the studio door.

A familiar voice said, "Come in!"

William, as usual in that room, was pottering about amid oils, canvasses and varnish. He was in shirt sleeves, he wore a large apron, his shock of fair hair, which gave him the look of a poet, was rumpled, there was a smudge on his cheek, but the absorption of his eyes, their look of intensity, half filled her with awe.

She had really come to tell him that she was going to be sent away. But as soon as she found herself in his presence she was overcome by sheer pride. From the first this young man had treated her with a deference which implied that she was of a clay superior to his own. His bearing towards her always stressed the fact that she was the niece of his good master, and that he was a servant humbly grateful for his fifteen shillings a week.

At first this attitude had fed her vanity in a subtle way. But now, in present circumstances, it seemed almost to enrage her. It was quite absurd that a man of such distinguished talent should place her upon a pedestal. The truth of the matter was she was unfit to lace his shoes, and it was amazing that he did not know it.

Upon her entrance William had immediately risen from his stool, and had bowed slightly over the pot of varnish he held in his hand, with a half-humorous air of homage, as some famous chemist might have done when disturbed by a great lady in the midst of his wonderful researches. "I know it's not me you have come to see," his gentle manner seemed to say; "it is this marvellous thing on the easel at my elbow."

All the same it was William she had come to see. She had come to him for countenance and sympathy. And it did not help her at all that she should be treated with a shy reserve. She craved to be told that she had come to mean something to him; she craved to be told that his fastidious concern for her hands, and the regard he had for a beauty in which she herself did not believe was more than mere chivalry towards women in general. Alas, in spite of the eager friendliness of her reception this was not apparent. In the eyes of William she was just the master's niece, and the incident of the pumice stone was without significance, beyond the fact that he was no more than the least of her servants.

It was very exasperating.

"But if you are wise," said a voice within, "you will not let this Gaby know that you think so."

XVII

JUNE spent a worried and disconsolate night. She had very little sleep. Time and again she listened to the melancholy drip-drip of rain on the eaves just over her head. Never in her life had she felt so wretched. She was horribly lonely, without resources or friends. How she was to live through the endless years of servitude and dependence on the will of others that lay ahead she did not know.

To keep on telling oneself to bear up seemed of little use. She had had to do that each hour of each day since her mother's death. The prospect of being cast upon the world was indeed dispiriting, yet in the end it might turn out better than to sacrifice one's youth upon the altar of such a Moloch as Uncle Si.

As people who sleep ill are apt to do, she fell into a comfortable doze just about the time she ought to be getting up. Thus, to her dismay, she entered upon the trying institution known as Monday morning at a quarter past seven instead of half past six.

"Uncle Si will be growling for his breakfast in another quarter of an hour," was the thought that urged her into her clothes with a frantic haste. One twist she gave and no more, without so much as a glance in the glass, at the mane of brown gold hair, and then she flew downstairs, buttoning the front of her dress.

A fire was burning in the kitchen grate, and upon it slices of bacon were sizzling in a frying-pan; the cloth was laid for breakfast; moreover, the parlour was already swept and dusted. In fact, at the precise moment of June's belated appearance upon the scene, William, with a businesslike air, was returning from a visit to the dustbin.

When they met in the passage by the scullery she came within an ace of rebuking him. "Even if I oversleep myself you've no right to be so officious," was the sharp phrase which rose to her lips. But a saving sense of justice, not always at the service of the female soul, held it back. After all, such kindness and devotion were worthy of respect; he had saved, besides, an unpleasant scene with Uncle Si.

"Oh, thank you, William, ever so much," she had the grace to murmur, hoping as she hastily disposed of the last button of her dress, that he wouldn't notice she had come down, "half undone."

"Please don't mention it, Miss June," he said, with the politeness of a courtier, as he returned the empty dustpan to its home beneath the scullery sink. "As you didn't seem quite yourself last night I was hoping you would not get up at all this morning. I was going to bring your breakfast up to you, and set it outside your door."

"Oh, but you are much too kind." A sudden fierce rush of colour made her cheeks burn horribly. He was a very nice fellow, even if he was not so bright in some things as he ought to be.

Uncle Si, by the grace of providence, was a few minutes late for his breakfast. This seldom happened for, as a rule, he was the soul of punctuality. However, he was going down to Newbury by the nine o'clock from Paddington to attend a sale; in consequence, he had bestowed far more pains upon his appearance than was usual at this early hour. He was in a fairly good humour. The fact that the charwoman's return would enable him "to fire" his niece had cheered him so much that for once he had slept like a just man.

"Don't expect me until supper time," he said to June, as he put on his high felt hat and his macintosh, and grasped the knobbed stick, as ugly as himself, which invariably accompanied his travels. "And my advice to you, my girl, is to think over very carefully what I said to you last night."

With an air of quiet satisfaction, S. Gedge Antiques stepped briskly forth into a soft autumn day where the sun as yet could not quite make up its mind to greet him.

It was to be a day of great events. And the first of these began to materialise shortly before eleven when June chanced to enter the shop. William, just at that moment, was fathoms deep in conversation with a customer. The customer was very tall, she was strikingly distinguished and, in the opinion of June, she was dressed exquisitely. Soft silk and faint blue Chinese embroidery clothed her with a dangerous beauty. But it was the coquetry of her hat, an artful straw wreathed wonderfully in flowers of many a subtle shade that gave the crowning touch.

The hat it was, no doubt, that completed William's overthrow. There was a look of rapture in the eyes with which the vain fellow regarded its wearer, for which June could have found it in her heart to slay him on the spot.

That tell-tale look was really a little too much. June could not help lingering on the threshold to watch these two. So shamelessly was William engrossed with this vision of pure beauty that there was not a chance of his eyes straying to look at her. And she would not have cared if they had. Such an irrational surge of jealousy was now in her heart that she would have welcomed his seeing what she thought of his gazing like that, even upon the grandest young woman in the land.

"So nice of you to take so much trouble," the fair customer said in a voice of such melody that June had to own that the celebrated Miss Banks, the daughter of Blackhampton's chief physician, whose charm of manner had ever remained in her mind as the high-water mark of human amenity, would now have to take second place.

"Not at all, madam," said William, in the William way. Even June had to admit that such fine courtesy, a little excessive, no doubt, was far removed from mere sycophancy. Had he not practised on her? For that reason she had a perfect right to feel furious; William's homage was far too inclusive. At the same time, there was no gainsaying that in this case he had every excuse. Regarded as the mirror of fashion and the mould of form, Miss Banks of Blackhampton was now a back number.

"The friend I sent it to liked it very much indeed," said the Super-girl. "It was so exactly what she wanted. And if by chance you are able to match it, I shall be most grateful."

William, with that divine air of his, promised quite simply and sincerely to do his best.

"The price, too, was very moderate," said the Super-girl with the geniality of one who owns a province. Then suddenly she half turned, and her merry glance, assisted by a Miss Banksian stick-eyeglass was trained full upon the Hoodoo. "What a delicious monster!" The voice had quite a Brahms trill in it, not that June had ever heard of Brahms. "It reminds one of Edgar Allan Poe or the Grand Guignol."

Unabashed by culture, William stood to his full height. June could only marvel at his coolness.

"So Oriental. So grotesque. Makes one think of Ali Baba and the Cave of the Forty Robbers. Very valuable, of course?"

"No, I wouldn't exactly call it valuable." June hardly knew whether to admire or to deplore this candour. "And it takes up a lot of room, and absorbs a lot of light. Almost needs the British Museum, as you might say, to show it to advantage."

Again the Brahms trill, as the eye of the Super-girl travelled from the Hoodoo to William. "Those fearful eyes and those grinning jaws studded with crocodile's teeth make it look absolutely alive. And it's so perfectly hideous that one feels sure there must be a curse on it."

"Mr. Gedge declares there is."

"Really?" The eyes, the blue eyes of the Super-girl grew round and merry. "I'd love to have a thing with a curse on it—if it's a real one?"

"Mr. Gedge would part with it for a very reasonable sum I feel sure," said William, with a judicious air that June admired the more for being hardly able to credit it in him.

With the casual air so becoming to riches, the young woman asked the price.

"Twenty pounds would buy it," she was informed.

"Curse and all?"

"Curse and all, madam." William had a nice sense of humour, which June had discovered before she had known him an hour, but in this big moment he did not relax a muscle.

For about a quarter of a minute the Super-girl looked again at the Hoodoo. And then with the air of one who takes a great decision, she gave the ugly chin a playful tap and said: "I believe the long gallery at Homefield is the very place for you, my friend. You may not be a thing of beauty, but at the far end I am sure you would be a joy for ever!" She made then such fine play with her stick-eyeglass, that Miss Banks was put off the map altogether. "And a real live curse given in, I think you said?"

William bowed a grave affirmative.

It was clear that Miss Blue Blood was intrigued. She folded, unfolded, refolded her stick-eyeglass; she looked the Hoodoo up, she looked the Hoodoo down, standing three paces back in order to do so. "Before I really decide"—addressing the monster in a voice of warm caresses—"I must get my father to come and look at you, my dear. He's wiser than I in these matters. You might kill all the pictures in the long gallery."

At this point William bowed again with exceeding deference. But here was not the end. The stick-eyeglass lit on the bowl of Lowestoft, which the Sawney who was turning out to be not quite such a sawney as he seemed, had picked up in his recent travels in Suffolk.

"I like that. What a charming piece!"

Mr. Half-Sawney held the charming piece to the light for Miss Stick-eyeglass to gaze upon.

"Yes—really quite charming!"

Their heads were so close while together they bent over its beauties, that June, without wishing real harm to either, could have found it in her heart to hope that the bowl might fall from the hands of William and break into a thousand pieces.

"What is the price?"

The bowl was turned on to its base while the young man glanced at the mystic code which had been traced by the hand of S. Gedge Antiques.

"Six guineas, madam," she was most deferentially informed.

"I collect Lowestoft. A charming piece. It will go so well with my others. Will you kindly send it to 39b, Park Lane?"

"Certainly, Miss Babraham."

The amazing Miss Babraham opened a vanity bag, took out a sheaf of notes, and chose six which, with the smile of a siren, she handed to William, who received them with one more bow from his full height, and proceeded to write out a receipt.

Somehow this transaction was altogether too much for June. Flashing one long last glance of immeasurable venom upon the stick-eyeglass who, all unconscious of the deadly passions it had aroused, had now returned to elegant and final contemplation of the Hoodoo, the niece of S. Gedge Antiques withdrew hurriedly to the scullery sink, filled a bucket of water, and proceeded with a kind of contained fury to scrub the floor of the larder.

XVIII

WHEN William came in to dinner there was music to face. But as there was no sure ground at the moment for real battle, the music opened *pianissimo*. It began with a few rather pointed enquiries.

"Had a rather busy morning, haven't you?"

"I don't think it has been anything out of the way," was the non-committal answer.

"Done any business?" The question was casual, but June fixed him with her eye.

"Oh, yes!" So light and airy was the tone that business might have mattered nothing. "I've sold the Lowestoft bowl."

"Uncle Si'll be pleased, I expect." She found it terribly difficult to keep a sneer out of her voice, but you never know what you can do till you try. "Fetch much?"

She knew perfectly well, of course, the price it had fetched.

"Six guineas!"

"Isn't that a pretty good profit on what you paid for it at Saxmundham?" said June, with the precision of the born head for affairs.

"I got it for thirty shillings at Saxmundham, but of course that was at a sale."

"Seems a fair profit, anyway."

"Yes, I suppose it is."

"Will you get any?"

"Oh no!" said William, trying to spear a pickled walnut in a glass jar.

"Then I think it's an infamous shame that the whole of that six guineas should go into the pocket of Uncle Si."

With a polite shake of the head, William dissented. "But don't you see, I couldn't have bought it unless the master had given me the money, and also marked the catalogue."

"It was your brains that bought it. And your brains sold it, too. I think you ought to see that Uncle Si is simply living upon them."

"No, no, Miss June," said William staunchly. "Please don't forget that it is the master who taught me everything."

June declined to argue the point. She knew it was no use. For the hundredth time she was up against his fixed idea. Besides, there was something else to talk about.

"To whom did you sell that beautiful bowl?" Her voice was that of the dove.

"I sold it to a Miss Babraham," said the Sawney in a voice of perfectly stupendous impersonality.

"To a Miss Who?"

She had caught the name quite clearly, and not for the first time that day, but there was a kind of morbid fascination in toying with a subject which was really without significance, and could lead nowhere. All the same she pined for an insight into the workings of the mind of this strange young man who was such a baffling mixture of the over-simple and the highly gifted.

"Her name is Miss Babraham."

"Who is she when she is at home?"

She tried hard to imitate a detachment which was a little uncanny, yet knowing all the time that she was making a sad hash of the performance. The trick seldom comes easy to the daughters of Eve.

"Who did you say she was?"

"Her father is Sir Arthur Babraham." The impersonality of William made her writhe.

"Oho!" said June, still trying her best to rise to William's level, and fully conscious that she was failing miserably. "One of the big bugs, eh?"

It was vulgar, she knew, to speak in that way. Among the things she had learned at the Blackhampton High School was a due and proper regard for baronets. Miss Preece, its august headmistress, would have been shocked, not merely by her tone, but also by her choice of words. But High School or no High School, the intrusion of Sir Arthur Babraham suddenly made her see red. She must be vulgar—or burst!

"What you'd call one of the smart set, I suppose?" said June abruptly breaking a long and rather trying pause. "Well, I don't think much of her stick-eyeglass, anyway."

Terrific disparagement of Miss Babraham, her works and her belongings was intended, yet to the queer creature seated opposite who by now was almost ready for the tapioca pudding, which had been so carefully prepared for him, it did not seem to imply anything at all.

"You take no stock of smart sets, I dare say," said June, with growing truculence. "You've never heard of them, have you? China tea sets are more in your line, aren't they?"

That was real wit, and people far less clever than this Sawney—a contradiction in terms and yet the only word which seemed to describe him after all!—must have seen the force of it. But not he! He solemnly rose and collected the plates, and then fetched in the tapioca pudding for all the world as if there was absolutely no point in the remark.

"Who did you say that tall girl was?" said June, returning mothlike to the flame, as she helped the Sawney very substantially to his favourite dish.

"Miss Babraham!"

"And who did you say her father was?"

"Sir Arthur Babraham!"

"And what might *he* do for a living?"

This was not ignorance. It was mere facetiousness. She knew quite well that no Sir Arthur Babraham since first invented by that ridiculous monarch, King James, had ever done anything for a living. But it was good to feel how such a "break" would have hurt Miss Preece.

"He's one of the richest men in England," said William, dipping his spoon into his tapioca with an impersonality which approached the sublime.

June knew that. There was the daughter of Sir Arthur Babraham to prove it.

"One of Uncle Si's best customers, I suppose?"

"Doesn't often come here. But he has wonderful taste."

"In daughters?" said June sardonically.

"In everything. Only last night I read in the paper that there isn't a better judge of pictures living."

June merely said "Oh!"

"He's one of the trustees of the National Gallery, you know."

"Oh!" said June.

"And owns a very fine private collection of the Dutch School."

"Does he?" It was June's turn now to be impersonal; in fact, it was up to her to let him see that it would take more than Sir Arthur Babraham and a private collection of the Dutch School to impress her.

"I suppose his daughter is what you'd call rather *fetching*?" She had once heard the word on the lips of the admired Miss Banks at a charity bazaar.

But in William's opinion it was not adequate to the occasion.

"To my mind," he said, and his voice fell, "she's a non-such."

June stepped midway in the act of bestowing upon him a second helping of tapioca.

"She's a what?" she demanded fiercely.

"A museum piece, Miss June." His enthusiasm was restrained but none the less absurd. "She's hallmarked. She walks in beauty." A blush, faint yet becoming, slowly overspread William's delicately tinted complexion.

June snorted. Had it been within the province of eyes to slay, this Gaby would have had no use for a second helping of tapioca.

"Glad to know that!" said June, homicidally. "As you are so set on beauty, you must have had an interesting morning."

A disgracefully impersonal silence was William's only answer. The deadliness of the observation seemed completely lost upon him. But was it?—that was the question for gods and Woman. Such a silence might mean anything.

"I suppose you'd say she had wonderful taste?"

"Miss Babraham?"

"No, Joan of Arc," said Woman, venomously.

"Her taste is very good indeed—that is, in some things."

"In hats, I suppose."

"I meant in old china," said the impersonal one. "I've never known her to make a mistake in old china."

"That's interesting." It was a weak remark, but June had seldom felt less conversationally brilliant.

Silence again. A third helping of tapioca was politely declined. June then pushed across the cheese. William removed its cover, and disclosed an extremely meagre piece of Leicestershire.

"Please may I give you a little?" he asked, with his inimitable air.

"There'll be none for yourself if you do. Besides, I don't want any. No thank you." She remembered her manners, although that was not easy just now. "I'll go out presently and buy some more. I'd quite forgotten the cheese."

"Please—please take this tiny piece."

"When I say no, I don't mean yes," said June, tempering strength of character with calm politeness. "I can't imagine Miss Babraham eating a piece of Leicestershire cheese in a dirty overall—can you?"

The remark was so irrelevant that it verged upon the grotesque. Heaven knows from what malign impulse it sprang. No girl in her senses would ever have made it. Giant Despair and the Hag Desperation must have been its sponsors.

It was quite open to William to follow the line of least resistance and ignore the question. A William less true-blue, a William less a gentleman right through to the core might without dishonour have done so. But this was a William of a nobler clay.

"Miss June, your overall isn't dirty."

The rich sincerity of these six and a half little words seemed gravely to imperil the whole sublime edifice of his impersonality.

He was contradicted flatly for his pains; yet she knew in her heart that whether the overall was dirty or whether it was clean, the renegade was already half forgiven.

"What did you think of her dress?" This new on-rush of irrelevance was despicable, but she seemed quite to have lost control of herself.

"It was perfect. To my mind, nothing is more becoming to a tall lady than a dress of soft dark blue silk."

Dyed-in-the-wool idiot! As though it was not his clear and obvious duty never even to have noticed whether Miss Babraham wore a dress of soft blue silk or a muslin with spots or a grey alpaca, or just a plain serge coat and skirt. Times there are when the stupidity of the human male has really no limit.

"Must have cost a pretty penny," said June acidly.

William shook his head, and boldly affirmed that it couldn't be bought for money.

"That's just nonsense," said June tartly. "There isn't a dress in the world that couldn't be bought for money."

"What I really mean is, to have a dress which looked like that, you would also have to buy the wearer," said William the amazing.

June expressed a ripe scorn by vehemently beginning to clear the table. High time, certainly. They had been discussing cold mutton and pickled walnuts and tapioca pudding and Leicestershire cheese and things and women for one solid hour by the Queen Anne clock, a real antique, in the middle of the chimneypiece, for which S. Gedge had lately refused the sum of forty guineas.

XIX

IN the course of the afternoon, June found herself immersed in the crisis of her fate. It began with a desire to own a dress of soft blue silk. This, she well knew, was insane. In the first place, she was still in mourning for her mother; in the second, she must hoard every penny of her slender means; in the third, was William's conviction that the success of a dress depended upon its wearer.

Not a shade of excuse could be found for this vaulting ambition. But it was fixed so firmly in the centre of her mind, that when she set out soon after three to order the cheese she could think of nothing else. The grocer was at the end of the street and two minutes did her business with him. And then in the toils of imperious desire she marched boldly down to Charing Cross and took a bus to Oxford Circus.

A yearning for a dress of blue silk was upon her like a passion. It was madness and yet it was very delicious. What could a blue silk dress avail when at any moment she was likely to be cast adrift? That thought hit hard as she sauntered slowly along the Street of Streets gazing wistfully upon its long array of too-fascinating drapers' windows.

Her store of worldly wealth was nineteen pounds and a few odd shillings. It was as certain as anything could be that she was about to enter upon the most critical period of her life, and this was all she had to tide her over. But do what she would to act like a reasonable being she was now at the mercy of a demon more powerful than common prudence. She was haunted by a passion for a blue silk dress and no matter what happened to her afterwards she must satisfy that craving.

It was a rather thrilling business to rake these forbidden windows in quest of a thing it was sheer madness to buy, yet within one's power to do so. Why was she going to buy it? Because she wanted it so badly? Why did she want it so badly? That was a question she could not answer.

Had she been really pretty this folly might have seemed less amazing. But she knew she was plain. At least, she always felt and always passed for plain at Blackhampton. But her pilgrimage along Oxford Street which, in the middle of a bright afternoon of early October, seemed the Mecca of fashion, beauty and good taste went some way to change the attitude she had taken up in regard to her personal appearance.

Plain she might be, her clothes might be severely provincial, their hue depressing, but she was clearly informed by the sixth sense given to Woman that she was not wholly unlooked at. It was nice to feel that such was the case; indeed, it was stimulating, yet so deeply was she occupied just then with large affairs that she didn't think much about it.

After many windows she had seen, she found herself drifting with the tide into a store of regal aspect. Here she was received by young women, elegant and gracious, with a courteous charm that made a search for five yards of blue silk fabric in its least expensive form a perfectly simple and yet delightful adventure. Moreover, it brought in its train a great idea. Was it necessary, after all, that domestic servitude should be her lot? Might it not be possible to become one of these smart and pleasant ladies in their very attractive clothes?

Expenditure of spirit, anxious care, went to the final purchase of four and a half yards of cotton silk material, more cotton than silk, at eight and elevenpence three farthings a yard; and then the new thought gained such a hold upon her, that before leaving the store she took an inventory of her person in one of the huge mirrors which made the place so enchanting. Standing boldly in front of the great glass, surveying herself with a curiosity that was half fear, she went over her "points" as might an Eastern merchant who buys a slave.

She was taller than she supposed. That was thought the first. And if she wore shoes with high heels, as so many girls did, she could look still taller. She could pass for slender, that was her second thought; and her chest was something to be proud of. She might not have much in the way of grace, and she might lack style, yet she didn't lack dignity. Her features were irregular, and there was no denying their freckles, but seeing her frontispiece this afternoon, with its fighting chin and determined eyes, the full effect was rather striking. But when all was said it was her hair that was important. This she had always known, but in the strong and subtle lights of the best mirror into which she had ever gazed, it ministered considerably to the sum and total of her charms. Perhaps her friend, Mr. Boultby the druggist, had not overshot the mark when he compared her hair to the Empress Eugenie's, and said it ought to be painted by an R. A.

A mop of russet gold hair was little enough for a girl who stood in her particular shoes. She felt that as she gazed upon it; felt it besides with something akin to resentment. But even a self-criticism, cool and stern, must allow that she made a better showing in Mr. Selfridge's mirror than could have been expected. She was far from being beautiful, but that hair in its subtle-tinted abundance saved her somehow from being ordinary. And to-day she looked very much alive with the bloom of youth and health.

Four and a half yards of blue material under her arm, she went out into Oxford Street, feeling rather better equipped for the battle of life. She drew back a pair of shoulders that were really not so bad, and defiantly lifted a chin that had looked uncommonly square in the mirror. It was good to feel that she had underrated herself. She must learn to dress in the London way, and then she might be able to hold her own.

Walking slowly back to Oxford Circus, head higher now, she began quite to like this new idea of becoming a shop assistant. At the worst, it would be a far easier and more dignified way of life than domestic service. So much was she engaged by it, and so great the pressure of her thoughts that at first she didn't notice that a man was following her.

The knowledge overtook her by degrees. Stopping to look in various windows, each time she did so brought a vague feeling that the eyes of a man were upon her. She crossed the Circus, but the feeling was still there; and at the corner of Berners Street, without quite knowing how, surmise entered the region of fact. Moreover, she even contrived to learn the style of man he was.

Out of the tail of an eye, as she stood by the edge of the kerb, she saw that he was pale and dark, neither short nor tall, that he had a slight moustache, and wore a hat of peach coloured velours. His presence gave her an odd feeling; in fact, it might be said to frighten her just a little, although there was certainly no reason why it should in broad daylight. But she had an idea that he was going to speak to her and that he was seeking an opportunity to do so.

Hastily she moved on, determined to give further shop windows "a miss" for the present. However, she had not gone far when it occurred to her that she was in need of a cup of tea, and that it would be very pleasant to have one.

Just across the road was an A. B. C. shop. The fear of pursuit still upon her, the sudden dash she made for this bourn was so ill-timed that her sovereign faculty of keeping her head in a crisis was needed to save her from being run over by Bus 13, which was going to the "Bell" at Hendon.

With quite a sense of adventure, she went to one of a row of vacant tables at the far end of the shop. She ordered a small pot of tea, a scone and a pat of butter. And then she realized that a pale, dark man, neither short nor tall, with a slight moustache, and wearing a hat of peach-coloured velours had followed her in, and was just about to take a seat at the table next her own.

XX

JUNE was not a timid girl. She had no lack of courage; and now that a chance had been given her to reason things out, a feeling akin to fear promptly yielded to mere annoyance. And even that emotion took wings when she had had time to glance at the hat of peach-coloured velours. Its owner looked harmless enough. He was a man of thirty, or perhaps a little more; he wore a well-cut black jacket, a pair of rather baggy trousers of a light grey check, a silk collar, a flowing bow tie, a diamond ring on the little finger of the left hand. The general effect of what to June was a decidedly interesting personality was somehow to fulfil her preconceived idea of an artist.

As soon as the man felt the gaze of June upon him, he swept off the hat of peach-coloured velours with a gesture at once easy and graceful, fortified it with a smile at which it would have been impossible to take offence, and said with a slight lisp,

"Miss Graham?"

"I am not Miss Graham," said June calmly. She always prided herself upon her self-possession. Just now it seemed to help her considerably.

The man carried off his question with such an air of tact that it must have ranked as a bona fide mistake had not June been aware that he had crossed the road and followed her into the shop. Rather strangely, as soon as he took it upon himself to speak to her, the lingering sense of vexation gave way to curiosity. The mere look of the man had the power to excite an immediate interest, but June was careful to keep strictly upon her guard.

He ordered a bottle of ginger beer, and when the waitress had gone for it, he turned to June and said, with the companionable air of an old friend: "It's funny, but you are exactly like a girl I used to know."

"Why funny?" asked June bluntly.

The nature of the question, and the look of June's keen eye made the man smile a little. Evidently she was a bit of a character. It appeared to stimulate him.

"It's always funny when you mistake someone for someone else."

"Is it?" said June, warily.

"Don't you agree," he said, with a laugh that sounded decidedly pleasant.

"It's a thing I should never think of doing myself."

"You are lucky." He was amused by her bluntness. "I wish I had your good memory."

The tea arrived, and June poured it out in a spirit of thankfulness. As soon as she had drunk half a cup, which was reviving, she forgot all about her annoyance in a new feeling of exhilaration tempered by quiet amusement.

"You are most remarkably like a Scotch girl I used to know in Paris," said the man, taking up the thread of conversation, after having drunk a little, a very little, ginger beer.

"Am I?" said June, coolly.

"She was an artist's model. Sometimes she used to sit for me."

"Are you an artist?" said June, allowing herself to become interested, for the reason perhaps that she simply could not help it.

"Of sorts," was the answer. "I studied several years in Paris before the war."

From the moment he had sat down at the next table and June had been able to get a clear view of him she had somehow known that art was his calling. He looked an artist so emphatically that there would have been something fatally wrong with the cosmos had he turned out to be anything else.

In spite of a determination to be cautious indeed, she was not equal to the task of repressing an ever growing curiosity. Art had lately come to have a magic meaning for her.

"What kind of pictures do you paint?"

"Portraits and the figure chiefly."

"Do you ever paint landscapes?"

"They are not quite my line of country," said the man. "Portraits and the figure are what I go for as a rule. I am looking for a model now. Would you like to sit to me?"

"I don't know." June spoke doubtfully. "I don't think I could."

"Haven't you ever sat?"

"No, I haven't."

"Time you began. You are just the sort of girl."

"Why am I?"

"For one thing you have personality."

This was a surprising and rather thrilling corroboration of Mr. Boultby. At the back of her mind the old druggist had always figured as "a bit of a gasbag" with a ready flow of conversation and a gift of easy compliment. But it would seem that this estimate did him less than justice. Mr. Boultby was better informed than she had thought. And at this moment a phrase he had used came back to her with a force that was a little startling. "A girl as good-looking as you can always get a living," Mr. Boultby had once said.

"I suppose you mean my hair?" said June naïvely.

He showed two rows of very white and level teeth in a smile which piqued her curiosity.

"Partly your hair, and partly your figure," he said, taking a second tiny sip of ginger beer. "Why not come and try? I have a studio in Haliburton Street, just out of Manning Square."

June shook a doubtful head. She then gave a glance sideways at the imbiber of the ginger beer. Her knowledge of the world was slender, but she was not a fool, and there was something about this "forthcomingness" which even exceeded that of Mr. Boultby himself, that warned her to be careful.

"You'd be well paid, of course."

"How much?" June had no false modesty when it came to a question of money. This was an aspect of the matter that had not struck her until then.

"I'd pay you five shillings an hour," he said lightly. "And ten for the altogether."

June's heart gave a leap. To a girl in her position it was a princely reward. Such an offer seemed most tempting. But a moment's consideration of the issues it raised brought on a sudden fit of shyness.

"I don't think I could," she said.

"Why not?" The eyes of the man were now fixed intently upon her face.

"Oh, I don't——"

"Not enough, eh?"

She felt his eyes so forcibly upon her that she coloured hotly.

"It isn't that."

"What's your reason then?"

"I've not been used to that sort of thing."

He smiled broadly.

"It's only a matter of keeping still. Of course, I shall not press you to sit for 'the altogether' if you had rather not."

"The altogether" was Greek to June.

However, she did not confess her ignorance, but was content to make a mental note to ask William what it meant. And at the moment she did so the thought of William brought the Van Roon to her mind.

"I suppose you know a lot about pictures?" An idea was forming already in that practical head.

"Perhaps I know as much about them as some people," said the man, beginning to roll a cigarette. June could not help feeling that his answer was in piquant contrast to what William's would have been had such a question been put to him. It had a self-complacency which even if it implied deep knowledge was also open to criticism.

"What do you think a Van Roon would be worth?"

"A Van Roon!" he said, offhandedly. "Well, you know, that might depend on many things."

"They are very valuable, I suppose," said June, trying to look innocent.

"Very valuable indeed, at the present time. Privately, I think they are overrated. The Flemish School is being run to death, but of course, that's only my opinion."

"Would it be worth a hundred pounds?"

"What! A Van Roon!" The man laughed. "My good girl, you might multiply a hundred pounds by a hundred, and then think you had got 'some' bargain if you found yourself the owner of a Van Roon."

"This mightn't be a good one." June spoke cautiously. She saw at once that it would be wise "to go slow."

"All Van Roons are good, you know. But some, of course, are a bit better than others."

"I've been told it is one of the best," said June, after a moment's deliberation.

"Which are you talking about? The one in the National Gallery, I suppose. That's the only Van Roon in this country. The Americans have robbed us of three within the last ten years."

"Yes, I've heard so," said June, with a wise air.

"In my humble opinion, it can't be compared with the chap in the Louvre, and they say that its stable companion, which was cut out of its frame back in the Nineties, and has never been found, is even finer."

"Still you think it's very valuable?"

"The one in the National Gallery? Sure! It wouldn't be there, you know, if it wasn't. The Flemish School is booming these days, and Van Roon is the pick of the bunch, and the least prolific. Tell me," the man's small and rather furtive eyes began to twinkle, "why are you so interested in Van Roons? Is it, by any chance, that you've got one for sale?" And he laughed very softly and gently at what he evidently considered a rich joke.

June looked at him gravely.

"It so happens that I have!" she said with a caution which seemed to give the value of drama to a simple announcement.

XXI

ADOLPH KELLER was the man's name. And as June was to learn later, he had never felt more amused in his life. It was really a jest that he should follow a countrified-looking girl into a teashop, get into conversation with her, and then be quietly told that she had a Van Roon to sell. There was something rather pathetic in a girl of her class making such a statement. All she could mean was that somehow she had got hold of a more or less "dud" copy of "Sun and Cloud," that much lithographed work in the National Gallery which in consequence was now familiar to the big public.

"So you've got a Van Roon for sale, have you?" said Adolph Keller, who was hardly able to keep from laughing outright. "Good for you! What's the size of it?"

"Sixteen inches by twelve," said June, with the patness of one who prided herself, and with reason, upon a most excellent memory.

"Without the frame?"

June nodded.

"Yes, that's about the size," said Keller. "It's called 'Sun and Cloud,' I suppose?"

"It's not called anything at present," said June, "as far as I know, although sun and cloud are in it."

"Bound to be—if it's a Van Roon."

"And there are trees as well."

"Trees, are there? A copy of the one in the National Gallery, I expect. Is there a windmill in the left hand corner?"

There was no windmill in the left hand corner, June declared with confidence. She remembered that at first William had thought there was, but had changed his opinion later.

"Then that washes out the National Gallery. I dare say it's a copy of 'L'Automne' in the Louvre. By the way, how did you come by it?"

"It was given to me by a gentleman, a friend of mine," said June, after a moment for reflection.

"A very good friend, too." The tone of the laugh had a little too much banter to be pleasant. "Isn't everybody, you know, who gives a Van Roon to his best girl? A bit of a plutocrat evidently."

June didn't know what a plutocrat was, but she was too proud to say so. She made a mental note to look up the word in the dictionary.

"How did your rich friend come by it? Do you happen to know?"

"He isn't rich," said June, with a wish for perfect honesty. "He found it in a shop."

"Where was the shop?"

"It was at a place called Crowdham Market."

"Down in Suffolk. Sounds a funny place to find a Van Roon."

"It was ever so dirty when it was found. And another picture seemed to have been painted on the top of it."

"Queer." The eyes of Adolph Keller narrowed in their intentness. "Who told you it was a Van Roon?"

"The man who gave it to me."

"Who told him?"

"He found the signature." June's quiet precision owed something to the fact that she was now fully and rather deliciously aware of the effect she was making.

"What!... The signature of Mynheer Van Roon?"

"Yes," said June.

The incredulity of Keller had yielded now to a powerful curiosity. He looked at June with a keenness he tried hard to veil. This was a very unlikely story, yet he knew enough of life to appreciate the fact that mere unlikelihood is no reason why a story should not be true. Besides, this girl had such an ingenuous air that it was impossible to believe her tale was a deliberate invention. At the same time, it had elements which were particularly hard to swallow.

"Why was the picture given to you?"

"I asked for it," said June, whose simple honesty now involved a tell-tale blush.

Mr. Keller looked her steadily in the eye, and then he laughed, but not unsympathetically.

"Your best boy, I suppose, and he could deny you nothing."

"That's it," said June awkwardly. This audacious irony was new to her, and she did not know how to meet it.

"By the way, what is this young chap of yours? An artist?"

"Yes," said June. "I suppose he is—in a way. He studies art and renovates pictures, and he knows a lot about them."

"Not so much as he thinks," said Adolph Keller, "else he would not be such a fool as to give away a Van Roon, even to a girl as nice and pretty as you are."

He had lowered his voice to a whisper of rare sweetness and carrying power. There was something about him that was powerfully attractive; at the same time, a look had crept into a pair of rather furtive eyes which was oddly repellent.

"Do you say you really have this picture in your possession?" His intentness when he put this question made June feel a little uncomfortable.

"Yes, it has been given to me."

"Could you let me see it?"

June hesitated.

"I think I could," she said, after a pause.

"Well, suppose you bring it round to my studio for me to look at?"

Again June hesitated.

"As you like, of course," said Keller, carelessly. "I was only thinking it might be worth your while, that's all. You see, I happen to know one or two dealers and people, and I might be able to find out for you just what it's worth."

June saw the force of this. She was in desperate straits, and this man had the appearance of a friend in need.

"Perhaps I will," she said.

"Very well," said the man. "When will you come?"

For a moment June thought hard. "I couldn't come before Thursday."

"The day after to-morrow—that'll suit me. What time?"

June continued to think hard. "It would have to be between three and four." She spoke with slow reluctance. "That's the only time I can really get away."

"All right," said the man, briskly. "You'll find me at the Haliburton Street Studios up till five o'clock on Thursday. Number Four. Give a good ring; the bell is a bit out of gear. My name is Keller. Can you remember it, or shall I write it down for you, with the address?"

"Write them down for me, please."

The man tore a leaf from a pocket book, and wrote his name and address with a fountain pen: Adolph Keller, 4 Haliburton Street Studios, Manning Square, Soho. When he had done this, and given it to her, he tore out another leaf and asked her to write down hers. This she accordingly did, and then the sudden thought of William's tea caused her to rise abruptly.

Mr. Keller wished to pay her bill, which was five-pence, but she declined to let him.

"Au revoir! Thursday afternoon. Manning Square is only about three minutes from here. Don't forget," were the words with which he took leave of her. "Bring it along. I dare say I'll be able to tell you whether it is genuine, and perhaps give you an idea of its value."

He laughed slightly, and then offered his hand in a very friendly manner. She took it with a reluctance she was rather ashamed of showing. He was so kind, so agreeable, so anxious to be of use that there seemed no warrant for the subtle complexity of feeling he had aroused in her.

XXII

JUNE'S way home to New Cross Street was beset with anxieties. Much would depend on what she did now. She felt that her whole life was about to turn on the decision she had to take in a very difficult matter.

There was no one to guide her, not a soul on whose advice she might lean. But before she had returned to the threshold of S. Gedge Antiques she had made a resolve to get immediate possession of the picture, and to let this Mr. Keller have a look at it. She did not altogether like him, it was true. But the feeling was irrational; she must be sensible enough not to let it set her against him without due cause. For he was a friend whom Providence had unmistakably thrown in her way, and there was no other to whom she might turn.

William was a broken reed. With all his perception and talent, he was likely to prove hopeless now that Uncle Si was setting his wits to work to obtain the picture for himself. William's devotion to his master's interest would be simply fatal to her scheme. For the sake of them both, June felt she must take a full advantage of the heaven-sent opportunity provided by this Mr. Keller.

Other decisions, too, would have to be made. As soon as Uncle Si knew the picture was hers, he would almost certainly carry out his threat of putting her in the street; at least she was no judge of character if the event proved otherwise. A means of livelihood must be sought at once. That afternoon's experience of Oxford Street had opened up new vistas, which, however, might lead nowhere. But even if she could not get employment in a shop Mr. Keller's offer of work as an artist's model at five shillings an hour must not be lightly put aside.

The first thing to be done, however, was to clinch William's gift of the picture once and for all. She made up her mind that it should be fully consummated before the return of Uncle Si from Newbury.

As soon as William had been given his tea she broached the subject. But when she asked for possession, there and then, his crest fell.

"I was still hoping, Miss June," the simpleton owned, "that you'd let the dear old master have this lovely thing. It has come to mean so much to him, you see. I will get another one for you."

"Not another Van Roon," said June, sharply.

"No, I'm afraid I couldn't promise a Van Roon." A cloud passed over William's face. "But I might be able to pick up something quite good, which perhaps you would come to like as much."

June shook a disconsolate head.

"I don't think," she said, in a slow voice, as she fixed her eyes on the wall in front of her, "there is another picture in the world I should value so much as that one. I simply love that picture."

William was troubled.

"The old master loves it, too."

"But you gave it me, you know." June was painfully conscious of a swift deepening of colour.

The plain fact was not denied.

"You mustn't think me very hard and grasping if I hold you to the bargain."

"No, Miss June. If you insist, of course the picture is yours."

"To do with just as I like."

"Why yes, certainly."

June proceeded to take the bull by the horns. "Very well," she said. "After supper, I shall ask you to hand it over to me, and I will put it in a place of safety."

William sighed heavily. He seemed almost upon the verge of tears. June simply loathed the part she was playing. The only consolation was that she was acting quite as much in his interest as in her own.

Uncle Si came in shortly before eight. He sat down to supper in quite a good humour. For once the old man was in high conversational feather.

It was clear that his mind was still full of the picture. Without subscribing for one moment to William's preposterous theory that the thing was a genuine Van Roon, he had had a further talk on the matter with his friend, Mr. Thornton, with whom he had travelled down to Newbury; and, he had arranged with that gentleman to bring his friend, Monsieur Duponnet, the famous Paris expert who was now in London, to come and look at it on Thursday afternoon. Monsieur Duponnet who knew more about Van Roon than anybody living, and had had several pass through his hands in the last ten years, would be able to say positively whether William was wrong, and S. Gedge Antiques was right, or with a devout gesture for which June longed to pull his ugly nose, vice versâ.

The time had now come for June to show her hand. Very quietly indeed her bolt was launched. William had given the picture to her.

The old man simply stared at her.

It was clear, however, that his thoughts were running so hard upon M. Duponnet and the higher potentialities that just at first he was not able to grasp the significance of June's bald statement.

So that there should be no doubt about the position June modestly repeated it.

"Given it to you!" said the old man, a light beginning to break. "How do you mean—given it to you?"

Calmly, patiently June threw a little more light on the subject. And while she did so her eyes were fixed with veiled defiance upon the face of Uncle Si. The thought uppermost in her mind was that he took it far better than could have been expected. "Given it to you," he kept on saying to himself softly. There was no explosion. "Given it to you," he kept on. He grew a little green about the gills and that was all.

At last he turned to William: "Boy, what's this? Is the girl daft?" The mildness of tone was astonishing.

William explained as well as he could. It was a lame and halting performance, and at that moment June was not proud of him. But she was even less proud of herself. The part she was playing, gloss it over as one might, was ignoble. And William's embarrassment was rather painful to witness. He stammered a good deal, he grew red and nervous; and all the while the voice of his kind and good master became more deeply reproachful, and melted finally in a note of real pathos. "How could you do such a thing?" he said. "Why you know as well as I do, my boy, that I would have given you anything in reason for that picture—anything in reason." And there he sat at his supper, the very image of outraged benevolence and enthusiasm, a Christian with a halo!

"Old Serpent" said the fierce eyes that June fixed upon his face. For a moment it looked as if the old wretch was going to shed tears. But no, he was content with a mild snuffle and that was all.

XXIII

By bedtime, when June went to her attic, she had fully made up her mind that there must be no half measures now. She feared Uncle Si more than ever. There was something in that snuffle at the supper table, in that whine of outraged feeling, in that down-gazing eye which was far more formidable than any mere outburst of violence. Here was such a depth of hypocrisy that she had got to look out.

A light was showing under the studio door. June's knock met with a prompt invitation to enter. William was affectionately lingering over a few final touches, which should prove beyond a doubt the authenticity of this masterpiece.

"Have you got it really clean at last?" said June, trying to speak lightly, yet not succeeding. Emotional strain could not be so easily concealed; and— uncomfortable thought—her acting was not so finished as that of Uncle Si.

"Yes," said William, with a little thrill of rapture. "And how wonderful it is!"

June agreed. "Yes, wonderful!" Also with a little thrill of rapture, yet loathing herself because her tone was so vibrant—Uncle Si was not to have a walk over after all! "And now if you don't mind I'll put it in a place of safety."

He flashed one swift glance at her. "But, Miss June, isn't it quite safe here?"

"I should just think it wasn't!" leapt to the tip of her tongue. But Uncle Si's masterly snuffle recalled to her mind the value of meiosis. Thus she had recourse to a gentle "I think I'll sleep better if I take care of it myself," which sounded quite disarming.

With one of his deep sighs which made her feel a perfect beast, William handed over the picture. "If you only knew, if you could only guess what pleasure this exquisite thing would give the dear old master——"

Overcome by a kind of nausea, June fled headlong to the room next door. She groped for her candle, found and lit it; and then she proceeded to bury the treasure at the bottom of her trunk. Heaping and pressing down as many things upon the picture as the trunk would hold, she locked it carefully, and put the key in her purse. Then she undressed, knelt and said her prayers; she then blew out the candle and crept into bed with a stifling sense of disgust, tempered by grim satisfaction.

XXIV

NEXT morning at the breakfast table, June looked for developments. To her surprise, however, things went their accustomed way, except that if anything Uncle Si was a little more amiable than usual. He made no reference to the Van Roon; but it was referred to in his manner, inasmuch that he bore bacon and coffee to his lips with the air of a known good man deeply wounded in his private feelings. Not a feather of this by-play was lost upon his niece; and no doubt what was of more importance, it was not lost upon William. But its impact was very different in the two cases. While June simply longed to hit the Old Crocodile upon his long and wicked nose, William seemed hard set to refrain from tears.

About midday, however, while June was in the back kitchen preparing a meal, Uncle Si came to her.

"Niece," he said, in the new voice, whose softness June found so formidable, "you remember the other day I told you to look for a job?"

June nodded.

"Have you got one?"

"No, I haven't."

"Well, Mrs. R. is coming back on Monday, so the sooner you get fixed up the better. Your best plan, I think, is to go this afternoon and have your name put down at a registry office as a cook-general. Cook-generals earn good money, and they live all found. Your cooking won't be the Carlton or the Ritz, of course"—a gleam of frosty humour played upon that subtle face—"but you seem strong and willing, and you know how to boil a potato, and no doubt you'll improve with experience."

June was inclined to curtsey. The old wretch plainly felt that he was giving her a handsome testimonial. But at the back of her mind was anger and contempt, and it was as much as she could do to prevent their peeping out.

After dinner, as soon as the table was clear, and the pots washed, she proceeded to take Uncle Si at his word. She decided to go out at once and look for a place which, however, except as a last resort, should not be domestic service. To begin with, she would try the shops, or perhaps the dressmakers, as her mother always said she was handy with her needle; or, failing these, she might consider the exciting proposal of becoming an artist's model.

Fixing her hat before the crazy looking glass the thought of Mr. Keller recurred to her mind. Had the day only been Thursday she could have taken the picture to him there and then, and had his opinion upon it. Not that such a course would have been altogether wise. She knew nothing about this new and rather mysterious acquaintance, beyond the fact that if speech and manner meant anything he was a gentleman. Certainly, to talk to he was most agreeable.

Before setting out on her pilgrimage, she had to make up her mind as to whether it would not be advisable to take the Van Roon with her, and put it in a place of safety. So long as it remained under that roof it was in jeopardy. Uncle Si was not to be trusted an inch. The fact, however, that she had nowhere to take the treasure decided her finally to let it stay where it was until the next day.

Anyway, it was under lock and key. That was something to be thankful for; yet as she came downstairs and passed through the shop into New Cross Street, drawing on her neat black gloves with a sinking heart, instinct told her that she was taking a grave risk in leaving the picture behind.

No, S. Gedge Antiques was not to be trusted for a moment. Of that she was quite sure. By the time she had gone twenty yards along the street this feeling of insecurity took such a hold upon her that she stopped abruptly, and faced about. To go back? Or not to go back? Indecision was unlike her, but never was it so hard to make up her mind. Could it be that Uncle Si was as wicked as she thought? Perhaps she had now become the prey of her own guilty conscience. In any case, she knew of nowhere just then in which to place the precious thing; and this fact it was that turned the scale and finally settled the question.

She went down to the Strand, and took a bus to Oxford Circus. That Mecca, alas, did not prove nearly so stimulating as the previous afternoon. As soon as she came really to grips with that most daunting of all tasks, "the looking for a job," her hopes and her courage were woefully dashed. Real pluck was needed to enter such a palace as David Jones Limited, to go up without faltering to some haughty overseer in a frock coat and spats and ask if an assistant was wanted.

Three times, in various shops, she screwed herself to the heroic pitch of asking that difficult question. Three times she met with a chilling response. And the only gleam of hope was on the last occasion.

"There is one vacancy, I believe," said Olympian Zeus. "But all applicants must apply by letter for a personal interview with the manager."

Sooner than renew the attempt just then, June felt she would prefer to die. A girl from the provinces, new to London and its ways, without credentials or friends, or knowledge of "the ropes" must not expect to be taken on, at any rate in Oxford Street.

Much cast down she returned to her teashop of yesterday. Seated at the same table, her mind went back to the fascinating acquaintance she had made there. Was it possible that a career had been offered her? Or was the suggestion of this new friend merely the outcome of a keen interest in the picture?

It could not be so entirely, because she clearly remembered that Mr. Keller had proposed her sitting to him as a model before she had mentioned the picture at all.

She went back to New Cross Street in a state of gloom; her mind was dominated by a sense of being "up against it." And this unhappy feeling was not softened by the discovery she made as soon as she entered that cold and uninviting garret. In her absence the lock of her trunk had been forced and the picture taken away.

The tragedy was exactly what she had foreseen. But faced by the bitter fact she was swept by a tempest of rage. It could only be the work of one person. Her fear and dislike of Uncle Si rose to hatred now.

In a surge of anger she went downstairs and in the presence of William charged Uncle Si.

"You've been at my box," she stormed.

He looked at her with a kind of calm pensiveness over the top of his spectacles.

"If you lock away things, my girl, that don't belong to you, I'm afraid you'll have to stand the racket." So lofty, so severe was the old man's tone that for the moment June was staggered.

"It's stealing," she cried, returning hectic to the attack.

Uncle Si waggled a magisterial finger in her face. "Niece," he said, with a quietude which put her at a disadvantage, "I must ask you not to make an exhibition of yourself. Have the goodness to hold your tongue."

June maintained the charge. "The picture's mine. William gave it me. You've broken open my box and stolen it."

S. Gedge Antiques, after a mild side glance in the direction of William, proceeded to fix a glacial eye upon his niece. "What I have to say is this." His tone was more magisterial than ever. "At present, my girl, you are under age, and as long as you live with me the law regards me as your guardian. And, as I have told William already, in my opinion you are not a fit and proper person to have the care of a thing so valuable as this picture may prove to be. Mind you,"—the old fox gave William a meaningful look—"I don't go so far as to say that it *is* valuable, but I say that it *might* be. And, in that case, I can't allow a mere ignorant girl from the country who, in a manner of speaking, doesn't know the letter A from a pig's foot to accept it from you, my boy. It's very generous of you, and I hope she's thanked you properly, but if I allow her to take it, some unscrupulous dealer is sure to bamboozle her out of it. That's assuming it's valuable, which, of course, I don't go so far as to say that it is."

"Thief!" stormed June. "Wicked thief!"

However, she knew well enough that it was a real pity to let her feelings get the better of her; it enabled the Old Crocodile to shine so much by comparison. He addressed himself to William in his most sanctimonious manner. For the good of all concerned, such a bee-yew-ti-ful thing—it sickened June to see the old humbug lift his eyes to heaven—must be cared for by him personally. An uneducated mawkin could not hope to appreciate a work of art of that quality, and if anything happened to it, as in such hands something inevitably must, William's master would never be able to forgive himself, he wouldn't really!

The old man spoke so gently and so plausibly and hovered at times so near to tears, that William would have been less than human not to have been moved by his words. Uncle Si had not the least difficulty in making clear to his assistant that he was swayed by the highest motives. His own private regard for the picture, which, of course, William must know was intense, did not enter into the case at all; but wisdom and experience declared that until Monsieur Duponnet of Paris had seen the picture it must remain in responsible hands.

"But I tell you the picture's mine, mine, mine!" cried June.

No, the picture was William's. That outstanding fact was emphasized again in his master's kindly voice. Was he not William's guardian also in the eyes of the law? Not for a moment could he think of allowing the young man in a fit of weak generosity to give away a thing that might prove to be a real work of art.

June was a little disappointed by William's attitude in the matter. The way in which he submitted to Uncle Si did him no credit. Surely the picture was his to do with as he chose; yet to judge by Uncle Si's handling of the affair the young man had no right to dispose of it. June deplored this lack of spirit. He should have fought for his own. At the same time, her mind was tormented by the unpleasant thought that he really wanted to revoke his gift.

The more she considered the position, the less she liked it. She could not rid herself of a feeling that she was playing an unworthy part. It was all very well to regard her actions as strictly in William's interest. But were they? She was haunted by a sense of having descended perilously near to the level of Uncle Si himself.

Anyhow, she had tried her best to outwit S. Gedge Antiques. And he had outwitted her. There was no disguising it. Both were playing the same game, the same crooked game, and it seemed that Uncle Si, as was only to be expected, was able to play it much better than could she. The artful old fox had bested her with her own weapons. Were they not equally unscrupulous? Was not William the toy of both?

XXV

IN the course of the next morning, June was informed by Uncle Si, with his most sanctimonious air that "he could not pass over her impudence, and that she had better pack her box and go." Moreover, that force might be lent to this ukase, he sternly summoned William from the lumber room, and ordered the young man to help her down with her box as soon as it was ready; and then he must fetch her a cab.

This was more than June had bargained for. She was expecting to be kicked out; but she had not looked for the process to be quite so summary. It did not suit her plans at all.

"Get a room for yourself in a decent neighbourhood," said the old man. "Mrs. Runciman will know of one, no doubt. You've money enough to keep you while you look for work."

June's swift mind, however, saw instant disadvantages. Secretly, she cherished the hope, a slender one, no doubt, of being able to discover where the picture was hid. Once, however, she left the house that hope would vanish. And it was painfully clear that it was Uncle Si's recognition of this fact which now made him so determined to be quit of her.

The old serpent was fully alive to what lay at the back of her mind. He knew that so long as she slept under his roof the picture could never be safe.

She was shrewd enough to size up the position at once. Reading the purpose in the heart of Uncle Si she told him plainly that much as she disliked her present address she did not propose to change it until her lawful property had been restored to her.

"You are going to leave this place within an hour, my girl, for good and all."

"I shall not," said June flatly. "Until you give me the picture, I don't intend to stir."

"The picture is not yours. You are not a fit person to have it. And if you don't go quietly your box will be put into the street."

"Dare to touch my box again, and I shall go straight to the police."

Uncle Si didn't care a straw for the police. She had not the slightest claim upon him; in fact she was living on his charity. As for the picture, it had nothing whatever to do with the matter.

At this point it was that William came out in his true colours. He had been standing by, unwilling witness of these passages. Anxiously concerned, he could no longer keep silent.

"Beg your pardon, sir," he said, stammering painfully, and flushing deeply, "but if Miss June leaves the house, I'm afraid I'll have to go as well."

This was a thunderbolt. S. Gedge Antiques opened his mouth in wide astonishment. He gasped like a carp. The atmospheric displacement was terrific. Slowly the old man took off his "selling" spectacles, and replaced them with his "buying" ones. Certainly the effect was to make him look a shade less truculent, but at the moment there was no other result. "Boy, don't talk like a fool," was all he could say.

William, however, was not to be moved. He never found it easy to make up his mind; for him to reach a decision in things that mattered was a slow and trying process. But the task achieved it was for good or ill. His stammers and blushes were a little ludicrous, he seemed near to tears, but the open hostility of his master could not turn him an inch.

"Never in my born days did I hear the like." S. Gedge Antiques seethed like a vipers' nest. "Boy, you ought to be bled for the simples to let a paltry hussy get round you in this way."

"Give me the picture, Uncle Si," cried the paltry hussy, with a force that made him blink, "and I'll take precious good care you don't see me again."

The old man whinnied with rage. But he had not the least intention of giving up the picture; nor had he the least intention of giving up that which was almost as valuable, the services of his right-hand man. William was irreplaceable. And the instant his master realised that this odd fellow was very much in earnest, he saw that there was only one line to take. He must temporize. With all the tact he could muster, and on occasion the old man could muster a good deal, the Old Crocodile proceeded to do so.

The "firing" of his niece should stand in abeyance for the time being. He gave solemn warning, however, that she must get a job right away, as his mind was quite made up that he was not going to find house room for the likes of her an hour longer than he could help. As for the boy, of whom he had always held such a high opinion ever since the day he had first picked him out of the gutter and upon whom he had lavished a father's kindness, he was really quite at a loss—with a snuffle of heart-melting pathos—to know how to put his deeply wounded feelings into words.

For June, all the same, the upshot was victory. The inevitable packing of her box could be postponed to her own good time. But well she knew that the reprieve was due to William and to him alone. It was his splendidly timed intervention that had enabled her to win the day.

The previous evening harsh thoughts of the Sawney had crept into her heart. After giving her the picture, surely it was his duty to take a stronger line upon the rape of it. But that phase of weakness was forgotten now. He had come out nobly. At a most critical moment he had fought her battle; and he had fought it with magical effect.

All was forgiven. He was O. K.

XXVI

JUNE was dominated now by a single thought. By hook or by crook she must get back the picture before she left that house. If she failed to do so, she would never see it again, and there would be an end of all her hopes. Exactly what these hopes were she did not venture to ask herself; in any case, they would not have been easy to put into words. But she felt in a vague way that William's future and her own were bound up in them.

It was clear that the picture was concealed somewhere upon the premises, because Mr. Thornton and his friend, M. Duponnet, were coming there the next day to look at it. June was quick to realize that this fact offered a measure of opportunity which, slender as it was, must certainly be used. No other was in the least likely to come her way.

Three o'clock on Thursday afternoon she had learned already was the hour of the appointment. It was now the afternoon of Wednesday. No matter what the penalty, if flesh and blood could contrive it, she must be present at this interview, and see what happened to the treasure.

Despair heavy upon her, she lay awake the best part of the night searching her mind for a plan of action. But the quest seemed hopeless. Uncle Si could so easily thwart any scheme she might evolve. And he would not have a scruple. She must outwit him somehow, but to outwit one of such cunning was a task for a brain far stronger and nimbler than hers.

Lying up there in her comfortless bed, wild thoughts flocking round her pillow like so many evil spirits, the whole sorry affair was as haunting as a bad dream. And, interwoven with it, in the most fantastic way, was the shop below, and more particularly the Hoodoo, the presiding genius, which now stood forth in June's mind as the replica of Uncle Si himself. He was surely possessed by a devil, and this heathen joss as surely embodied it.

On Thursday morning June rose early. She was in a mood of desperation. Little sleep had come to her in the long and dreary night hours. But, in spite of feeling quite worn out, her determination to "best" Uncle Si and regain her own property had not grown less. No ray was to be seen anywhere, yet defiant of fate as she still was, the time had not yet come to admit even to herself that all was lost.

As dustpan and brush in hand she began the day's work, more than one reckless expedient crossed her mind. In the last resort she might put the matter in the hands of the police. If she could have counted on William's support, she would have been tempted to do this, but the rub was, he could not be depended on at all. Nobly as he had fought her recent battle, it was clear that so far as the picture itself was concerned, his sympathies were wholly with Uncle Si. Even if he did not deny that the picture was her lawful property he had certainly done his best to revoke his gift.

No, she would gain nothing by calling in the police. She must find some other way. During the night a wild plan had entered her mind. And if in the course of the morning no scheme more hopeful occurred to her, she was now resolved to act upon it.

To this end, she began at once to throw dust in the eyes of Uncle Si. At the breakfast table he was told that she meant to spend the afternoon looking for a job if, with a modest eye on her plate, "he had no objection."

The Old Crocodile had not the least objection. With gusto he assured her that it was quite the best thing she could do. Privately he assured himself that he didn't want her hanging around the place while he was transacting business of great importance with Mr. Thornton and Monsieur Duponnet. Ever in the forefront of his mind was the fact that these gentlemen were coming to see him at three o'clock.

About an hour before the time appointed the old fox sent William on an errand which would keep him away most of the afternoon. And further to ensure that the coast should be quite clear, S. Gedge Antiques said sharply to his niece, "Go and put on your hat, my girl, and make yourself scarce. Get after that job you spoke about. I won't have you hanging around while these gentlemen are here."

June, however, had other views. And these, whatever they were, she was at great pains not to disclose. First she watched William go innocently forth on a long bus ride to Richmond. Next she made sure that Uncle Si was composing himself in his armchair for his usual "forty winks" after dinner. And then she proceeded boldly to develop her audacious design.

To start with, she crept into the front shop and surveyed the Hoodoo. The quaintly hideous vase was fully six feet tall, its body huge, its mouth wide. Was it possible to get inside? There was little doubt that if she was able to do so, this curious monster was quite large enough to conceal her.

She saw at once that the task before her was no light one. But by the side of the Hoodoo, inscrutable Providence had placed a genuine antique in the shape of a gate-legged table, £4.19.6—a great bargain. The sight of this was encouraging. She climbed onto it. And then wedging the Hoodoo most cunningly between the table and the wall, and artfully disposing her own weight, so that the monster might not tip over, she lowered herself with the caution and agility of a cat into the roomy interior.

It was almost a feat for an acrobat, but she managed it somehow. Keeping tight hold of the rim as she swung both legs over, her feet touched bottom with the vase still maintaining the perpendicular. The space inside was ample, and without even the need to bend, the top of her head was invisible. Near the top of the vase, moreover, was the monster's open mouth, a narrow slit studded with teeth, which not only afforded a means of ventilation, but also through which, to June's devout joy, she was able to peer.

For such a crowning boon on the part of Providence she had every reason to feel grateful. So far everything was miraculously right. Her daring had met with more success than could have been hoped for. One problem remained, however, which at that moment she did not venture to look in the face. To get into the vase was one thing; to get out of it would be quite another.

No friendly table could avail her now. In ascending that sheer and slippery face of painted metal-work, she must not expect help from outside when the time came to escape from her prison. Besides one incautious movement might cause the whole thing to topple. And if topple it did, the results would be dire.

This, however, was not the time to consider that aspect of the case. Let her be thankful for a concealment so perfect which allowed her to breathe and to see without being seen or her presence suspected. For such material benefits she must lift up her heart; and hope for the best when the time came to get out. With a sense of grim satisfaction she set herself "to lie doggo," and await the next turn in a game that was full of peril.

It was not long before Uncle Si shambled into the shop. June could see him quite clearly, as he came in with that furtive air which she had learned to know so well. First he took off his spectacles and applied to them vigorously a red bandanna handkerchief. Then he peered cautiously round to make sure that he was alone.

June had not dared to hope that the picture was concealed in the shop; and yet it offered every facility. There were many nooks and crannies, and the whole place was crammed with old pieces of furniture, bric-à-brac, curios. But June had felt that S. Gedge Antiques was not likely to run the risk of hiding his treasure in the midst of these. She thought that his bedroom, under lock and key, was the most likely place of all.

Howbeit, with a sharp thrill, half torment, half delight, she saw that this was not the case. Within a few feet of the Hoodoo itself was an old oak chest which Uncle Si cautiously drew aside. The very spot whereon it had rested contained a loose board. He took a small chisel from a drawer in the counter, prised up the board and from beneath it took forth the buried treasure.

Long and lovingly the old man looked at it, hugging it to his breast more than once in the process, and as he did so June was reminded irresistibly of the Miser Gaspard in "Les Cloches des Corneville," that famous play she had once seen at the Theatre Royal, Blackhampton. To hide such a thing in such a place was a regular miser's trick. It was just what she had expected of him. Presently a grandfather clock, with a Westminster Abbey face, "guaranteed Queen Anne," chimed the hour of three. June could scarcely breathe for excitement. Her heart seemed to rise in her throat and choke her.

At five minutes past three came Mr. Thornton and Monsieur Duponnet. The Frenchman was a small and dapper personage, with a keen eye and a neat imperial. In manner he was much quieter than tradition exacts of a Frenchman, but it was easy to tell that Uncle Si was much impressed by him. Louis Quinze-legs, too, was full of deference. That gentleman, whose face was almost as foxy as that of Uncle Si himself, and about whose lips a thin smile flitted perpetually, had an air of tacit homage for the smallest remark of M. Duponnet, who was clearly a man of great consequence if the bearing of Mr. Thornton was anything to go by.

June, at the back of the shop, inside the Hoodoo and her keen eyes hidden by its half-open jaws, which, in addition to other advantages was partly masked by a litter of bric-à-brac, was in a position to gain full knowledge of all that passed between these three. To begin with, S. Gedge Antiques ceremoniously handed the picture to Louis Quinze-legs who, with a fine gesture, handed it to Monsieur Duponnet.

The Frenchman examined the canvas back and front through his own private glass, scratched portions of it with his nail, pursed his lips, rubbed his nose, and no doubt would have shrugged his shoulders had not that been such a jejune thing for a Frenchman to do.

With a deference that was quite impressive, Mr. Thornton and S. Gedge Antiques waited for M. Duponnet to say something.

"Ze tail of ze R. is a little faint, hein!" was what he said.

"But it is a tail, Mussewer," said S. Gedge Antiques in a robust voice.

"And it is an R," said polite Mr. Thornton, as he bent over the picture.

"You can bet your life on that," said S. Gedge Antiques.

M. Duponnet did not seem inclined to wager anything so valuable as his life. After a little hesitation, which involved further minute examination through his glass, he was ready to take the 'R' for granted. But he went on to deplore the fact that the picture was without a pedigree.

"A pedigree, Mussewer!" It was now the turn of S. Gedge Antiques to rub his nose.

M. Duponnet succinctly explained, with the air of a man expounding a commonplace in the world of art, that Van Roons were so few, their qualities so rare, their monetary value so considerable, that as soon as one came into the market its history was eagerly scrutinised. And should one suddenly appear that previously had not been known to exist it would have to run the gauntlet of the most expert criticism.

"May be, Mussewer!" S. Gedge Antiques wagged a dour head. "But that's not going to alter the fact that this be-yew-ti-ful thing is a genuine Van Roon."

In a manner of speaking it would not, agreed M. Duponnet, but it might detract considerably from its market value.

"That's as may be." The old man suddenly assumed quite a high tone.

M. Duponnet and Mr. Thornton took the picture to the other side of the shop and conferred together. So low were their voices that neither Uncle Si nor June could hear a word of what passed between them. Times and again they held the canvas to the light. They laid it on a tallboys, and pored over it; they borrowed the microscope of one another and made great show of using it; and then finally Mr. Thornton crossed the floor and said to Uncle Si, who was handling a piece of Waterford glass with the most pensive unconcern: "What's your price, Mr. Gedge?"

"Heh?" said the old man, as if emerging from a beautiful dream. "Price? You had better name one."

Excitement at this point seemed to cause June's heart to stop beating.

"The trouble is," said Mr. Thornton, "our friend, M. Duponnet, is not quite convinced that it is a Van Roon."

"But there's the signature."

"It seems to have been touched up a bit."

"Not by me," said S. Gedge Antiques, austerely.

"We don't think that for a moment," said Mr. Thornton, in a voice of honey. "But the signature is by no means so clear as it might be, and in the absence of a pedigree M. Duponnet does not feel justified in paying a big price."

There was a pause while the old man indulged in a dramatic change of spectacles. And then he said rather sourly, in a tone that M. Duponnet could not fail to hear: "Pedigree or no pedigree, I shall have no difficulty in selling it. You know as well as I do, Mr. Thornton, that American buyers are in the market."

"Quite so, Mr. Gedge," said Mr. Thornton suavely. And then while Uncle Si glared at both gentlemen as if they had been caught with their hands in his pocket, they conferred again together. This time it was M. Duponnet who ended their discussion by saying: "Meester Gedge, name your figure!"

"Figure?" said Uncle Si dreamily; and then in his odd way he scratched his scrub of whisker with a thumbnail and rubbed a forefinger down his long and foxlike nose.

"Your price, Meester Gedge?"

"Mussewer!" said the old man solemnly, "I couldn't take less than five thousand pounds, I couldn't really."

June held her breath. For some little time past she had been convinced that the picture was valuable, but she was hardly prepared for this fabulous sum.

M. Duponnet shook his head. "Meester Gedge, if only we had its 'istory!"

"If we had its history, Mussewer, I should want at least twice the money. Even as it is I am taking a big chance. You know that as well as I do."

This seemed to be true. At all events, M. Duponnet and Mr. Thornton again talked earnestly together. Once more they fingered that rather dilapidated canvas. Head to head they bent over it yet again; and then suddenly M. Duponnet looked up and came abruptly across to the old man.

"Meester Gedge," he said, "I can't go beyond four t'ousand pounds. That is my limit!"

"Five, Mussewer Duponny, that is mine," said Uncle Si, with a dark smile.

It was a jejune thing for a French gentleman to do, but at this point M. Duponnet really and truly gave his shoulders a shrug, and advanced three paces towards the shop door. Uncle Si did not stir a muscle. And then M. Duponnet faced about and said: "Guineas, Meester Gedge, I'll give four t'ousand guineas, and that's my last word."

Uncle Si having no pretensions to be considered a French gentleman, did not hesitate to give his own shoulders a shrug. It was his turn then to confer with the discreet and knowledgeable Mr. Thornton, who it was clear was acting the difficult part of a go-between.

June heard that gentleman say in an audible whisper: "A fair price, Mr. Gedge, for the thing as it stands. It hasn't a pedigree, and to me that signature looks a bit doubtful. In the market it may fetch more or it may fetch less, but at the same time four thousand guineas is a fine insurance."

Finished dissembler as Uncle Si was, even he did not seek to deny the truth of this. There could be no gainsaying that four thousand guineas *was* a fine insurance. True, if the picture proved to be a veritable Van Roon it might fetch many times that sum. In that shrewd mind, no bigger miracle was needed for the thing to turn out a *chef d'œuvre* than that it should prove to be worth the sum offered by M. Duponnet. Either contingency seemed too good to be true. Besides, S. Gedge Antiques belonged to a conservative school, among whose articles of faith was a certain trite proverb about a bird in the hand.

It went to the old man's heart to accept four thousand guineas for a work that might be worth so very much more. June could hear him breathing heavily. In her tense ear that sound dominated even the furious beating of her own heart. A kind of dizziness came over her, as only too surely she understood that the wicked old man was giving in. Before her very eyes he was going to surrender her own private property for a fabulous sum.

"Four t'ousand guineas, Meester Gedge," said M. Duponnet, with quite an air of nonchalance. But he knew well enough that the old man was about to "fall."

"It's giving it away, Mussewer," whined Uncle Si. "It's giving it away."

"Zat I don't t'ink, Meester Gedge," said the French gentleman, quietly unbuttoning his coat and taking a fountain pen and a cheque book from an inner pocket. "It's a risque—a big risque. It may not be Van Roon at all—and zen where are we?"

"You know as well as I do that it's a Van Roon," Uncle Si verged almost upon tears.

"Very well, Meester Gedge, if you prefer ze big chance." And cheque book in hand the French gentleman paused.

June was torn. And she could tell by the strange whine in the rasping voice that the Old Crocodile was also torn.

At this moment of crisis, Mr. Thornton interposed with masterful effect. "In my humble opinion," he said, "it's a very fair offer for the thing as it stands."

"You are thinking of your ten per cent. commission, my boy," said S. Gedge Antiques with a gleam of malice.

"Well, Meester Gedge," said M. Duponnet, "take it or leave it." And the French gentleman began to fold up his cheque book.

With a groan to rend a heart of stone, S. Gedge Antiques brought himself suddenly to accept the offer. Half suffocated by excitement, June watched M. Duponnet cross to the desk and proceed to write out a cheque for four thousand guineas. And as she did so her heart sank. She was quite sure that she was looking upon the picture for the last time.

In jumping to this conclusion, however, she had not made full allowance for the business capacity of Uncle Si. When M. Duponnet had filled in the cheque and handed it to him, the Old Crocodile scrutinised it very carefully indeed, and then he said: "Thank you, Mussewer Duponny. The bank closes at three. But to-morrow morning I'll take this round myself as soon as it opens. And if the manager says it's all right, you can have the picture whenever you like."

"*Bien!*" The Frenchman bowed politely. "Meanwhile, take good care of the picture. There are many thieves about." M. Duponnet laughed. "Mind you lock it up in a safe place."

"You can trust Mr. Gedge to do that, I think," said Louis Quinze-legs dryly.

"I hope so, I'm sure," said the old man with a frosty smile.

"*Soit!*" M. Duponnet smiled too. "I'll call for it myself to-morrow morning at twelve."

"Thank you, Mussewer!"

S. Gedge Antiques gave his visitors a bow as they went up to the shop door, and ushered them ceremoniously into the not particularly inviting air of New Cross Street.

XXVII

JUST at first June was unable to realise that M. Duponnet had not taken the picture away with him. The blood seemed to drum against her brain while she watched Uncle Si turn over the cheque in his long talon fingers and then transfer it to a leather case, which he returned to his breast pocket with a deep sigh. Afterwards he took up the picture from the table on which he had set it down and then June grasped the fact that the treasure was still there.

The face which bent over it now was not that of a happy man. It was a complex of emotions, deep and stern. The price was huge for a thing that had cost him nothing, but—and there it was that the shoe pinched!—if it should prove to be a real Van Roon, he might be parting with it for a song.

June could read his thoughts like an open book. He wanted to eat his cake and have it too. She would have been inclined to pity him had her hatred and her scorn been less. In his cunning and his greed he was a tragic figure, with a thing of incomparable beauty in his hand whose sole effect was to give him the look of an evil bird of prey. Utter rascal as she knew him to be now, she shivered to think how easy it would be for herself to grow just like him. Her very soul was fixed upon the recovery of this wonderful thing which, in the first place, she had obtained by a trick. And did she covet it for its beauty? Or was it for the reason which at this moment made Uncle Si a creature so ill to look upon? To such questions there could only be one answer.

For the time being, however, these things were merged in the speculation far more momentous: What will the Old Crocodile do now? She was feeling so uncomfortable in her narrow hiding place, which prevented all movement, and almost forbade her to breathe, that she hoped devoutly the old wretch would lose no time in putting back the treasure.

This, alas, was not to be. The picture was still in the hand of Uncle Si, who still pored over it like a moulting vulture, when a luxurious motor glided up to the shop door. Almost at once the shop was invaded by two persons, who in the sight of June had a look of notable importance.

The first of these, whom June immediately recognised, was the tall, fashionable girl whose visit had caused her such heart-burning the week before. She was now accompanied by a gentleman who beyond a doubt was her distinguished father.

"Good morning, Mr. Gedge!" It was twenty past three by the afternoon, but June was ready to take a Bible oath that Miss Blue Blood said "good morning." "I've persuaded my father to come and look at this amazing vase." And with her *en-tout-cas* Miss Blue Blood pointed straight at the Hoodoo.

Feeling herself to be a rat caught neatly in a trap, June at once crouched lower. The Hoodoo being fully six feet tall and her own stoop considerable, she was able to take comfort from the fact that just then no part of her own head was showing. But how long was she likely to remain invisible? That was a question for the gods. And it was further complicated by the knowledge that the Hoodoo's mouth was open, and that the point of Miss Blue Blood's green umbrella might easily find a way through.

A-shiver with fear June tried to subdue her wild heart, while Miss Babraham, her father, Sir Arthur, and S. Gedge Antiques gathered round the Hoodoo. She hardly dared to breathe. The least sound would betray her. And in any case, one of the three had merely to stand on an adjacent coffin stool and peer over the top for the murder to be out.

The tragedy which June so clearly foresaw was not permitted to take place at once. Plainly the fates were inclined to toy with their victim for a while. Miss Blue Blood's laugh—how rich and deep it was!—rang in her ears and made them burn as she gave the Hoodoo a prod and cried out in her gay Miss-Banks-like manner, "Papa, I ask you, did you ever see anything quite like it?"

"By George, no!" laughed that connoisseur.

"It's such a glorious monster," said his enthusiastic daughter standing on tiptoe, "that one can't even see over the top."

"Puts one in mind," said Sir Arthur, "of the Arabian Nights and the Cave of the Forty Robbers."

"The long gallery at Homefield is the very place for it!"

"I wonder!" The connoisseur tapped the Hoodoo with his walking stick and turned to S. Gedge Antiques. "Do you happen to know where it came from?" he asked.

"From a Polynesian temple in the South Sea Islands, I believe, sir," said Uncle Si, glibly.

"What do you want for it?" And Sir Arthur tapped the Hoodoo again.

"I'll take thirty pounds, sir." It was the voice of a man bringing himself to part with a valuable tooth. "Sixty was the sum I paid for it some years ago. But it isn't everybody's fancy, and it swallows a small place."

Sir Arthur observed with pleasant humour that such a monstrosity ought to be taken over by the nation. S. Gedge Antiques, with a humour that strove to be equally pleasant, concurred.

At this point, to June's mortal terror, Miss Babraham made a second attempt to look over the top.

"Stand on this coffin stool, Miss," said S. Gedge Antiques, politely producing that article from the collection of bric-à-brac around the Hoodoo.

June's heart stood still. The game was up. Sickly she closed her eyes. But Providence had one last card to play.

"Thank you so much," said Miss Babraham. "But it won't bear my weight, I'm afraid. No, I don't think I'll risk it. There's really nothing to see inside."

Uncle Si agreed that there was really nothing to see inside; and June breathed again.

"Thirty pounds isn't much, papa, for such a glorious monstrosity." Miss Blue Blood had evidently set her heart on it.

Sir Arthur, however, expressed a fear that a thing of that size, that hue, that contour would kill every object in the Long Gallery. Great argument ensued. And then to June's relief, Miss Babraham, her father, Sir Arthur and S. Gedge Antiques, arguing still, moved away from the Hoodoo.

The upshot was that Sir Arthur, overborne at last by the force of his daughter's reasoning, agreed to buy the monster, for what in the opinion of the seller, was a ridiculously inadequate sum. It was to be carefully packed in a crate, and sent down to Homefield near Byfleet, Surrey. So much for the Hoodoo. And then the eye of a famous connoisseur lit on the picture that the old dealer had laid on the gate-legged table.

"What have we here?" said Sir Arthur, fixing his eyeglass.

Uncle Si became a sphinx. The connoisseur took the picture in his hand, and while he examined it with grave curiosity he too became a sphinx. So tense grew the silence to June's ear that again she was troubled by the loud beating of her heart.

At last the silence was broken by the light and charming note of Miss Babraham. "Why, surely," she said, "that is the funny old picture I saw when I was here the other day."

"We have cleaned it up a bit since then, madam," said Uncle Si in a voice so toneless that June could only marvel at the perfect self-command of this arch dissembler.

Sir Arthur, it was clear, was tremendously interested. He turned the picture over and over, and used the microscope very much as M. Duponnet had done. Finally he said in a voice nearly as toneless as that of Uncle Si himself. "What do you ask for this, Mr. Gedge?"

"Not for sale, sir," was the decisive answer.

The nod of Sir Arthur implied that it was the answer he expected. "Looks to me a fine example." A true amateur, he could not repress a little sigh of pleasure. There was no concealing the fact that he was intrigued.

"Van Roon at his best, sir," said S. Gedge Antiques.

"Ye-es," said the connoisseur—in the tone of the connoisseur. "One would be rather inclined to say so. If the question is not impertinent,"—Sir Arthur fixed a steady eye upon the face of deep cunning which confronted his— "may I ask where it came from?"

The old man was prepared for the question. His answer was pat. "I can't tell you that, sir," he said, in a tone of mystery.

Again Sir Arthur nodded. That, too, was the answer he had expected. In the pause which followed Sir Arthur returned to a loving re-examination of the picture; and then said S. Gedge Antiques in a voice gravely and quietly confidential: "Strictly between ourselves, sir, I may say that I have just turned down an offer of five thousand guineas."

"Oh—indeed!"

It was now the turn of the Old Crocodile to gaze into the impassive countenance of the famous connoisseur.

XXVIII

"FIVE thousand guineas, sir, I have just refused," said Uncle Si, "for this little thing, as sure as God's in the sky."

So shocked was June by this adding of blasphemy to his other crimes, that she shivered audibly. Miss Babraham cocked up her head at the sound. "You've a cat somewhere, haven't you?" she said, looking around the shop.

"No, madam," said Uncle Si shortly. So like a woman to butt in at such a moment with such a remark!

"In my humble opinion," said Sir Arthur, gazing solemnly at the picture, "this is a finer example of Van Roon than the one—and the only one!—we have in the National Gallery."

"There, sir, I am with you," said S. Gedge Antiques with unction.

"One would like to know its history."

The old man became a sphinx once more. "I can only tell you, sir, I didn't buy it as a Van Roon," he said cautiously.

"Really!" Sir Arthur grew more intrigued than ever. "Well, Mr. Gedge, whatever you bought it as, I think there can be no doubt that you've made a lucky purchase."

"I am wondering, sir," said S. Gedge Antiques, "whether the National Gallery would care to acquire this fine example?" It was a sudden inspiration, but those measured tones and calculating eyes gave no indication of the fact.

Sir Arthur Babraham, in his own capacity of a National Gallery trustee, began sensibly to moderate his transports. "More unlikely things, Mr. Gedge," at last he brought himself reluctantly to say. "Van Roons are very scarce, and if this one is all that he appears to be at a first glance, it will be a pity to let him leave the country."

Piously, S. Gedge Antiques thought so, too.

Sir Arthur turned to the picture again. Like M. Duponnet he seemed to have difficulty in keeping his expert gaze off that fascinating canvas.

"Reminds one," he said, "of that choice thing that was stolen from the Louvre about twenty-five years ago. The size is similar and, as I remember it, the whole composition is in some ways identical."

The old man was startled, but not visibly. "Was there one stolen from the Loov, sir?" he said, with a polite air of asking for information.

"Why, yes! Don't you remember? There was a great stir at the time. It was cut out of its frame. The French Government offered a big reward, but the work has never been recovered."

"Indeed, sir." All at once the Old Crocodile began to gambol a little. "Let's hope this ain't the boy." He gave a mild snigger. But as his next words proved there was more in that snigger than met the ear. "In the event of this little jool turning out to be stolen property, what, sir, do you suppose would be the position of the present owner?"

"Difficult to say, Mr. Gedge."

"He'd receive compensation, wouldn't he?"

"Substantial compensation one would think—if he was able to prove his title."

If he was able to prove his title! Those blunt little words had a sinister sound for S. Gedge Antiques, but he did not turn a hair. "No difficulty about that, sir," he said, robustly.

"Quite!" Evidently Sir Arthur had no doubt upon the point. "But as the question might arise it may be well to have it settled before disposing of the picture."

S. Gedge agreed.

"And in any case, before parting with it," said Sir Arthur, "it will be wise, I think, to take advice."

Again S. Gedge agreed. "You mean, sir, it may be very valuable indeed?"

"Yes, I quite think it may be. At a cursory glance it has the look of a fine example of a great master. I remember at the time that 'L'Automne' disappeared from the Louvre, it was said to be worth at least two hundred and fifty thousand francs, and since then Van Roons have more than doubled in price."

"In that case, sir"—there was a tremor of real emotion in the voice of the old dealer—"this be-yew-ti-ful thing ought not to be allowed to leave the country."

"Unfortunately the French authorities may compel it to do so." And the connoisseur sighed as he fingered the canvas lovingly.

Affirmed S. Gedge Antiques: "I don't believe, sir, for a moment that it is 'L'Automne.'"

"One wouldn't like to say it is," said the cautious Sir Arthur. "And one wouldn't like to say it isn't."

"It'll be up to the Loov to prove it, anyhow."

"Quite. In the meantime, before you let it go, I hope you'll give me an opportunity of looking at it again."

This modest request caused the old man to rub his nose. He was not in a position, he said mysteriously, to give a promise, but certainly he would do his best to meet the wishes of Sir Arthur.

"Thank you, Mr. Gedge. If this picture is not claimed by other people, and of course one doesn't for a moment suggest that it will be, steps might be taken to keep it here. We are so poor in Van Roons—there is only one, I believe—to our shame!—in this country at the present time—that we can't afford to let a thing like this slip through our fingers. Therefore, as I say, before you decide to sell I hope you'll take advice."

S. Gedge Antiques gravely thanked Sir Arthur Babraham. He would keep those wise words in mind. And in the meantime he would pack *That* in a crate—he pointed a finger straight at June's eyes—and send it to Homefield.——

"——near Byfleet, Surrey, I think you said, sir?"

XXIX

THE distinguished visitors were bowed into the street. And then S. Gedge Antiques, with the face of a man whose soul is in torment, returned to contemplation of the picture, and also of M. Duponnet's cheque which he took out of his pocket book. It was clear that his mind was the prey of a deep problem. The bird in the hand was well enough so far as it went, but the bird in the bush was horribly tempting.

At last with a heavy sigh the old man returned the cheque to his pocket, and then cautiously lifting up the loose board, put back the picture whence it came and drew the oak chest over the spot. He then shambled off to the room next door, which was full of odds and ends mingled with a powerful smell of oil and varnish.

June at once made an attempt to get out of prison. But she now found her position to be as she had already surmised. To enter without help had been no mean feat, to escape in the same fashion was impossible. Wedged so tightly inside the Hoodoo, there was neither play nor purchase for her hands; and frantic as her efforts were, they were yet subordinated to the knowledge that it would be quite easy for the thing to topple over. Should that happen the consequence would certainly be alarming and possibly ghastly.

Frantically wriggling in the jaws of the Hoodoo, it did not matter what she did, she was firmly held. And the fear of Uncle Si, who was pottering about quite close at hand, while imposing silence upon her, intensified the growing desperation of her case. She was a mouse in a trap.

Too soon did she learn that only one course was open to her. She must wait for William's return. Irksome and humiliating as the position was, it was clear that she could do nothing without help.

Would William never come? The minutes ticked on and her durance grew exceedingly vile. She became conscious of pains in her shoulders and feet, she felt as if she could hardly draw breath, her head throbbing with excitement seemed as if it must burst. It was a horrible fix to be in.

Suffering acutely now, she yielded as well as she could to the inevitable. There was simply nothing to be done. She must wait. It was imprisonment in a most unpleasant form and she was frightened by the knowledge that it might continue many hours. Even when William did return, and there was no saying when he would do so, he was quite as likely to enter by the back door as by the shop. So terrible was the thought that June felt ready to faint at the bare idea.

This was a matter, however, in which fate was not so relentless after all. June was doing her best to bear up in the face of this new and paralysing fear when the shop door opened and lo! William came in.

Great was her joy, and yet it had to be tempered by considerations of prudence. She contrived to raise her lips to the mouth of the Hoodoo, and to breathe his name in a tragic whisper.

As he heard her and turned, she urged in the same odd fashion: "For Heaven's sake—not a sound!"

"Why—Miss June!" he gasped. "Where are you?"

She checked him with wild whisperings that yet served to draw him to her prison.

He was dumbfounded, quite as much as by her fiercely tragic voice as by the amazing predicament in which he found her.

"Help me out!" she commanded him. "And don't make the least sound. Uncle Si is next door, and if he finds me here, something terrible will happen."

Such force and such anxiety had one at least of the results so much to be desired. They forbade the asking of futile questions. Every moment was precious if she was to make good her escape.

William in this crisis proved himself a right good fellow. His sense of the ludicrous was keen, but he stifled it. Moreover, a legitimate curiosity had been fully aroused, but he stifled that also as he proceeded to carry out these imperious orders. But even with such ready and stalwart help, June was to learn again that it was no easy matter to escape from the Hoodoo.

Without venturing to speak again, William mounted the gate-legged table and offered both hands to the prisoner. But the trouble was that she was so tightly pinned that she could not raise hers to receive them. And it was soon fatally clear that so long as the Hoodoo kept the perpendicular it would be impossible for any external agent to secure a hold upon the body wedged within its jaws.

After several attempts at dislodgement had miserably failed, June gasped in a kind of anguish: "Do you think you can tip this thing over—very gently—without making a sound?"

This was trying William highly indeed, but it seemed the only thing to be done. Happily he was tall and strong; much was said, all the same, for his power of muscle and the infinite tact with which it was applied that he was able to tilt the Hoodoo on to its end. Keeping the vase firmly under control, he then managed to regulate its descent to the shop floor so skilfully as to avoid a crash.

Such a feat was really a triumph of applied dynamics. June, however, was not in a position to render it all the homage it deserved, even if she was deeply grateful for the address that William brought to bear upon his task. Once the Hoodoo had been laid full length on the shop floor she was able to wriggle her body and her shoulders with what violence she pleased, without the fear of disaster. A series of convulsive twists and writhings and she was free!

As soon as she knew that she was no longer pinned by the jaws of the monster, the action of a strong mind was needed to ward off a threat of hysteria. But she controlled herself sufficiently to help William restore the Hoodoo to the perpendicular; and then she said in a whisper of extreme urgency which was barely able to mask the sob of nerves overstrung: "Not one word now. But go straight into the kitchen—just as if you hadn't seen me. And remember whatever happens"—the whisper grew fiercer, the sob more imminent—"if Uncle Si asks the question you *haven't* seen me. I'm supposed to be looking for a job. You understand?"

To say that William did understand would have been to pay him a most fulsome compliment; yet the stout fellow behaved as if the whole of this amazing matter was as clear as daylight. Such was June's fixity of will, the sheer force of her personality, that he left the shop at once like a man hypnotised. Excited questions trembled upon his lips, but in the face of this imperiousness he did not venture to give them play.

He made one attempt—one half-hearted attempt.

"But Miss June——!"

The only answer of Miss June was to cram one hand over his mouth, and with the other to propel him towards the door which led to the back premises.

XXX

As soon as William had passed out of the shop, June stood a moment to gather nerve and energy for the task before her. Feeling considerably tossed, above all she was devoured by a horrible form of excitement whose effect was like nothing so much as a bad dream. But this was not a time for dreams. The situation was full of peril; not a moment must be lost.

The picture was her immediate concern. She set herself at once to the business of moving the oak chest aside. This presented no difficulty, for there was nothing in it; but the loose board beneath it did. Fingers unhelped could not prise it up; they must have a chisel. She knew that such an implement was to be found in one of the drawers of the desk, but she had stealthily to open three or four before she came upon the right one.

While all this was going on, she could hear the voices of William and Uncle Si in the room next door. It seemed that no matter what her caution or her haste, she would almost certainly be interrupted before she was through with her task. But luck was with her. She was able to lift the board, take forth the picture, replace the chest and return the chisel to its drawer without the voices coming any nearer.

Picture in hand, she tiptoed out of the shop as far as the stairs. Through the open door of the inner room the back of Uncle Si was visible as she crept by. It was taking a grave risk to attempt the stairs at such a moment, but she was wrought up to a point when to go back and wait was impossible. She must continue to chance her luck.

Up the stairs she crept, expecting at every second one to hear a harsh voice recall her. To her unspeakable relief, however, she was able to gain sanctuary in her own room without hindrance. She bolted the door against the enemy, although so far as she was aware, he was still in the room below in total ignorance of what had happened.

Shivering as if in the throes of fever, she sat on the edge of her narrow bed. The treasure was hers still. She held it to her bosom as a mother holds a child; yet the simple act gave rise at once to the problem of problems: What must be done with the thing now? There could be no security for it under that roof. And not to the picture alone did this apply, but also to herself. Anything might happen as soon as the old man found out that the Van Roon was not, after all, to be his. Meanwhile, the future hardly bore thinking about; it was like a precipice beyond whose edge she dare not look.

One act, however, did not admit of a moment's delay: there and then the treasure must be smuggled out of the house and put in a place of safety. Rowelled by this thought, June rose from the bed, took a piece of brown paper and some string from her box, and proceeded to transform the picture into a neat parcel. She then slipped off her dress, which was considerably the worse for contact with the dusty interior of the Hoodoo, performed a hasty toilette, put on her walking-out coat and skirt and changed her shoes. Finally, she put on the better of the only two hats she possessed, slipped her mother's battered old leather purse into her coat pocket, and then, umbrella in one hand, parcel in the other, she turned to the hazard of stealing downstairs and making good her escape.

In the middle of the twisty stairs, just before their sharpest bend would bring her into the view of persons below, she stopped to listen. The voices had ceased; she could not hear a sound. Two ways lay before her of reaching the street: one via the parlour to the kitchen and out along the side entry, the other through the front door of the shop. Either route might be commanded at the moment by the enemy. With nothing to guide her, June felt that the only safe course just then was to stay where she was. In the strategic position she had taken up on the stairs she could not be seen from below, yet a quick ear might hope to gain a clue to what was going on.

She had not to wait long. From the inner room, whose door opposite the foot of the stairs was still half open, although its occupant was no more seen, there suddenly came the strident tones of Uncle Si. They were directed unmistakably kitchenward. "Boy, you'd better get the tea ready. Seemin'ly that gell ain't home."

"Very good, sir," came a prompt and cheerful response from the back premises.

June decided at once that the signs were favourable. Now was her chance; the way through the front shop was evidently clear. Deftly as a cat she came down the remaining stairs and stole past the half-open door of what was known as "the lumber room," where, however, old chairs were sometimes fitted with new legs and old chests with new panels.

Uncle Si was undoubtedly there. June could hear him moving about as she passed the door; indeed she was hardly clear of it when she received a most unwelcome reminder of this fact. Either he chanced to turn round as she crept by, or he caught a glimpse of her passing in one of the numerous mirrors that surrounded him. For just as she reached the shop threshold she heard his irascible bark: "That you, niece?"

The road clear ahead, June did not pause to weigh consequences. She simply bolted. Even if the old man was not likely to guess what her neat parcel contained, it would surely be the height of folly to give him the chance.

Never in her life had she been quite so thankful as when she found herself in the street with the treasure safely under her arm.

XXXI

JUNE went swiftly down New Cross Street to the Strand. Until she reached that garish sea of traffic she dare not look back lest hot on her heels should be Uncle Si. Such a discovery was not at all likely she well knew; the feeling was therefore illogical, yet she could not rid herself of it until she was merged in the ever-flowing tide.

Taking refuge at last in a jeweller's doorway from the maelstrom of passers by, June had now another problem to face. The Van Roon must find a home. But the question of questions was—where?

Apart from William and Uncle Si, and her chance acquaintance, Mr. Keller, she did not know a soul in London. Mr. Keller, however, sprang at once to her mind. Yet more than one reservation promptly arose in regard to him. She knew really nothing about him beyond the fact that he was a man of obviously good address, belonging to a class superior to her own. He was a man of the world, of a certain breeding and education, but whether it would be wise to trust a comparative stranger in such a matter seemed exceedingly doubtful to a girl of June's horse sense. Still there was no one else to whom she could turn. And recalling the circumstances of their first meeting, if one could ignore the means by which it had come about, there was something oddly compelling, something oddly attractive, about this Mr. Keller.

In the total absence of other alternatives, June found her mind drawn so far in the direction of this man of mystery that at last she took from her purse a slip of paper on which he had written his name and address: "Adolph Keller, No. 4, Haliburton Studios, Manning Square, Soho."

Could she trust him with the care of a Van Roon? Now that she had been a witness of its terrible effect on Uncle Si, she was forced to ask whether it would be right to trust any man with such a talisman. Luckily, the world was not peopled exclusively with Uncle Sis. She would have to trust somebody with her treasure, that was certain; and, after all, there was no reason to suspect that Mr. Keller was not an honest man.

She was still in the jeweller's doorway, wrestling with the pros and cons of the tough matter, when a passing bus displaying the name Victoria Station caught her eye. In a flash came the solution of the problem.

Again she entered the sea of traffic, to be borne slowly along by the slow tide as far as Charing Cross. Here she waited for another bus to Victoria. The solving of the riddle was absurdly simple after all. What place for her treasure could be safer, more accessible than a railway station cloak room?

She boarded Bus 23. But hardly had it turned the corner into Whitehall when a thin flicker of elation was dashed by the salutary thought that her brain was giving out. The cloak room at Charing Cross, from the precincts of whose station she had just driven away, was equally adapted to her need. Along the entire length of Whitehall and Victoria Street she was haunted by the idea that she was losing her wits. A prolonged scrutiny of her pale but now collected self in a confectioner's window on the threshold of the London and Brighton terminus was called for to reassure her. And even then, for a girl so shrewd and so practical, there remained the scar of a distressing mental lapse.

It did not take long to deposit the parcel in the cloak room on the main line down platform. But in the act of doing so, occurred a slight incident which was destined to have a bearing on certain events to follow. When a ticket was handed to her, she could only meet the charge of three pence with a ten shilling note.

"Nothing smaller, Miss?" asked the clerk.

"I'm afraid I haven't," said June, searching her purse, and then carefully placing the ticket in its middle compartment.

"You'll have to wait while I get change then."

"Sorry to trouble you," June murmured, as the clerk went out through a door into an inner office. Ever observant and alert, she noticed that the clerk was a tallish young man, whose freely curling fair hair put her in mind of William, and that he wore a new suit of green corduroy.

The likeness to William gave *bouquet* to her politeness, when the young man returned with the change. "Sorry to give you so much trouble," she said again.

"No trouble, miss." And Green Corduroy handed the change across the cloak room counter with a frank smile that was not unworthy of William himself.

XXXII

THE treasure in a safe place, June had to consider what to do next. One fact stood out clear in her mind. She must leave at once the sheltering roof of S. Gedge Antiques. There was no saying what would happen when the Old Crocodile discovered that the Van Roon was missing.

The sooner she collected her box and her gear, and found another lodging the better. Her best plan would be to go back to New Cross Street and get them now. Uncle Si was hardly likely as yet to have made the discovery. It would be wise, therefore, to take advantage of this lull, for at the most it was only a matter of a few hours before the truth was known. And when known it was, Number Forty-six New Cross Street was the very last place in London in which she would choose to be.

There was a chance, of course, that "the murder" was out already. But she would have to take the risk of that. All that she had in the world beyond the six paper pounds, nine shillings and ninepence in her purse, was in the box in the garret. Her entire resources were about seventeen pounds in money, a scanty wardrobe, and a few odds and ends of jewellery of little value, but if she could get hold of these they might suffice to tide her over a sorely anxious time.

In the present state of her nerves, courage was needed to return to New Cross Street. But it had to be. And it was now or never. If her box was to be got away, she must go boldly back at once and claim it. How this was to be done without arousing suspicion she did not quite know, but the most hopeful method was to announce that she had been able to find a job, and also good lodgings, and that she did not care to lay the burden of her presence upon Uncle Si one hour longer than was necessary.

She had been brought up with a strict regard for the truth, but fate was driving her so hard that she could not afford to have scruples. Hanging by a strap on the Underground to Charing Cross, which seemed the quickest route, and time was the essence of the matter, she rehearsed the part she had now to play. Certainly the playing itself would not lack gusto. Nothing life so far had given her would yield quite so much pleasure as saying good-bye to the Old Crocodile, and ironically thanking him for all his kindness. At the same time, the job and lodgings story must be pitched in just the right key, or his suspicions would be aroused, and then something horribly unpleasant might occur.

By the time June had turned out of the Strand into New Cross Street, a heavy autumnal dusk had fallen upon that bleak thoroughfare. Somehow the dark pall struck at her heart. In a sense it was symbolical of the business upon which she was engaged. She felt like a thief whose instinct welcomes darkness, and whose conscience fears it.

Never in her life had she needed such courage as to turn up that gloomy and dismal street and accost the forbidding threshold of S. Gedge Antiques. The shop was still open, for it was hardly more than six o'clock, and two gas jets lit the interior in a way that added to its dolour.

She stood a moment with the knob of the shop door in her hand. All the nerve she could muster was wanted to venture within. But she did go in, and she felt a keen relief when a hasty glance told her that Uncle Si was not there.

XXXIII

JUNE had a further moment of indecision while she thought out what her line must be. She resolved to go direct to her room and pack her box. Afterwards she must find William and enlist his help in bringing it downstairs, and then she would get a taxi and drive off with her things before Uncle Si discovered his loss. Otherwise...!

Her mind had not time to shape the grisly alternative, before the immediate course of events shaped it for her. Suddenly she was aware of a presence lurking in the dark shadows of the shop interior. It was couchant, vengeful, hostile. Almost before June could guess what was happening it had sprung upon her.

With astounding force her right wrist was grasped and twisted behind her back. She gave a little yelp of pain. A second yelp followed, as she struggled to free herself, only to find that she was locked in a vice, and that to fight against it would be agony.

"Now, where is it?" The low voice hissing in her ear was surely that of a maniac. "Where's the picture?" The grip upon her had the strength of ten. "Where is it—eh?" As the question was put, her captor shook her fiercely. "Tell me." He shook her again. "Oh, you won't—won't you?" And then she realized that there was something in his hand.

She called wildly for William, but there was no response.

"No use lifting up your voice. The boy's out."

She fought to get free, but with a wrist still locked, she was at his mercy. "Now then, where's that picture? Won't tell me—eh?" There was madness in that depth of rage.

Quite suddenly there came a sickening crash upon her shoulders. She let out with her heels and found the shin of the enemy, she fought and screamed, yet pinned like that, she felt her wrist must break and her arm be wrenched from its socket.

"Where is it—you thief?" The stick crashed again, this time in a series of horrible blows. So severe was the pain that it seemed to drive through her whole being. She began to fear that he meant to kill her; and as the stick continued to descend she felt sure that he would.

She was a strong, determined girl, but her captor had her at a hopeless disadvantage. His strength, besides, was that of one possessed. Her cries and struggles merely added to his savagery.

"Tell me where it is or I'll knock the life out of you."

Utterly desperate, she contrived at last to break away; and though with the force of a maniac he tried to prevent her escape, somehow she managed to get into the street. He followed her as far as the shop door, brandishing the stick, hurling imprecations upon her, and threatening what he would do if she didn't bring the picture back at once.

Bruised and gasping, June reeled into the darkness. Feeling more dead than alive, she lingered nearby after the old man had gone in, trying to pull her battered self together. She badly wanted her box, yet the only hope of getting it now was by means of the police. As things were, however, it would not be wise to ask their help. The old wretch was so clever he might be able to make her out a thief; besides, for the time being she had had more than enough of this horrible affair.

Cruelly hurt she moved at last with slow pain towards the Strand. By now she had decided that her most imperative need was a night's lodging. Before starting to look for one, however, the enticing doors of a teashop gave her a renewed sense of weakness. Gratefully she went in and sat down, ordering a pot of tea and a little bread and butter which she felt too ill to eat.

Nearly half an hour she sat in the company of her thoughts. Hard, unhappy thoughts they were. Without one friend to whom in this crisis she could turn, the world which confronted her now was an abyss. The feeling of loneliness was desolating, yet, after all, far less so than it would have been were she not fortified by the memory of a certain slip of paper in her purse.

A slow return of fighting power revived a spark of natural resolution within her. After all, a potent weapon was in her hands. She must think out a careful plan of turning it to full account. And at the worst she was now beyond the reach of Uncle Si. Even if he kept her box and all its contents, weighed in the scale of the picture's fabulous worth, her modest possessions amounted to very little.

Stimulated by this conclusion, she began to forget her aches. When a waitress came June asked for her bill. It was sixpence. She put her hand in the pocket of her coat. Her purse was not there.

With a little thrill of fear, she felt in the pocket on the other side. The purse was not there either. She was stunned. This was a blow far worse than those she had just received. She grew so dazed that as she got up she swayed against the table, and had to hold on by it to save herself from falling.

The waitress who had written out the bill caught a glimpse of scared eyes set in a face of chalk.

"Aren't you well?" she asked.

"I—I've lost my purse," June stammered. "It's fallen out of my pocket, I think." As with frantic futility she plunged her hand in again, she was raked by the true meaning of such a fact in all its horror. Unless her purse had been stolen on the Underground, and it was not very likely, it had almost certainly fallen out of her pocket in the course of the struggle with Uncle Si.

It was lying now on the shop floor unless the old wretch had found it already. And if he had he would lose no time in examining its contents. He had only to do so for the cloak-room ticket to tell him where the Van Roon was deposited, and to provide him with a sure means of obtaining it.

"You may have had your pocket picked."

June did not think so. Yet, being unable to take the girl into her confidence, she did not choose to disclose her doubts.

"Perhaps I have," she gasped. And then face to face with the extreme peril of the case, her overdriven nerves broke out in mutiny. She burst into tears. "I don't know what I'll do," she sobbed.

The waitress was full of sympathy. "Your bill is only sixpence. Come in and pay to-morrow."

Through her tears June thanked her.

"'Tisn't my bill, although it's very kind of you. There was something very important in my purse."

"Where did you have it last?"

"In the booking hall, when I took a ticket from Victoria to Charing Cross."

"Your pocket's been picked," said the waitress with conviction. "There's a warning in all the Tubes."

The comfort was cold, yet comfort it was of a kind. June saw a wan ray of hope. After all, there was a bare possibility that inexorable Fate was not the thief.

"I'd go to Scotland Yard if I were you," said the waitress. "The police often get back stolen property. Last year my sister's house was burgled, and they recovered nearly everything for her."

June began to pull herself together. It was not hope, however, that braced her faculties, but an effort of will. Hope there was none of recovering the purse, but she was now faced by the stern necessity of getting back the picture. In the light of this tragedy it was in most serious peril. Delay might be fatal, if indeed it had not already proved to be so. She must go at once and get possession of the treasure lest it be too late.

The waitress was a good Samaritan. Not only could the bill wait until the next day, but she went even further: "Is your home far from here?" she asked.

"My home—far?" said June, dazedly. For the moment she did not understand all that was implied by the question.

"If you live on the District, and you haven't a season, I don't mind lending you a shilling to get you home."

June accepted a shilling with earnest thanks. In the circumstances, it might be worth untold gold: "You can give it me back any time you are passing," said the waitress, as June thanked her again and made her way unsteadily out into the street.

The chill air of the Strand revived her a little. She had decided already that she must go at once to Victoria. Every minute would count, and it now occurred to her that if she took the Underground, several might be saved.

To the Underground in Trafalgar Square she went. It was the hour of the evening rush. Queues were lining up at all the booking office windows. And at the first window she came to, some three persons or so ahead of her, was a figure oddly familiar, which, however, in her present state of disintegration she did not recognize at once. It was clad in a sombre tail coat of prehistoric design, jemima boots, frayed shepherd's plaid trousers braced high and a hard square felt hat which gave a crowning touch of oppressive respectability. Moreover, its progress was assisted by a heavy knotted walking stick, at the sight of which June gave an involuntary shiver.

An instant later the shiver had developed into a long and paralyzing shudder. Uncle Si was just ahead of her; in fact she was near enough to hear a harsh voice demand almost with menace a ticket to Victoria.

June's worst fears were realized. The purse had fallen from her pocket to the shop floor in the struggle; the old wretch had found it, deciphered the precious ticket, put two and two together, and was now on his way to claim the parcel. All this was crystal clear to her swift mind. She felt a strong desire to faint, but she fought her weakness. She must go on. Everything was as good as lost—but she must go on.

She took her ticket. And then in the long subway to the platform she raced on ahead of Uncle Si. He was so near-sighted that even had he been less absorbed in his own affairs he would not have been likely to notice her.

June reached the platform well in front of the old man. But the train to Victoria was not in. It arrived two minutes later; by then, Uncle Si had appeared, and they boarded it together. She was careful, however, not to enter the same compartment as the enemy.

Short as the journey was, June had ample time to appreciate that the odds were heavily against her. The mere fact that the cloak-room receipt for the parcel was in the custody of Uncle Si would confer possession upon him; it had only to be presented for the Van Roon to be handed over without a question.

The one chance she had now was to get on well ahead of the old beast, and convince the clerk that in spite of the absence of the ticket the parcel was hers. She knew, however, only too well that the hope of being able to do this was frail indeed—at all events before the holder of the ticket arrived on the scene to claim it.

At Victoria, June dashed out of the train even before it stopped. Running past the ticket collector at the barrier and along the subway she reached the escalator yards in front of Uncle Si, and, in spite of being unused to this trap for the unwary, for Blackhampton's more primitive civilization knew escalators not, she ascended to the street at a pace far beyond the powers of the Old Crocodile. By this means, indeed, she counted on gaining an advantage of several minutes, since it was hardly likely that Uncle Si would trust himself to such a contrivance, and in ignorance of the fact that she was just ahead, would choose the dignified safety of the lift.

So far as it went the thought was reassuring. Alas, it did not go far. As June ran through the long station to the cloak-room at its farthest end, she had but a very slender hope of being able to recover the parcel. She had no intention, however, of submitting tamely to fate. In this predicament, whatever the cost, she must make one last and final effort to get back her treasure.

At the cloak-room counter she took her courage in both hands. A man sour and elderly had replaced the wearer of the green corduroy, who was nowhere to be seen. This was a piece of bad luck, for she had hoped that the nice-looking young man might remember her. Happily, no other passengers besieged the counter at the moment, so that without loss of time June was able to describe the parcel and to announce the fact that the ticket she had received for it was missing.

Exactly as she had foreseen the clerk raised an objection. Without a ticket she couldn't have the parcel. "But I simply must have it," said June. And spurred by the knowledge that there was not one moment to lose in arguing the case, she boldly lifted the flap of the counter and entered the cloak-room itself.

"No use coming in here," said the Clerk, crustily. "You can't take nothing away without a ticket."

"But my purse has been stolen, I tell you," said June.

"Then I should advise you to go and see the station-master."

"I can't wait to do that." And with the defiance of despair, expecting each moment to hear the voice of Uncle Si at her back, June ignored the Clerk, and proceeded to gaze up and down the numerous and heavily burdened luggage racks for her property.

XXXIV

"NOT a bit o' use, don't I tell you." The Clerk was growing angry.

June pretended not to hear. Her heart beating fast she went on with her search for the parcel; yet in the midst of it she grew aware that somebody was approaching the counter. She dare not pause to look who it was, for she knew only too well that it was almost bound to be Uncle Si.

The Clerk uttered another snarl of protest as he turned away to attend to the new comer. As he did so, June breathed a prayer that her eye might fall on the parcel in that instant, for her only hope now was to seize it and fly. That, however, was not to be. She had omitted to notice the place in which it had been put, and do as she would she could not find it now.

At this crucial moment, there emerged from the inner office her friend of the green corduroy. She simply leapt at what was now her one remaining chance.

"Oh, I'm so glad you've come," cried June, in a voice that was a little frantic: "You remember my bringing a brown paper parcel here, don't you—about two hours ago?"

The tone, tinged as it was with hysteria, caused Green Corduroy to look at June with mild astonishment. "I've lost the ticket you gave me for it, but I'm sure you remember my bringing it." Her brain seemed on fire. "Don't you remember my giving you a ten shilling note? And you had to go and get the change."

Green Corduroy was a slow-brained youth, but a knitting of the brow seemed to induce a hazy recollection of the incident. But while the process was going on, June gave a glance over her shoulder, and behold there was Uncle Si the other side of the counter. A second glance told her, moreover, that Crusty Sides already had the fatal ticket in his hand.

What must she do? It was not a moment for half measures. While she was stirring the memory of Green Corduroy, the treasure would be gone. She did not hesitate. Observing Crusty Sides wheel, paper in hand, with the slow austerity of one of the Company's oldest and most respected servants towards a luggage rack near by, June seized the clue. Of a sudden her eyes lit on the parcel at the top of the pile. Already the responsible fingers of Crusty Sides were straying upwards, yet before they could enclose the Van Roon, June made a dash for it, and managed to whisk it away from under his nose.

Her brain was like quicksilver now. She had a mad impulse to rush off with the treasure without further explanation; all the same she was able to resist it, for she realized that such a course would be too full of peril.

"Yes—this is it," she said in an urgent whisper to Green Corduroy. And as she spoke, with a presence of mind, which in the circumstances was a little uncanny, she slipped behind a large pile of boxes out of view of Uncle Si.

"Surely you remember my bringing it?"

Green Corduroy seemed to think that he did remember. At this point Crusty Sides, with an air of outrage, sternly interposed. "But a pawty claims it. And here's his ticket."

"The ticket's mine," said June, in a fierce whisper. "It's been taken from my purse."

"Nothin' to do with us, that ain't," said Crusty Sides.

"But you *do* remember my bringing it, don't you?" Beseechingly June turned to Green Corduroy. And he, that nice-looking young man, with a frown of ever-deepening perplexity, slowly affirmed that he thought he did remember.

"The ticket's what we've got to go by," said Crusty Sides, sternly. "Nothin' else matters to us."

"If you'll look at it," said June to Green Corduroy, "you'll see that it's made out in your writing."

Green Corduroy looked and saw that it was. As far as he was concerned, that seemed to clinch the argument. And even Crusty Sides, a born bureaucrat, was rather impressed by it. "You say this here ticket's been taken off on you?" he asked.

"Yes," said June in an excited whisper. "By my wicked thief of an uncle."

Instantly she regretted the imprudence of her words.

"Uncle a thief, eh?" proclaimed Crusty Sides, in a voice of such carrying power that to June it seemed that the Old Crocodile could hardly fail to hear him.

"Anyhow, this gentleman knows that it was I who brought the parcel," she said, determinedly to Green Corduroy.

That young man looked her straight in the eye, and then declared that he did know. Further, like many minds "slow in the uptake," when once in motion they are prone to deep conclusions. "Seems to me, Nobby," he weightily affirmed, under the stimulus no doubt of being addressed as a gentleman, in the Company's time, by such a good-looking girl, "that as this lady has got the parcel, and we have got the ticket for it, she and Uncle had better fight it out between 'em."

"I don't know about that," growled Nobby.

Green Corduroy, however, stimulated by the fiery anguish of June's glance, and no doubt still in thrall to the fact that she considered him a gentleman, was not to be moved from the statesmanlike attitude he had taken up. "You let 'em fight it out, Nobby. This lady was the one as brought it here."

"I gave you a ten shilling note, didn't I?" The voice of June was as honeyed as the state of her feelings would permit.

"Yes, and I fetched the change for you, didn't I?"

Crusty Sides shook a head of confirmed misogyny. "Very irregular, that's all I've got to say about it."

"Maybe it is, Nobby. But it's nothing to do with you and me."

Green Corduroy, with almost the air of a knight errant, took the all-important slip of paper from his colleague. Flaunting it in gallant fingers, he moved up slowly to the counter.

S. Gedge Antiques, buying spectacles on nose, knotted cudgel in hand, was impatiently waiting. "The parcel is claimed by the lady who brought it," June heard Green Corduroy announce.

She waited for no more. Following close behind Crusty Sides, who also moved up to the counter, she slipped quietly through an adjacent door to the main line platform before Uncle Si grew fully alive to the situation.

Clasping the parcel to her bosom, she glided swiftly down the platform, and out by the booking hall, travelling as fast as her legs would take her, without breaking into a run, which would have looked like guilt, and might have attracted public notice. She did not dare to glance back, for she was possessed by a fear that the old man and his stick were at her heels.

Once clear of the station itself, she yielded to the need of putting as much distance between Uncle Si and herself as a start so short would permit. There was now hope of throwing him off the track. Thus, as soon as she reached the Victoria Street corner, she scrambled on to a bus that was in the act of moving away.

One seat only was vacant and, as in a state of imminent collapse she sank down upon it, she ventured for the first time to look behind her. She quite expected to find Uncle Si at her elbow already, but with a gasp of relief she learned that the old man was nowhere in sight.

XXXV

JUNE did not know in which direction the bus was going. And when the conductor came for her fare, which he did as soon as the vehicle began to move, she was quite at a loss for a destination. There was nothing for it but to draw a bow at a venture. She asked for Oxford Circus, the only nodal point of the metropolis, besides Charing Cross, with which she was familiar. By a rare piece of luck, Oxford Circus was included in its route, and what remained of the shilling the girl at the teashop had given her was sufficient to get her there, and leave four pence in hand.

Alighting at Oxford Circus, she stood under a lamp to consider what she should do now. There was nowhere she could go, there was not one friend to whom she could turn. Battered and spent in body and spirit by all that had happened to her during the last few hours she was now in a flux of terror to which she dare not yield.

At first she thought of seeking advice of a policeman, but it would have been extremely difficult just then to tell her strange story. Its complications were many and fantastic; besides, and she trembled at the idea, it was by no means clear that she would be able to establish her claim to the Van Roon in the eye of the law.

Still, something would have to be done. She must find a home of some kind not only for her treasure, but for herself. Feeling desperately in need of help, she decided as a preliminary measure to spend three of her four remaining pence on a cup of tea. She had a vague hope that in that magic beverage inspiration might lurk.

The hope, as it chanced, was not vain. Near by was an A.B.C. shop; and she had hardly sat down at one of its marble-topped tables when, by an association of ideas, her mysterious acquaintance, Mr. Adolph Keller, sprang again into her mind. He had given her his address. Alas, the slip of paper on which it was written was in her purse, but she had a particularly good memory, and by raking it fiercely she was able to recall the fact that his place of domicile was Haliburton Studios, Manning Square.

She did not like trusting any man on an acquaintance so slight, especially as it had come about in so odd a fashion, but Mr. Keller had shown himself very friendly, and there was no one else to whom she could turn. Sipping her cup of tea, in slow and grateful weariness, she began to develop this idea. Horse sense, Mr. Boultby had always said, was her long suit; therefore she well understood the peril of taking a comparative stranger into her confidence. But very cogently she put to herself the question: What else could she do?

Of sundry policemen, who were very obliging, June asked the way to Manning Square. It was in Soho, not so very far from Oxford Circus, as she remembered Mr. Keller saying, and, in spite of a local fog which had come on in the last twenty minutes, the police were so helpful that she had no great difficulty in getting there. During the short journey her mind was much engaged in settling just what she would and would not say to Mr. Keller. She decided that as far as might be practicable she would leave the picture out of the case. It might not be possible to exclude it, but at any rate she would begin by offering to sit to him as a model, in accordance with his suggestion; and with that the pretext of her visit she would see if she could get him to lend her a little money to tide over immediate needs.

By the time she had come to Manning Square it was a few minutes past seven. Two complete circuits had to be made of this dingy, ill-smelling gap in the heart of Soho, before she came upon Haliburton Studios, which were not in the Square itself, but in a dismal by-street debouching from it. The tall block of buildings which comprised the studios was equally dismal, and as June entered a vestibule that shewed no light, she felt a sudden chill strike at her heart.

This, however, was not a moment to quail. It was a case, if ever there was one, of any port in a storm. The hazard of her errand fell upon her like a pall, but the knowledge that she had only a penny left with which to obtain a night's lodging was a veritable barb in the flesh.

Try as she would she could not recall the number of Mr. Keller's studio; nor was the information to be found upon the walls of the vestibule which she was not able to see. But while she stood at the foot of a winding flight of stone steps, striving to meet the difficulty which faced her now, she heard someone coming down. At the sound she went back to the door by which she had entered, where a lamp contending feebly against the fog, would enable her to see anyone who passed out of the flats.

The person who did so proved to be one of June's own sex, a youngish woman whose fur coat seemed to accentuate a note of tawdry and flamboyant finery. Even in the semi-darkness June could see that her face was rouged.

She had no illusion as to the kind of person she addressed:

"You want Mr. Keller's studio?" The woman peered into June's face in a manner which she felt to be decidedly objectionable. "It's the second door on the first landing." The tone, offhand, and more than a little contemptuous, was like a blow in the face.

XXXVI

IT was not until the woman had passed out of the vestibule into the street that June could find courage to mount the stone stairs.

The knocker on the second door was so crazy that it threatened to break off in her hand. Tact and skill were called for to draw sound from it at all; bell there was none; but a faint light percolated through the fanlight and it was a glimpse of this which heartened June to persevere. By dint of application she was able to coax a few sounds out of the knocker, a feat which at last brought reward. The beam beyond the fanlight expanded; there was a shuffle of approaching slippers; and then the door came open.

Mr. Keller, wearing a dressing gown in lieu of a coat, stood before her.

"Hulloa!" he said.

Before June could find words of her own she had been recognized: "Why— it's you!" The gentlemanly voice sounded most agreeable. "Walk right in. You're welcome as the flowers in May."

Tossed by the tempest as Mr. Keller's visitor still was, she could not help contrasting such a welcome with the air and manner of Uncle Si.

XXXVII

THE geniality of Adolph Keller had a tonic effect upon June's depression. She crossed his threshold with a sense of extreme relief, as one who finds a refuge from the storm. He closed the door of the flat, and then led the way into a spacious room with a high ceiling which was fixed up as a studio.

It was not without an air of comfort. The main part had been screened off; within a small but seductive inner space a bright fire mingled pleasant gleams with the radiance of the electric lamp. Two low wicker chairs were set invitingly near the hearth, and a table piled with books and magazines was between them. Amid these, however, space had been found for a tobacco jar, a siphon, a glass and a bottle of whisky. On the floor was a French novel, which he had laid down open to let her in.

Mr. Keller, evidently, was making himself comfortable for the night. The contrast between this snug and cheerful room and the rising fog, from which June had just escaped, struck her at once as delightful. With a little sigh of gratitude, she sank at the cordial invitation of her host into the first of the easy chairs.

He remembered her quite well, of course, yet for the moment he had forgotten her name, and what to June was the more surprising, the appointment she had made with him for that very afternoon seemed to have passed right out of his mind. Yet she was quick to see, for her wits were now working at high pressure, that this strange forgetfulness was in her favour. At any rate, it was going to help her in the task of keeping, as far as possible, the Van Roon out of the case.

"Lyons', wasn't it, we met at? One day last week? Your name's——?"

"I'm Miss Gedge." June's tone was a shade "stand off," for that appeared to be correct in the circumstances.

"Miss Gedge—yes—of course. Stupid of me to forget." He fixed the eye of a man with a sense of humour upon this odd visitor. "I've a shocking memory for names. Very glad to see you, anyhow, Miss Gedge." He took the low chair opposite with the calm and easy air of a model host. "And very nice of you to come on a damp and foggy night."

The tone, rather than the words, put it up to June to explain her coming. She did so rather awkwardly, with a touch of "nerves." Yet before committing herself to any positive statement as to why she was there, she was careful to dispose the parcel she carried as far beyond the range of his eyes as was possible at the side of the wicker chair in which she sat.

"You told me the other day"—She found it impossible to control the queer little tremble in her voice—"that you wanted an artist's model, and that my hair was just the colour you were looking for."

"By Jove, yes," he laughed. "Your hair's topping." The laugh deepened to enthusiasm. "It's the colour I want, to a hayseed." An eye of veiled appraisement passed slowly over her. "And what's almost as important there's stooks of it."

"Yes, there is," said June, doing her best to pick up his light tone of intimacy. "It is important, I suppose, for an artist's model to have hair long and thick."

"Ra-ther!" As he looked at her sideways, out of the corner of one eye, his tone seemed to change a little; and then he got up alertly from his chair, the mantle of the model host again upon him. "I'm afraid there's not much to offer you in the way of refreshment. There's only whisky. If you'll excuse me a minute, I'll fetch another glass."

"Oh, no, please, not for me," said June quickly. She was very tired and horribly depressed, but she had been strictly brought up.

The host seemed a little amused by her vehemence. He looked at her keenly with a pair of curious, small, near-set eyes, which June liked even less now than when she had noticed them first. "Well, have a cigarette, anyhow. These are like mother's milk." And he offered a box of Virginia.

June also declined a cigarette, in the same odd, rather fluttered tone which caused him to smile in a way that added to her nervousness.

"No? Well, make yourself comfy, anyhow. Draw your chair up to the fire."

She thanked him in a voice which, in spite of itself was a little prim, and which assured him that she was quite warm enough where she was. The attempted lightness and ease had gone; a subtle sense of fear, bred of hidden danger yet without any root in fact or logic, was rising in her. The position itself was embarrassing, yet so far Mr. Keller had shown no wish to presume upon it. Up till now he had been easy and charming; but June, in spite of worldly inexperience, had the intuitions of her sex to guide her; and she felt instinctively that there might be a great deal behind these graces. She was grateful all the same; they were much needed balm for many bruises.

When Mr. Keller sat down again in the wicker chair, about two yards away from her, a sense of languor crept upon June. The warmth of the fire, the glow of the lamp, the notes of a singularly quiet voice were like a subtle drug. Alive to danger as she was, its caress was hard to resist. Such a position was one of acute peril, for she was literally throwing herself upon the mercy of a person who was very much an unknown quantity, yet what alternative was there?

"Don't mind a pipe, I hope?" The polite voice from the chair opposite was not really ironical; it was merely kind and friendly, yet feminine intuition shivering upon the dark threshold of a mighty adventure knew well enough how easily a tone of that kind could turn to something else.

"Oh no, I don't mind at all." She tried again to get the right key, but a laugh she could not control, high-pitched and irrelevant, was horribly betraying.

"That's all right then."

For about a minute, Mr. Keller puffed away in a sort of whimsical silence. Then he said with a soft fall, whose mere sweetness had the power to alarm, "Your hair's jolly. Very jolly indeed!"

June nervously muttered that she was very glad he liked it.

"So much of it, don't you know. Awfully useful to me just now. Quantity's almost as valuable as the colour. Does it reach your waist when you let it down?"

June, not without a little pride, said that her hair when let down reached below her waist.

"Capital!" said Mr. Keller, with a laugh. "The very thing I'm looking for just now. You'll make a stunning Andromeda."

June had not heard of Andromeda. She had read some Dickens, and a little George Eliot, and she could remember bits of Shakespeare learned at school, but her tastes were not literary. She pretended to know all about Andromeda, yet the next words of Mr. Keller were a proof that he was not deceived. June did not know, however, that he had pierced clean through her ignorance.

"She's the altogether. A classical subject."

"I like classical subjects myself." Abruptly June's mind went back to Miss Preece, the revered head mistress of the Blackhampton High School where it had been her privilege to spend one term. Her voice rose a whole octave, in its involuntary desire to approximate as closely as possible to that of a real lady.

"So do I." Mr. Keller's humorous purr was that of a man well pleased. "That's capital."

"You can't beat classical subjects, can you?" said June, making a wild attempt to achieve the conversational.

Again Mr. Keller looked across at her out of those near-set eyes of which by now she was rather afraid. "No, you can't," he said. "So large and so simple, and yet they strike so deep. They are life itself. A sort of summing up, don't you know, of all that has been, all that can be, all that will be."

June responded with more composure than she had yet shewn that she supposed it was so. It was nice to listen to talk of this kind from a man of Mr. Keller's polish. The chair was most comfortable, and how good it was to be in front of the bright fire! Her nerves were being lulled more and more as if by a drug; the sense of her peril amid this sea of danger into which she had plunged began to grow less.

"I expect," said Mr. Keller, in a tone so friendly and so casual that it fed the new sense of peace which was now upon June, "I expect you are pretty well used to the altogether?"

Even if she did not know in the least what was meant by "the altogether," it did not seem to be quite wise to confess such ignorance. "Ye-es, I suppose I am." And in a weak attempt to rise to his own agreeable plane of intimacy she laughed rather foolishly.

"Capital!" said Adolph Keller. "You are a well built girl." He sipped a little whisky. "Excellent shoulders. Figure's full of fine lines. Bust well developed. Plenty of heart room. Everything just right."

She coloured at the literal way in which he catalogued her points; even if it was done in the manner of an artist and a gentleman, one was a little reminded of a dog or a horse.

"I'll fix you up a screen. And then you can get ready." He sipped a little more whisky, and rose briskly and cheerfully. "Near the fire; it's real chillsome to-night. And when you pose you can sit on top of it if you like." He opened the lid of the coal box, and replenished the fire. "We must take care you don't catch cold. If you feel a draught, you can have a rug round your knees. I only want to make a rough sketch of the lines of the figure, to begin with; the shoulders chiefly. It won't take long. Quite sure you won't have a finger?" He pointed to the whisky. "Buck you up a bit. You look rather down."

June was quite sure that she would not have a finger. Mr. Keller passed beyond the screen into the studio itself to procure a second screen. June felt this activity to be alarming. It brought her up against the fact that she was there in the capacity of an artist's model. Suddenly it dawned upon her that she was expected to take off her clothes.

XXXVIII

MR. KELLER cleared a space near the fire, and elaborately arranged a second screen, which June did not fail to notice was decorated with nude figures.

"There you are," he said. "That'll keep you snug. And if you sit on a stool by the fire with a rug over your knees, you'll be as warm as a kitten."

June paled, but she did not speak.

"Begin as soon as you like, the sooner the better. Are you quite sure you won't have just a spot?" Again he pointed to the bottle on the table. "You look as if you want a drop of something."

Once more June declined the offer in a voice which in her own ear seemed absurdly small and faint.

"Pity," said Mr. Keller cheerfully, as he looked at her. "It'd put some life in you." And then, as she was still inert, he went on in a tone which pleasantly mingled gentlemanliness and business, "I always pay a sovereign an hour, you know—for the altogether."

A light of fear came into June's large eyes. "Does it mean," she asked, shyly and awkwardly, as she looked away from him, "that I shall have to take off my clothes?"

"Why, of course," he said, matter-of-factly. Her obvious embarrassment was not lost upon him, but the knowledge did not appear in his manner.

June shivered slightly. In that shiver a deep instinct spoke for her. "I couldn't do that," she said.

"Why not?" He lit a cigarette. "Aren't you well?"

June was very far from well. She felt within an ace of being overcome by all that had happened to her. Besides her bruised shoulders were still aching horribly. Even without the deep instinct that governed her, it would not have been possible to expose them.

"No-no," she said, "I—I'm not well."

As she spoke, she had to fight a powerful desire to burst into tears. But her latent fear of this man had suddenly grown. Overdriven as she was, however, she was yet conscious of a stern need to keep a hold upon herself. She knew nothing, less than nothing of her host, beyond the fact that he was smooth of speech. On the surface he was a gentleman, but as he stood looking down at her now she glimpsed in his dark eyes that which seemed to countervail everything.

Again she shivered. The sense of helplessness was paralyzing. It was as if a chasm had abruptly opened right under her feet. She was at his mercy. But she must not give one thought, so long as a spark of will remained with her, to the possibility of throwing herself upon it.

He continued to stand looking at her while she fought against a welling weakness that must have been only too patent. Then, as if a little puzzled by her, he went and fetched a glass from another part of the studio. He poured out a small quantity of spirit and offered it neat.

"Drink this. It'll do you good."

His voice, for the first time, had the grip of authority. He held the glass to her lips, but as if containing deadly fumes they shrank from contact with it.

"Don't be a little fool." The sharp tone was like the touch of a whip. "Why don't you do as you are told?"

She had not the strength to resent the command even if she was able to muster the power to resist it.

"Look here," he said, confronted by a limit to patience. "Why have you come? What's the matter with you? Tell me."

She remained mute. There was nothing she could tell. A lodging for the night, food, advice, protection were what she sought. Dominated completely as she was by hard necessity, she yet dare not confide in Keller. The subtle change that had come upon him since he had fixed up the screen and poured out the whisky filled her with an intense longing to get away. In spite of a growing weakness, which now threatened dire collapse, the subtle feelers of her mind were on the track of danger.

With a slow gathering of will that was a form of agony, she tried to collect the force to rise from the perilous comfort of the low wicker chair. But she was not able to rouse herself to action before the effort had been nipped by his next remark.

"If you've no intention of sitting to me, you'd better say in two words why you've come here."

The voice was no longer smooth; there was a cutting edge to it, lacerating to June's ear.

"I wanted you to lend me a sovereign."

It was the literal truth. But the unguarded words slipped from her before she could shape or control them. Almost before they were uttered she realized their bitter unwisdom.

"You can have a sovereign—if that's all you want." His tone grew light again. "But it's only fair and reasonable that you should earn it first."

Strive as she would, she was not able to keep a faint dew of tears from filming her eyes.

"No need to take off more than your bodice, if that's what's troubling you."

With her shoulders on fire, she could not take off her bodice, even had she wished to do so.

She sat inert while he continued to stand before her. The thread of will she still had, fully concentrated though it was on getting away from him, was now unequal to the ugly challenge of his voice and eyes.

"Let me go," she half whimpered.

Suddenly, in her own despite, her defences had begun palpably to fail. The blunder was fatal—if the cry of nature overdriven can be called a blunder. His eyes pinned hers. Trembling under the spell of their hard cunning she began to perceive that it was now a case of the serpent and the bird.

A frown darkened his face as he cast back to the first meeting with this girl. He tried to recall their conversation in the teashop two days ago. At the time it had interested him considerably, but he had laughed over it since, and decided to dismiss it from his mind. She had told him a cock-and-bull story about a picture. He could not recall the details of an absurd yarn which had not seemed worth his while to remember. At the best it was a bald and unconvincing narrative. But it concerned a Rembrandt. No, not a Rembrandt. A Van Roon!

With a heightening of curiosity, Adolph Keller gazed at the hunted creature now shrinking from his eyes. By Jove, she looked as if she had been through it! Something pretty bad must have happened to her quite recently. But why had she come to him?

Thoughts of the picture set his active mind to work. She had come to him because she was in want of money. So much, at least, was clear. To judge by the look of her, she had probably, at a moment's notice, been turned out of house and home. A domestic servant, no doubt, and no better than she should be, although a certain taste about her much-rumpled clothes and an attempt at refinement of manner suggested the wish to rise above her class.

In the midst of this quick mind process, Adolph Keller saw the brown paper parcel. It was in the place where his visitor had laid it when she had first sat down. He noticed that she had cunningly reared it by the farther side of her chair, so that it might be beyond the immediate range of his eye.

Keller's pulse quickened, yet he allowed no hint of his intriguing discovery to shew in his manner. Once again it changed towards his guest. The tone of sharp authority vanished. Twisting a dark moustache round strong, yet delicate fingers, his air of extreme gentlemanliness verged upon the sugary, as he said: "I don't like to see you like this. I don't really."

The tone's unexpectedness, perhaps even more than its kindness, moved June to further tears.

"You had better tell me, hadn't you, just what's upset you?"

She shook miserably. And then, thrown off her guard, by this new note of concern, she found the courage to venture again: "Please lend me a sovereign and let me go. I promise solemnly to pay it back."

He smiled in a way obviously to reassure. "What's your hurry, my dear girl?" Soft, as were the words, they yet caused the design to fail.

Their non-effect was clearly visible in the girl's tragic eyes. She was caught in a trap; all his trimmings and posturings seemed only to emphasize the fact that she had no means of getting out.

Like a powerful drug the brutal truth attacked her brain. It was as if its higher nerve centres could no longer act. She was completely in the power of this man. And only too well did she know that he knew it.

Inevitably as fate, those slim fingers dipped towards the side of her chair. "What have we here?" The inflexion was lightly playful, yet it drove all the blood from her heart. "May I look?" His hand closed on the parcel before she could muster one futile finger to stay it.

Galvanized, as if by electricity, she sprang up from her chair without knowing what she did. "Please—it's mine!" Without conscious volition she tried weakly to defend her property.

He put her off with the cheery playfulness of a teasing brother. "Just one little peep," he said. The treasure was yielding its wrappings already to those deft fingers. Smiling all the time, he treated the thing as a mere joke. And he was able to give the joke full effect, because, not for an instant did he expect it to turn out anything else.

XXXIX

ADOLPH KELLER gave a low whistle. He took in his breath quickly. The treasure, in its rare incredible beauty, had declared itself to his eyes. And to the eyes of an artist, wholly unready for the revelation, it came in a single devastating flash.

"My God!" he said, in a whisper, half rapture, half surprise.

Aglow with excitement he removed the shade from the electric lamp. Holding the picture beneath the light, an arm's length away from his eyes, he turned it over several times in that fashion of the expert which June had now learned to dread. And then humming softly, and with his fingers still enclosing it, he passed beyond the screen to a table on which lay a microscope.

With a feeling of nausea, June watched everything he did. Only too well she knew that the microscope would simply feed his excitement. In a fresh spasm of weakness, she reeled against the chimneypiece. She had now the sensation of having fallen over a precipice into a bottomless pit. Already she was sinking down, down, down into night and damnation.

Keller soon returned, microscope in hand; and while he plied it under the lamp she dare not glance at his face. Passively she waited for his next words. The power of action had left her.

When, at last, he did speak, his voice was calmer and gentler than she looked for. "Tell me," he said, "how did you come by this rather jolly old thing?"

The tone of playfulness was almost silly. But she was not deceived, for striking through it was the oiliness of Uncle Si. And she knew that she had only to glance at that face shining pale under the lamp, which was a thing she dare not do, to carry the resemblance farther.

"Tell me," he repeated softly.

A sense of destiny seemed to weigh her down.

"It has been given to me." Her voice was hardly audible.

"Given to you." He smiled a little, as his mind went off in search of the half forgotten fragments of their talk two days ago. "Let me see—your best boy, wasn't it?—who made you a present of a picture—by a well known R. A.?"

June did not know how to answer, yet she was able to realize that an answer of some kind was imperative.

"That's it," she said. There was nothing else she could say.

"I rather like this thing, do you know." His voice was acquiring a sort of growing brightness which seemed quite to admit her to his confidence. "It might almost have been painted by the snuffy old Scotsman—one MacFarlane by name—who first shewed me how to draw. It's just in his manner. By Jove!"—The voice of Adolph Keller seemed to glow with humour—"I can almost see that cantankerous whiskyfied old fool daubing that water and those trees. But in his day not a bad painter, you know, not a bad painter." And the voice of the pupil tailed off in a note of reluctant affection of which he seemed half ashamed.

It was June's turn to say something, but her frozen lips could not utter.

Keller, holding the picture in both hands, gave her a side look, which he tried, as far as he could, to conceal. In the midst of this scrutiny, he said: "To you, I expect, one picture is very much the same as another?"

"I know what I like," June was able to answer, perhaps for no better reason than that by now she understood only too well that it hardly mattered what she answered.

"Well, anyhow, that's something," said Keller, with a forced laugh. "Great thing to know your mind in these little matters. Nice of your best boy—was your best boy, wasn't it?—to give you this. Not that it's worth much to the ordinary buyer. Pictures are like lovers, you know. Their beauty, sometimes, is in the eye of the beholder."

It sickened her to hear him lie in this way. The deadly sensation of falling, falling, falling came over her again. But she let him run on. For one thing she lacked the power to check him; and even had the power been hers it would have been worse than futile to try to do so.

XL

"LOOK here," said Adolph Keller, in the midst of his prattle. "I've taken rather a fancy to this bit of a thing. Suppose you let me have it. I'll give you a landscape in exchange; I've one or two that are not so bad, and you shall have your pick. Moreover," and he fixed June with a steady eye, "you shall have your sovereign as well."

She shook her head tensely. Inclination now wished to tell him the fabulous worth of the picture; but prudence said no. The calculated way in which he had lied was proof enough that he knew its value already. She held out her hand. In a voice dry and choking she said: "Please give it to me. I ought to be going."

He gazed at her with the eye of a condor. "Much better take what you can get for it, hadn't you? It'll be a difficult thing to sell, you know. This is quite a fair offer."

"Give it me, please," June gasped miserably.

"Don't be a little fool."

The tone was like the closing of a door. She knew at once that he had not the remotest intention of giving it back to her. And what followed immediately upon the words made the fact only too clear. He laid the picture on a table some little distance away, and then pouring out a quantity of spirit he drank it neat. His next act was to produce a case from which he took forth a pound note.

"Here you are," he said roughly. "Take this and be jolly thankful. And then make yourself scarce, as soon as you like."

It was an intimation that there was going to be no more pretence. The tone was that of a cynical bully who judged it to be best for both parties that the owner of the Van Roon should now be given an unmistakable perception of reality.

Overdriven as June was, the knowledge that at the very last she was to be robbed of the fruits of her hard-won victory was more than she could bear. Faced by this man's cool insolence and mean cunning, she was swept by a tide of rage. He knew that she could have no proof of ownership, and he was going to reap a full advantage from the fact. At that moment, of an unendurable bitterness, she was spurred and lashed by the same Devil which two hours ago had driven Uncle Si to frenzy.

"The picture's mine," she cried hoarsely. And then, advancing towards the table. "Give it me ... you thief!"

At the ugly word he recoiled a step, but the next instant he grabbed her by the wrists. In the struggle to get free, she felt his evil breath upon her face. Many a dram must have gone to so much foulness; as his powerful grip slowly fastened upon her there came swift knowledge of a new and more urgent peril.

She was alone with this man in his own flat. Utterly without a means of defence as she was, she had been mad enough to offer him a physical challenge. In a few seconds she would be at his mercy. And then, inflamed by drink, and being the kind of beast that he was he would insist upon the spoils of the victor.

Before she was fully alive to what was taking place she found herself forced slowly backwards to the wall. She knew then that she was fighting for her life, and for that which in this unspeakable moment implied so much more.

"I'll teach you to come here, you——!" His face was that of a maniac.

She gave a shriek of terror and lashed out wildly at his shins. Fighting like a tigress, at first she kept him at bay. The power of his hands was terrific, but she did not scruple to use the weapons nature had given her. After a long and horrible minute of claws, teeth and feet, in the course of which she bit him savagely, it grew reasonably clear to Adolph Keller that if only she cares to use it, the female of the species does not lack a means of defence.

"You beauty!" he gasped, as he struggled to shift his grip upon her.

Goaded by the furies he found his way at last to her throat. And then she felt that he was going to kill her. Moreover, as his madman's grip began slowly to distil her life through its fingers, he perceived how simple a matter it was going to be.

XLI

KELLER'S own defences were almost down, but just in the nick of time was he able to realize this fact. And man of calculation that he was, even in this moment of madness, when each devil in his soul conspired for his final overthrow, he was able, by dint of underlying coolness of blood to make a powerful effort to save himself.

He longed to kill this wretched girl, but as he pressed his fingers into the soft and delicate throat, he was stayed by thoughts of the price that would have to be paid for wreaking an insane passion upon her.

For a wild instant he feared that the premonition had come too late; the primordial beast in his heart had slipped its chain. Already it had tasted blood. In this frenzy of revolt, the fetters imposed by centuries of civil life were hardly likely to be submitted to again.

Gasping and helpless June felt that she was dying. The clutch upon her was that of the garotte. Her eyes began to darken. Clawing the air for the breath she could not draw, the end that seemed inevitable now was yet far off.

At last, as if responding to her prayer, a kind of stupor came upon her. But how tardily! Brain, heart, soul, body contended no more against a power beyond their own; at last her slow life was ebbing. The end of torment indescribable would be akin to joy.

Æons seemed to pass. A flicker of summer lightning, ages off, came and was not. So faint it was and so far that it could only be reckoned in terms of eternity. More light flickered which, of a sudden, grew miraculously near. The vivid sense of pain returned; she grew alive to the fact that the harsh glare of the electric bulb, which was still unshaded, was beating down upon her eyes.

Powerful arms were about her, she was being supported. The fumes of raw spirit were in her nostrils, a glass was pressed against her lips. She fought again to get free, only feebly now, for this was but a last reaction of a dying will. Yet the final word of all was nature's. When mind itself had ceased to count, the life-force grasped wildly at the proffered means of life.

"Thank God!" she heard a thick voice mutter. "I felt sure you were a goner."

A livid face, whose eyes seemed to blind her own, materialized suddenly before her. "Drink it up, damn you!" said the voice hoarsely. "And then get out—you——!"

It was insult for the sake of insult, and therefore the full measure of her victory. But it meant less than nothing to June now. She scarcely heard, or hearing did not comprehend. Beyond pain and suffering, beyond good and evil her torn spirit only craved release.

As soon as the fire in the glass had kindled her veins this desire was met, less, however, by the operation of her own will than by the will of Keller. As if she had been a noisome reptile whom his flesh abhorred, and yet had a superstitious fear of killing, he dragged her out of the room, along the short passage as far as the door of the flat. Slipping back the catch, he flung her out on to the landing.

As she fetched up against the iron railing opposite the door, which guarded the well of the staircase, she heard a low hiss: "Take yourself off as soon as you like, you——, or you'll find the police on your track."

XLII

JUNE had no idea of the time that she lay in a huddle against the railing. But it may not have been so long in fact as it was in experience. Shattered she might be, yet unknown to herself, there was still a reserve of fighting power to draw upon.

Cold iron, moreover, and raw air had a magic of their own. Clear of that mephitic room and the foul presence of Keller, a fine human machine began slowly to renew itself. Except for a faint gleam from the room out of which she had just come, stealing through the fanlight of the door out of which she had been flung, there was not a sign of light upon the staircase. The entire building appeared to be deserted. Its stone-flagged steps were full of echoes as soon as she ventured to move upon them; and when clinging to the railing for support she had painfully descended two she entered a region of total darkness.

It was like going down into a pit. Could she have only been sure that death awaited her below, she might have been tempted to fling herself into it headlong. But she knew that the ground was not far off.

Three or four steps more brought her to the vestibule. At the end of it was a door, open to the street. Outside this door shone a faint lamp, round which weird shadows circled in a ghostly witch-dance. The night beyond was a wall of horrors, which she had lost the will to face.

Met by this pitiless alternative, she recoiled against the wall of the vestibule, huddling in its darkest corner, behind the stairs. Crouching here, like a hunted thing at bay, she fought for the courage to go out and face her destiny.

She fought in vain. Half collapsed as she now was, a spur was needed to drive her into the grim wilderness of the open street. One glance at the crypt outside sufficed to tell her that with no point to make for, it would be best to stay where she was and hope soon to die.

Why had she not had the sense to throw herself down the stairs and kill herself? A means would have to be found before the night was out. She could bear no more. A terrible reaction was upon her. It was as if a private door in her mind had suddenly given way and a school of awful phantoms had rushed in and flooded it.

She was living in a nightmare that was too bad to be true. But it was true and there lay its terror. Adrift in the dark canyons of that vast city, penniless and alone, with the marks of thieves and murderers upon her bruised body, and her treasure stolen, there was only one thing to look for now.

Death, however, would not be easy to come by. As she huddled in cold darkness in the recess behind the stairs she felt that her will was going. To enter the night and make an end would need courage; but a miserable clapping together of the jaws was sign enough that the last hope of all was slipping away from her.

XLIII

COWERING in body and spirit in that dark corner, time, for June, became of no account. Perhaps, after all, she might be allowed to die where she was. As a kind of inertia crept upon her she was able to draw something of comfort from the thought. It would be better than the river or being run over in the street.

She grew very cold; yet a lowering of the body's temperature induced a heightened consciousness. Aches and pains sprang into life; the forces of her mind began to reassert themselves; the phantoms about her took on new powers of menace. Gradually it became clear to June, under the goad of this new and sharper phase of suffering, that mere passivity could not induce the death she longed for.

No, it was not in that way the end would come. She would have to go into the shadow-land beyond the lamp, and seek some positive means of destroying herself. For that reason she must hold on to the fragment of will that now remained to her. It alone could release her from the awful pit in which she was now engulfed.

She gathered herself for an effort to move towards the fog-encircled light at the entrance to the street. But the effort, when made, amounted to nothing. Her limbs were paper, all power of volition was gone.

The October raw struck to her blood. She began to whimper miserably. To pain of mind was added pain of body, but the delicate apparatus from whose harmony sprang the fuse of action was out of gear. Something must be done; yet no matter how definite the task, any form of doing was beyond her now.

At this dire moment, however, help came. It came, moreover, in an unlooked-for way. She heard a door slam over head. There was the sound of a match being struck, and then came a gingerly shuffle of feet on the stone stairs.

Someone was coming down. June cowered still lower into the dark recess at the back of the stairway. A man was approaching. And by the flicker of the match which he threw away as he reached the floor of the vestibule she saw that the man was Keller.

Faint and but momentary as was the glimpse afforded, June, with every sense strung again to the point of intensity, saw that under Keller's arm was a brown paper parcel. The sight of it was like a charm. Some fabulous djinnee might have lurked in that neat package, who commanded a miraculous power of reaction upon the human will.

Keller struck a second match and peered into the shadows. June knew that he was looking to see if she had lingered there, but the light could not pierce to the corner in which she crouched; and it burnt itself out, leaving him none the wiser.

Without striking another match Keller moved away from her towards the doorway, and as he did so June felt a swift release of heart and brain. A thrill of new energy ran through her. No sooner had Keller passed out of the vestibule, beyond the lamp into the fog, than without conscious impulse or design she began to follow him.

It may have been the reasoned act of a lucid being, but at first it did not appear to be so. Once, however, her limbs were moving, all her faculties, now intensely awake, seemed as if by magic to bear them company. As soon as she reached the open street, with Keller a clear ten yards ahead, the keen air on her face had an effect of strong wine. Her nerves felt again the sense of motion; the impulse of the natural fighter unfurled strong pinions within her. All the virile sense and the indomitable will of a sound inheritance rallied to her need.

Growing sensibly stronger at every yard, she followed Keller round the corner into Manning Square. The mist was thick, the lamps poor and few, but as well as she could she kept on his track. Lurking pantherlike in the deep shadows of the house-walls, she had approached within five yards of him by the time he had turned the corner into a bye-street. He went a few yards along this, and then zigzagged into a squalid ill-smelling thoroughfare whose dismal length seemed unending.

June had no difficulty in keeping up with these twists and winds, for Keller, impeded by the fog, moved slowly. For her, however, the fog had its own special problem, since there was a danger of losing him if he was allowed to get too far ahead; and yet if his steps were dogged too closely there was always the fear that he might turn round suddenly and see her.

At last the interminable street seemed to be nearing its end. For June, whose every faculty was now strung up to an unnatural acuteness, saw but a short distance in front the brightly lit awning of the Underground looming through the fog.

In a flash she realized the nature of the peril. Only too surely was this the bourn for which Keller was making. Once within its precincts and her last remaining hope would be gone.

It must be now or never. The spur of occasion drove deep in her heart. She knew but too well that the hope was tragically small, but wholly desperate as she was, with the penalty of failure simply not to be met, she would put all to the touch.

Closer and closer she crept up behind the quarry. But the entrance to the Tube loomed now so near that it began to seem certain that she must lose him before she could attempt what she had to do. Abruptly, however, within ten yards or so of his goal, Keller stopped. He began to search the pockets of his overcoat for a box of matches to relight his pipe which had gone out. While so doing, and in the preoccupation of the moment, he took the parcel from under his right arm, and set it rather carelessly beneath his left.

Providence had given June her chance. Like a falcon, she swooped forward. Aim and timing incredibly true, at the instant Keller struck a match and bent over his pipe, her fingers closed on the Van Roon, and whisked it out of his unguarded grasp.

XLIV

AS June turned and ran she heard a wild and startled oath. Before her was the eternal fog-laden darkness of the narrow street. But now it struck her with a thrill of pure terror that the mist was not thick enough to conceal her flight. The swift surprise of the onset had gained for her a start of a few yards, but instantly she knew that it would not suffice.

She ran, all the same, as if her heart would burst. But her legs seemed to wear the shackles that afflict one in a dream. Her most frantic efforts did not urge them on, and yet, in spite of that, they bore her better than she knew. Not a soul was in sight. She could hear Keller's boots echo on the damp pavement as they pounded behind her. It could only be a matter of seconds before his fingers were again on her throat. But this time, before robbing her of the Van Roon and getting clear, he would have to kill her.

The vow had hardly been made, when at the other side of the street she saw a thread of light. It came from a house whose door was open. Instinctively she turned and made one final dash for it. This was the last wild hope there was.

A man, it seemed, was in the act of leaving the house. Wearing overcoat and hat, he stood just within the doorway peering into the murk before venturing out. June flung herself literally upon him.

"Save me! Save me!" she was able to gasp. "A man! A man is after me!"

The house was of the poverty-stricken kind whose living room opens on to the street. June had a confused vision of a glowing lamp, a bright fire, a dingy tablecloth and several people seated around it. Her wild impact upon the man who was about to put off from its threshold drove him backwards several paces into the room. At the same instant a female voice, loud and imperious, rose from the table.

"Shut the door, Elbert, can't yer? The fog's comin' in that thick it'll put out the perishin' fire."

The bewildered Elbert, raked fore and aft by fierce women, automatically obeyed the truculent voice at his back, even while he gave ground in a collision which seemed to rob him of any wit that he might possess. With a deft turn of the heel, he dealt the door a kick which effectually closed it in the murderous face of the halting and hesitating Keller.

June, shuddering in every vein, clung to her protector.

"Gawd-love-us-all!" Cries and commotion arose from the table, yet almost at once the imperious voice soared above the din. "Set her down, can't yer, Elbert? Didn't yer see that bloke?"

"Ah—I did," said Elbert, stolidly pressing his queer armful into a chair near the fire.

"Better git after him lively," said the voice at the table. "He's the one as did in Kitty Lewis last week."

Elbert, a young man six feet tall and proportionately broad of shoulder, was not however a squire of dames. With a scared look on a face that even in circumstances entirely favourable could hardly rank as a thing of beauty, he moved to the door and slipped a bolt across. "Not goin' near the——" he said, sullenly. "Not goin' to be mixed up wiv it—not me."

The voice at the table, whose owner was addressed as Maw, proceeded "to tell off" Elbert. He was a skunk, he was no man, he was a mean swine. In the sight of Maw, who ran to words as well as flesh, Elbert was all this and more. She rose majestically, threatening to "dot him" if he didn't "'op in," and she came to June with an enormous bosom striving to burst from its anchorage, an apron that had once been white, and with her entire person exuding an odour peculiar to those of her sex who drink gin out of a teacup.

Three other people were at the table, and they were engaged upon a meal of toasted cheese, raw onions and beer. Of these, two were girls about sixteen, scared, slatternly and anæmic; the third was a toothless hag who looked ninety; and as the whole family, headed by Maw, suddenly crowded round June, the terrified fugitive, shuddering in the chair by the fire, hardly knew which of her deliverers was the most repulsive.

June fought with every bit of her strength against the threat of total collapse that assailed her now. In the desperate hope of warding off disaster, she gathered the last broken fragment of will. But nature had been driven too hard. For the second time within the space of one terrible hour, she lost the sense of where she was.

XLV

THE faces, with one exception, had receded into the background, when June returned slowly and painfully to a knowledge of what was happening. Maw was bending over her, and holding a cracked cup to her lips, and also "telling off" the others with a force and a scope of language that added not a little to June's fear.

Perhaps the smell of its contents had quite as much effect upon the sufferer as the cup's restorative powers. It was so distasteful to one who had been taught to shun all forms of alcohol, that a sheer disgust helped to bring her round.

At first, however, her mind was hardly more than a blank. But when, at last, a few links of recognition floated up into it out of the immediate past and hitched themselves to this strange present, a shock of new terror nearly overwhelmed her again. Recollection was like a knife stab. The Van Roon! The Van Roon! Where was it? Oh, God—if she had not got it after all!

The thought was pain, pure and exquisite. But the case did not really call for it. She was clutching the Van Roon convulsively to her breast like a child holds a doll. As she wakened slowly to this fact her brain wonderfully cleared.

The mind must be kept alive, if only to defend this talisman for whose sake she had already suffered so outrageously. She did not know where she was, and the evil presence holding the foul cup to her lips, and those other evil presences filling the background beyond gave her an intense apprehension.

Maw, however, in spite of a general air of obscenity, meant well. It was not easy for this fact to declare itself through that loud voice and ruthless mien; but gradually it began to percolate to June's violated nerves, and so gave her a fleck of courage to hold on to that sense of identity which still threatened at the first moment again to desert her.

"Where was you goin', deery?"

Rude the tone, but when June's ear disentangled the words, she was able to appreciate that they were spoken in the way of kindness. But if the knowledge brought a spark of comfort it was quickly dowsed. Where was she going? To that grim question there was no possible answer.

"Scared out of her life, poor lamb!" said Maw. With furtive truculence she announced the fact to the rather awed spectators who gathered once more about the sufferer.

"Where you come from?"

June's only answer was a shiver. The frozen silence was so full of the uncanny that Maw shook her own head dismally and tapped it with a grimy finger.

In the view of Maw, for such a calamity there was only one remedy. Once more the cup was pressed to June's lips; once more it was resisted, this time with a hint of fierceness reassuring to the onlookers, inasmuch that it implied a return of life.

"Looks respectable," said the cracked voice of the crone, who was now at Maw's elbow.

"Where was you goin'?" demanded Maw again.

June was beyond tears, or she would have shed them. Now that the facts of the situation in all their hopelessness were streaming back to her, a feeling of sheer impotence kept her dumb.

"Off her rocker," said Elbert gloomily.

XLVI

AMID the silence which followed Elbert's remark, June fought hard to cast her weakness off. She wanted no longer to die. The recovery of the talisman inhibited, at least for the time being, that desire. Acutely aware that the Van Roon was still miraculously hers, she felt that come what might she must go on.

But her position was hopeless indeed. She dare not venture out of doors, with a murderous thief waiting to spring upon her. And if venture she did, there was nowhere she could go. Besides, had there been any place of refuge for such a weary bundle of frightened misery, without money and with a sorry ignorance of the fog-bound maze of bricks and mortar in which she was now lost, there would have been no means of getting to her destination.

At the same time, she had no wish to stay with these uncouth, ill-looking, evil-smelling people one moment longer than was necessary. In a curiously intimate way she was reminded of that grim story Oliver Twist, which had so powerfully haunted her youth. To her distorted mind, this squalid interior was a veritable thieves' kitchen, the crone a female Fagin, the angel of the cup, a counterpart of Bill Sikes, and the gloomy, beetle-browed Elbert a kind of Artful Dodger grown up. She and her treasure could never be safe in such a place, yet at the other side of the door nameless horrors awaited her.

In June's present state it was far beyond her power to cope with so dire a problem. Keeping a stony silence as those faces, devoured by curiosity, pressed ever closer upon her, she half surrendered to her weakness again.

Amid the new waves of misery which threatened to submerge her, she was wrenched fiercely back to sensibility. The Van Roon was torn by a strong hand from her grasp. As if a spring had been pressed in her heart she rose with a little cry. Maw was in the act of handing the picture to Elbert. "There's a label on it, ain't there?" she said.

Still half stupefied, June clung to the table for support, while Elbert, who was evidently the family scholar, read out slowly the name and address that was written upon the parcel: "Miss Babraham, 39b Park Lane, W."

June was hardly in a state just then to grasp the significance of the words. Her mind was wholly given up to concern for the treasure which had passed to alien hands. And yet the words had significance, even for her, as the mind-process they induced soon began to reveal.

A locked door of memory, of which she had lost the key, seemed to glide back. Thoughts of William, of his friend, the tall, beautiful and distinguished wearer of the blue crepe de chine, and of Sir Arthur, her father, came crowding into her brain. And with them came a perceptible easing of spirit, as if they had been sped by the kindly hand of that Providence, of whom she had never been so much in need.

The recognition of this acted upon her like a charm. Girt by the knowledge that she was not alone in the world after all, and that friends might be at hand if only she could reach out to them, her mind began once more to function.

Even while Maw and Elbert were occupying themselves with the parcel's address and its specific importance, June was fain to inquire of an awaking self how such magic words came to be there at such a moment. Casting back to recent events, over which oblivion had swept, she was able to recall certain strands in the subtle woof of Fate. Days ago, years they seemed now, Miss Babraham had sent to William a picture frame to be restored. The stout brown paper in which it had been wrapped appealed to June's thrifty soul, and she had stowed it away in her box for use on a future occasion. Her mind's new, almost dangerous clarity, enabled her to remember that upon the paper's inner side was an old Sotheran, Bookseller, Piccadilly label which bore the name and address of Miss Babraham.

The piecing together of this slender chain gave June the thing she needed most. At this signal manifestation of what Providence could do, hope revived in her. If only she could get to Park Lane—wherever Park Lane might be!— to Miss Babraham.

As if in answer to the half-formed wish, Maw's dominant voice took up the parable. "Elbert, you'd better see this lidy as fur as Park Lane."

XLVII

ELBERT did not welcome the prospect with open arms. Nature had not designed him for such a task. All the same, Maw was imaged clearly in his mind as one whose word was law.

At the best of times, Elbert's obedience to that word was apt to be grudging. And to-night, with murder lurking outside in the darkness, he was full of a disgusted reluctance at having to face such a prospect. Even in circumstances wholly favourable to it, the countenance of Elbert was not attractive; to June at this moment it was very much the reverse. She felt that its owner was not to be trusted an inch.

Meanwhile her mind was growing very active. Miss Babraham's name and address, that magic omen, was like an elixir; it quickened the blood, it strengthened the soul. If only she could bear her treasure to Park Lane all might yet be well!

Urged by this spur, native wit sprang to her aid. The first thing to be done was to get clear of present company. She was haunted still by the likeness to Fagin's kitchen; but also there was a recollection of the fact that a Tube Station was only a few yards along the street. That was the haven wherein salvation lay.

Pressing hard upon the hope, however, was the dismal knowledge that only one penny remained in her pocket. This sum could not take her to Park Lane, unless that Elysium was close at hand. Alas, it was not at all likely. Her ignorance of London was so great, moreover, that she would need help to find her way there; and in the process of obtaining it in her present state of weakness she might be caught by new perils. For it was only too likely that Keller was lurking outside in the fog, waiting to spring upon her and tear the Van Roon from her grasp at the first chance that arose.

Beset by such problems, June felt that she was between the devil and the deep sea. Perhaps the best thing she could do was to dash along the street to the Tube, and then put herself in the hands of the nearest policeman. But even to attempt such a feat was to run a grave risk.

Elbert, in the meantime, scowling and disgruntled, was bracing himself under further pressure from Maw to brave the perils of the night. June felt, however, that it would be wise not to saddle herself with this reluctant champion if it could be avoided. To this end, she was now able to pluck up the spirit to ask what was the best means of getting to Park Lane.

Maw did not know, but Elbert when appealed to said that she could take the Tube to Marble Arch, or she might turn the corner at the end of the street and pick up a bus in Tottenham Court Road.

How much was the fare? Twopence, Elbert thought. Alas, June had only a penny. She was painfully shy about confessing this difficulty, but there was no help for it.

"Don't you worry, Miss. Elbert is goin' to see you all the way." And Maw fixed a savage eye upon her son.

Much as June would have preferred to forego the services of this paladin, Maw's ferocious glance settled the matter finally.

"And you'll carry the pawcel for the lidy," said Maw, as Elbert, scowling more darkly than ever turned up the collar of his overcoat.

XLVIII

THE Van Roon, at that moment, was in the hand of Maw. And although June was on fire to get it back, her natural faculties had the authority to tell her that undue eagerness would be most unwise. She must be content to await her chance, yet there was no saying when that chance would come; for Maw was careful to hand personally the parcel to Elbert.

Before June set out on her journey one of the girls pressed a cup of tea from the family brew upon her. It was lukewarm and thrice-stewed, but June was able to drink a little and to feel the better for it. She was in a high state of tension, all the same, when Elbert opened the street door, her treasure under his arm, and she followed close behind him into the darkness.

Surely Keller must be out there in the fog, waiting to attack them. Her heart beat wildly as she marched side by side with Elbert along the street towards the Tube. Distrust of her cavalier was great. Should he guess the value of the thing he bore, as likely as not he would play her a trick. But for the moment, at any rate, this fear was merged in the sharper one of what was concealed by the fantastic shadow shapes of that dark thoroughfare. Less than a hundred yards away, however, was the Tube Station. And to June's unspeakable relief they gained its light and publicity without misadventure. Here, moreover, was her chance. While Elbert searched his pockets for fourpence to purchase two tickets for Marble Arch, she insisted on relieving him of the parcel. Once restored to her care, she clung to it so tenaciously that the puzzled Elbert had reluctantly to give up the hope of getting it back again.

Going down in the lift to the trains, with the surge of fellow passengers guaranteeing a measure of safety, June allowed herself to conclude that Elbert, after all, might be less of a ruffian than he looked. If he had no graces of mind or mansion, he was yet not without a sort of rude care for her welfare. By no wish of his own was he seeing a distressed damsel to her home, yet the process of doing so, once he grew involved in it, seemed to minister in some degree to a latent sense of chivalry. At all events he had a scowl for anyone whose elbows came too near his charge.

Arriving at Marble Arch in due course, the heroic Elbert piloted the fugitive out of the station and across the road into Park Lane. Here, under a street lamp, they paused a moment to examine the label on the parcel for the number of the house they sought. Thirty-nine was the number, and it proved to be not the least imposing home in that plutocratic thoroughfare.

Elbert accompanied June as far as its doorstep. Before ringing the bell she said good-bye to her escort with all the gratitude she could muster, begging him to give her his name and address, so that she might at least restore to him the price of her fare. Yet the squire of dames saw no necessity for this. His scowl was softened a little by her thanks, but his only answer was to press the electric button and then, without a word, to slink abruptly away into the fog.

XLIX

JUNE felt a wild excitement, as she stood waiting for the answer to her ring. The stress of events had buoyed her up, but with Elbert no longer at her side and the door of a strange house confronting her, trolls were loose once more in her brain. A fresh wave of panic surged through her, and again she feared that she was going to faint.

The prompt opening of the door by a gravely dignified manservant acted as a strong restorative. June mustered the force of will to ask if she could see Miss Babraham. Such a request, made in a nervous and excited manner, gave pause to the footman, who at first could not bring himself to invite her into the large dimly lighted hall. Finally he did so; closed the door against the fog, and then asked her name with an air of profound disapproval, which at any other time must have proved highly embarrassing.

"I'm Miss Gedge," said June. "From the second-hand shop in New Cross Street. Miss Babraham'll remember me."

The servant slowly repeated the fragmentary words in a low voice of cutting emphasis. "I'm afraid," he said, while his eye descended to June's shoes and up again, "Miss Babraham will not be able to see you to-night. However, I'll inquire."

Superciliously the footman crossed the hall, to discuss the matter with an unseen presence in its farthest shadows. The conference was brief but unsatisfactory, for a moment later the unseen presence slowly materialized into the august shape of a butler, who seemed at once to diminish the footman into a relative nothingness.

"Perhaps you'll let me know your business," said the butler, in a tone which implied that she could have no business, at any rate with Miss Babraham, at such an hour.

June, alas, could not explain the nature of her errand. These two men were so imposing, so unsympathetic, so harsh, so frightening that had life itself depended upon her answers, and in quite a special degree she now felt that it did, she was yet unequal to the task of making them effective.

"Miss Babraham cannot see you now," said the slow-voiced butler, with an air of terrible finality.

"But I must see her. I simply must," wildly persisted June.

"It's impossible to see her now," said the butler.

The words caused June to stagger back against the wall. In answer to her tragic eyes, the butler said reluctantly: "You had better call again some time to-morrow, and I'll send in your name."

"I—I must see her now," June gasped wildly.

The butler was adamant. "You can't possibly see her to-night."

"Why can't I?" said June, desperately.

"She is going to a ball."

The words were like a blow. A vista of the fog outside and of herself wandering with her precious burden all night long in it homeless, penniless, desolate, came upon her with unnerving force. "But—please!—I must see her to-night," she said, with a shudder of misery.

Faced by the butler's pitiless air, June felt her slender hope to be ebbing away. She would be turned adrift in the night. And what would happen to her then? She could not walk the streets till daybreak with the Van Roon under her arm. Already she had reached the limit of endurance. The dark haze before her eyes bore witness to the fact that her strength was almost gone. No matter what the attitude of the butler towards her she must not think of quitting this place of refuge unless she was flung out bodily, for her trials here were nought by comparison with those awaiting her outside.

June's defiance was very puzzling to the stern functionary who quite plainly was at a loss how to deal with it. But in the midst of these uncertainties the problem was unexpectedly solved for him. A glamour of white satin, jewels and fur appeared on the broad staircase. Miss Babraham descended slowly.

Once more was June upheld by a sense of Providence. Hope flickered again, a painful, fluctuating gleam. She sprang forward to intercept this vision of pure beauty, wildly calling the name "Miss Babraham! Miss Babraham!"

The dazzling creature was startled out of her glowing self-possession: "Why, who *are* you?" she cried.

In a gush of strange words, June strove to make clear that she was the girl from the antique shop in New Cross Street, and that her uncle, its proprietor, was a very wicked old man who was trying to steal a valuable picture that had been given to her. She pressed the Van Roon upon the astonished Miss Babraham and besought her to take care of it.

After that, June had only a very dim idea of what happened. She found herself in a sort of anteroom without knowing how she got there, with faces of a surprised curiosity around her. Foremost of these was the lovely Miss Babraham, a thing of sheer beauty in her ball-dress, who asked questions to which June could only give confused replies, and issued orders that she was not able to follow.

Everything began to grow more and more like a wild and terrible dream. Other people appeared on the scene, among whom June was just able to recognize the tall form of Sir Arthur Babraham. By then, however she no longer knew what she was doing or saying, for deep blanks were invading her consciousness; even the treasure in which her very soul was merged had somehow slipped from her mental grasp, and like everything else had ceased to have significance.

L

AT eleven o'clock the next morning, Sir Arthur Babraham, looking worried and distrait, was pretending to read the "Times." If ever a man could be said to have "been born with a silver spoon in his mouth" it was this soft-voiced, easy-mannered, kindly gentleman. The rubs of a hard world had hardly touched his unflawed surfaces. He sat on committees, it was true, and played Providence at third or fourth hand to less happily situated mortals; yet scarcely, if at all, had he been brought face to face with the stark realities of life.

It is never too late, however, for some new thing to occur. The previous evening an experience had happened to this worthy man; and he could not rid his mind of the fact that it was disconcerting. On a table at his elbow was a picture without a frame, and more than once his eyes strayed from the newspaper to this object, which at a first glance was so insignificant, and yet as if cursed with an "obi" it had the power to dominate him completely.

In the midst of this preoccupation, Laura Babraham entered the room. She had returned late from the dance, and this was her first appearance that morning. Hardly had she saluted her father when her eye also fell on the picture, and a look of deep anxiety came into her eyes.

"Have you heard anything from the hospital?" she asked eagerly.

"I rang them up half an hour ago," said Sir Arthur. "The girl is very ill indeed. I gather from the tone of the person with whom I talked that the case is pretty serious."

"Yes," said Laura Babraham, in a low voice. "One felt sure of that. Never again do I want to see a human creature in the state that poor thing was in last night. I've been haunted by her ever since."

"Pretty bad, I must say." Sir Arthur plucked sharply at his moustache. "According to the Hospital, she's been knocked about and generally ill-used. There are marks on her throat, and they want my opinion as to whether they should communicate with the police."

"What do you advise, papa?" said Laura, with a growing concern.

"One doesn't know what to advise." Sir Arthur's moustache continued to receive harsh treatment. "We are faced with rather a problem, it seems to me."

"You mean that it will be a matter for the police if she doesn't get better?"

"Yes, certainly that. And it may be a matter for the police if she does get better."

Laura Babraham agreed; yet even then she did not see the problem in its full complexity. Sir Arthur, taking the first step towards her enlightenment, pointed to the Van Roon: "My dear, beyond any doubt that is a most precious thing. And, ignoring for the moment the state in which this young woman turned up last night, the question we have to ask ourselves is: What is she doing with it at all? And why was she ranging the streets alone, in the fog, at that hour?"

"From what one gathered," said Laura, "the picture is hers, and her uncle, the old curio man in New Cross Street, with whom she lives, is determined to steal it."

"Quite. That's her story, as far as one can get at it. But I put it to you, isn't it far more likely—prima facie at any rate—that the girl is trying to steal it from the old dealer?"

"I believe the poor thing is speaking the truth," said Woman in the person of Miss Laura Babraham.

"You mean, my dear," said her logical parent, with a sad little smile, "that you *hope* she is speaking the truth. With all my heart I hope so, too, even if it proves this old man—Gedge you say his name is—to be a terrible scoundrel. One of them certainly is not playing straight—but prima facie, as I say—if we call in the police, it is almost certain that it is this wretched girl who will find herself in prison."

"There I don't agree, papa," said Woman staunchly. "The poor thing says that William the assistant gave her the picture; and in all the dealings I have had with William in the course of the past year, he has been honesty itself."

Her father shook his head gently. "All very well, but Master William is the part of the story I like least. Is it probable, in the first place, that a young man who almost certainly has no money of his own, would be able to get possession of such a thing; and, again, assuming him to be clever enough to do so, is he going to be such a fool as to give it away to this girl? Let us look all the facts in the face. To my mind, the more one thinks of it the more inevitable the plain solution is."

"I'm absolutely convinced that William, at any rate, is honest."

Sir Arthur frowned and opened his cigar case. "And I for my part am convinced," he said, with a sigh as he cut off the end of a Corona, "that our friend William is a cunning scoundrel, who has been deep enough to get this young woman to do the dirty work and run all the risks, because he must know as well as anybody that a great deal of money is at stake."

Laura Babraham had a considerable respect for her father's judgment, yet she knew the value of her own. She did not think it was possible to be so deceived; her dealings with William had left her with the highest regard for his straightforwardness; if he proved to be the despicable creature Sir Arthur's fancy painted him, never again would she be able to hold an opinion about anyone. Yet her father's analysis of the case, as it presented itself to her clear mind, left her on the horns of a dilemma. Either this young man was a fool, or he was a rogue. Beset by two evils, she chose without hesitation that which to the feminine mind appeared the less.

"He's always struck one as rather simple in some ways and too much under the thumb of the old dealer, yet he's really very clever."

Sir Arthur drew mental energy from his Corona. "Not clever enough to keep honest, my dear."

"Please don't prejudge him. That wicked old man is at the back of all."

"Well, that is just what we have now to find out."

Laura assented; yet then arose the question as to the means by which the truth could be won. It was likely to resolve itself into an affair of William's word against the word of his master. Whoever could tell the more plausible tale would be believed; and William's friend saw from the outset that Circumstance had already weighted the scales heavily against him. On the face of it, the story as disclosed by the poor girl who was now in the Hospital, was frankly incredible.

Recollection of the pitiful scene of the previous night brought to Laura Babraham's mind her own urgent duty in the matter. The girl had begged her not on any account to give up the picture. So long as sense and coherence remained the unlucky creature had declared it to be her own lawful property. Laura had solemnly promised to see justice done, and it behooved her now to be as good as her word.

"I suppose, papa, you have telephoned already to Mr. Gedge?"

"The Hospital has, I believe," said Sir Arthur. "I particularly asked them to do so. The old fellow must be very anxious about the girl, and perhaps even more anxious about his Van Roon."

"Please don't say 'his Van Roon' before he's proved the ownership."

"That won't be difficult, I fear."

"We must make it as difficult for him as we can," said the tenacious Laura.

Sir Arthur shook his head. As a man of the world, he had but scant hope that the mystery would be cleared up in the way Laura desired.

———————————————————

LI

AT Number Forty-six, New Cross Street, the bottom seemed to have fallen out of the world. June's flight with the picture, as soon as it became known to William, caused him not only intense pain, but also deep concern. The news was a tragic shock for which he was quite unprepared; and the behaviour of his master seemed, if possible, to make it worse. The old man was distraught. Now that it was no longer necessary to mask his intentions, prudence slipped from him like a veil. On his return, baffled and furious, from Victoria he at once accused William of being in the plot against him.

William, hurt and astonished, was at a loss. He did not know all that had happened; he had only the broad facts to go upon that June had run off with the picture at an instant's notice, without a word as to her plans and leaving no address; and the bitter reproaches of his master appeared to him the outpourings of a mind not quite sane.

Such indeed they were. The truth was that upon one subject S. Gedge Antiques was a little unhinged. The love of money, an infirmity which had crept upon him year by year had begun to affect reason itself; and now that, as it seemed, he had thrown away, by his own carelessness, the one really big prize of his career, this dark fact came out.

William, who found it very difficult indeed to think ill of anyone, could only accept the broad fact that the picture had meant even more to the old man than he had supposed; therefore this good fellow was inclined to pity his master. It was not for a mind such as his, which took things on trust, to fill in the details of a tragic episode. He did not look for the wherefore and the why, yet he was very deeply grieved by what had occurred.

The old man could not rid his brain of the illusion that William had connived with June. Under the lash of an unreasoning rage he did not pause to consider the improbability of this, nor did he try to attain a broad view of the whole matter; it was almost as if his resentment, craving an outlet, must wreak itself upon the thing near at hand. Yet in the course of a few hours this dangerous obsession was to bring its own nemesis.

About twelve o'clock the next day, M. Duponnet came to fetch the picture. It had been arranged that Mr. Gedge should present the cheque at the Bank in the meantime, and if duly approved, as there was every reason to expect that it would be, the Van Roon should be handed over at once.

To the Frenchman's surprise, he was now greeted by his own cheque, backed by a livid countenance of tragic exasperation. The treasure had been stolen.

"Stolen!"

The face of S. Gedge Antiques forbade all scepticism.

"When? By whom?"

Mussewer Duponny might well ask by whom! It had been stolen by the girl who did the housework—the old man could not bring himself, in such circumstances, to speak of her as his niece—and he had not the least doubt in his own mind that the youth who helped him in the business who, at that moment, was in the next room polishing chairs, had put her wise in the matter, and was standing in with her.

S. Gedge Antiques, still in a frenzy of frustration, was hardly able to realize the gravity of this charge. Had he been in full command of himself, he must have weighed such a statement very carefully indeed before it was made. But remorselessly driven by his greed, he threw discretion to the wind.

The disgruntled purchaser was quick to seize upon the accusation. To his mind, at least, its import was clear. Even if the seller did not perceive its full implication, the buyer of the Van Roon had no difficulty in doing so.

"We must call in ze police, hein?"

The words brought the old man up short. He proceeded to take his bearings; to find out, as well as his rage would let him, just where he stood in the matter. Certainly the police did not appeal to him at all. It was not a case for publicity, because the picture was not his: that was to say, having now reached a point where the law of *meum* and *tuum* had become curiously involved, it might prove exceedingly difficult and even more inconvenient to establish a title to the Van Roon. No, he preferred to do without the police.

M. Duponnet, however, unfettered by a sense of restraint, argued volubly that the police be called in. The assistant was guilty or he was not guilty; and in any event it would surely be wise to enlist the help of those who knew best how to deal with thieves. Nothing could have exceeded the buyer's conviction that this should be done, yet to his chagrin he quite failed to communicate it to S. Gedge Antiques.

From that moment, a suspicion began to grow up in the Frenchman's mind that the seller was not laying all his cards on the table. Could it be that he was telling a cock and bull story? According to Mr. Thornton, who was acting as a go-between, this old man had long had the name of a shifty customer. Undoubtedly he looked one this morning. Jules Duponnet had seldom seen a frontispiece he liked less; and the theory now gained a footing in his mind that the old fox wanted to go back on his bargain.

There were two drawbacks, all the same, to M. Duponnet's theory. In the first place, as no money had yet changed hands, it would be quite easy for S. Gedge Antiques to undo the bargain by a straightforward means; and further, beyond any shadow of doubt, the old man was horribly upset by his loss.

"Let us go to ze bureau, Meester Gedge," he said, as conviction renewed itself in the light of these facts.

"No, no, no," cried the old man, whose brain, capable at times of a surprising vigour, was now furiously at work.

"But why not?"

S. Gedge Antiques did not reply immediately, but at last a dark light broke over the vulpine face. "Why not, Mussewer Duponny? I'll tell you. Because I think there may be a better way of dealing with that damned young scoundrel yonder." William's master pointed towards the inner room. "Happen the police'll need all sorts of information we don't want to give them; and my experience is, Mussewer, their methods are slow and clumsy, and out of date. They may take weeks over this job, and long before they are through with it, the picture will be in America."

"You may be right, Meester Gedge. But where's the 'arm in seeing what they can do?"

With the air of one whose faculties have been braced by a mental tonic, the old man shook his head decisively. "Mussewer Duponny," he said, in a slow voice which gave weight and value to each word, "I'm thinking with a little help from yourself and Mr. Thornton I can deal with this—this scoundrel much better than the police."

"At your sairvice, Meester Gedge," said Jules Duponnet, with a dry smile. He could not have been the man he was, had he remained insensitive to the depth of cunning which now transfigured the face of the old dealer. "But for Meester Thornton of course I cannot spick."

"You can't, of course," said the old fox, briskly. "But we'll go right now, and have a word with Mr. Thornton on the subject."

Like one in whom a change sudden and mysterious has been wrought, S. Gedge Antiques stepped through the house door into the passage, took his hat and coat from the peg, and his heavy knotted walking stick out of the rickety umbrella stand, put his head into the room next door and said, in a harsh tone to the polisher of chairs, "Boy, I'm going along as far as Mr. Thornton's, so you'd better keep an eye on the shop."

LII

THE old man, contrary to his practice, was a little late for the midday meal, and he had a poor appetite for it. As he tried to eat the cold mutton and the potato William had baked for him, his thoughts seemed a long way from his plate. William himself, who was too full of trouble to give much attention to food, now saw that the old man's earlier ferocity, which had hurt him even more than it had puzzled him, had yielded to a depth of melancholy that was hardly less disturbing. But the master's manner, on his return from the visit to Mr. Thornton, was far more in accordance with his nature, at least as William understood that nature; indeed, his voice had recaptured the note of pathos which seemed natural to it whenever the Van Roon was mentioned.

"I ought to tell you, boy," he said, in a husky tone, towards the end of the meal, "that it looks as if there'll be the dickens to pay over this job. A French detective from Paris has been here, and he's coming again this afternoon to have a word with you."

"With me, sir?"

The old man, whose eyes were furtively devouring the face of William, was quick to observe its startled look. "Yes, boy, you're the one he wants to see. The Loov authorities have managed to get wind of this Van Roon of ours, and they say it's the feller they've been looking for since 1898."

Easy to gull William in some respects was, yet, he could not help thinking that the French Government took a little too much for granted.

"I think so, too—but there it is," said the old man. "They have to prove the Van Roon is theirs, and that won't be easy, as I told the detective this morning. But I understand that the question of identity turns upon certain marks, as well as upon similarity of subject."

William allowed that the subject had an undoubted similarity with that of the picture stolen from the Louvre, but then, as he explained, every known Van Roon had a strong family likeness. In size they varied little, and they always depicted trees, water, clouds, and in some cases a windmill.

"Ours, I believe, had no windmill."

"No, sir, only water and trees, and a wonderful bit of cloud."

"I understand," said the old man mournfully, "that the one that was stolen from the Loov had no windmill."

"The other one in the Louvre has no windmill; there are two at Amsterdam that have no windmill; and there's one at The Hague, I believe, that hasn't a windmill."

"May be. These are all points in our favour. But, as I say, the whole question will turn upon certain identification marks, and this French detective is coming here this afternoon to examine it. So it seems to me that the best thing you can do is to go off at once, and get it back from that hussy, because you can take it from me, boy, that we are going to be held responsible for the picture's safety by the French police; and if when the detective calls again all we have to say is that it has vanished like magic, and we are unable to produce it, we may easily find ourselves in the lock-up."

This speech, worded with care and uttered with weight, had the effect of increasing William's distress. Underlying it was the clear assumption that he was in league with June, and this was intolerable to him, less because of her strangely misguided action, than for the reason that the master to whom he had been so long devoted found it impossible to believe his word.

"If only I knew where Miss June was, sir—" he said, miserably.

The old man, with the fragment of caution still left to him, was able to refrain from giving William the lie. It wasn't easy to forbear, since he was quite unable to accept the open and palpable fact that his assistant was in complete ignorance of June's whereabouts. So true it is that the gods first tamper with the reason of those whom they would destroy!

S. Gedge Antiques was in the toils of a powerful and dangerous obsession. He saw William in terms of himself; indeed, he was overtaken by the nemesis which dogs the crooked mind. For the old man was now incapable of seeing things as they were; the monstrous shadow of his own wickedness and folly enshrouded others like a pall. One so shrewd as William's master, who had had such opportunities, moreover, of gauging the young man's worth, should have been the last person in the world to hold him guilty of this elaborate and futile deceit; but the old man was in thrall to the Frankenstein his own evil thoughts had created.

He was sure that William was lying. Just as in the first instance the young man had given the picture to "the hussy", he was now in collusion with her in an audacious attempt to dispose of it. S. Gedge Antiques was not in a frame of mind to sift, to analyze, to ask questions; it seemed natural and convenient to embrace such a theory and, urged by the demon within, he was now building blindly upon it.

About three o'clock William was engaged in the lumber room putting derelict pieces of furniture to rights, when his master came with a long and serious face, and said that the French detective wanted to see him. William put on his coat and followed the old man into the shop where he found two persons awaiting him. With only one of these was William acquainted. Mr. Thornton was well known to him by sight, but he had not seen before the French dealer, M. Duponnet.

With a nice sense of drama on the part of S. Gedge Antiques the Frenchman was now made known to William as M. Duplay of the Paris police. Midway between a snuffle and a groan, the old man, raising his eyes in the direction of heaven, besought his assistant to tell Mussewer all that he knew as to the picture's whereabouts.

William, alas, knew no more than his master; and he found no difficulty in saying so. He was not believed, since the old man had had no scruple in the blackening of his character, and the Frenchman, with a skilful assumption of the manner of an official, which the others solemnly played up to, proceeded to threaten the assistant with the terrors of the law.

The French Government was convinced from the description, which had been given of the Van Roon by those who had seen it, that there could be little doubt it was their long missing property. Such being the case, the police were only willing to allow the young man another twenty-four hours in which to produce it for examination. If he failed to do that within the time specified, a warrant would be applied for, and he might find himself in prison.

In the face of this intimidation, William stuck to his story. He knew no more than the dead where the picture was; Miss June, to whom it had been given, had suddenly disappeared with it the previous night.

"Who is Mees June?" said the Frenchman sharply.

Miss June was the niece of Mr. Gedge.

"And he gave the picture to her?" The disappointed buyer, who felt that his suspicions in the matter were being confirmed, looked keenly from the young man to the old.

"No, sir," said William, with the utmost simplicity. "I gave it to her myself."

There was a pause, in which astonishment played its part, and then Mr. Thornton gravely interposed: "How do you mean you gave her the picture? It isn't yours to give. It is the property of your master."

"You are forgetting, boy," said the old man in a voice in which oil and vinegar were wonderfully mingled, "that I would not allow my niece to have such a valuable thing, and that you then made it over to me to dispose of to the best advantage."

"I gave it to Miss June," persisted the young man simply, "but I told her that, as you had set your heart upon it, I hoped very much she would let you have it."

While this odd conversation went on, the two dealers exchanged glances. Both were greatly puzzled. They were as one in being a little suspicious of the absolute bona fides of S. Gedge Antiques. Either this was a very clumsy method of establishing them, or there was more behind the picture's disappearance than met the eye.

S. Gedge Antiques, whose brain was working at high pressure, was not slow to read their minds. He closed the discussion with a brevity which yet was not lacking altogether in persuasion. "There's no time, boy, to go into all that," he said. "The girl's gone off with the picture, and wherever she's to be found, you must go right away, and get it back from her, and bring it here to me, or we may both find ourselves in the lock-up. That is so, Mussewer Duplay—what?" And with a lively gesture the old fox turned to the Frenchman.

Puzzled that gentleman certainly was, yet he heartily agreed. If the Van Roon was not produced within the next four and twenty hours, a warrant would be issued.

"Where is the hussy? That's what we want to know," said the old man. "Tell us what has become of her."

Frankly William did not know. He was not believed, at any rate, by his master who by now was deeper than ever in the coil of his own crookedness. As for the two dealers who, between them, had contrived, as they thought, to acquire one of the world's treasures for an absurd sum, they did not know what to think. The comedy they were performing at the instance of S. Gedge Antiques was designed to bemuse the assistant, yet both men had an uneasy feeling at the back of their minds that master and man were engaged in a piece of flapdoodle for their private benefit. If so, the old man was a fool as well as a rogue, and the young one was a rogue as well as a fool. Scant was the comfort to be got out of this reflection. They seemed very far from the goal on which their hearts were set; and impatience of such methods was just beginning to show itself in the bearing of Messrs. Duponnet and Thornton when the affair took a new and remarkable turn.

LIII

A TALL man, quietly dressed, yet wearing a silk hat and an eyeglass, with a pleasant air of authority, came into the shop. For a moment he stood by the door, a rather cool gazed fixed upon the group of four; and then, an odd mingling of alertness and caution in his manner, he advanced to the proprietor.

"May I have a word with you," said the visitor, with an air of apology for the benefit of the others whom he included in a smile which expressed little.

"Certainly you may, Sir Arthur," said S. Gedge Antiques, an odd change coming into his tone. Taken by surprise, the old man had been slow to reckon up the situation. He was not able to detach himself from the group, and lead the rather unwelcome visitor out of earshot before that gentleman had divulged the business which had brought him there.

"You must be anxious about your niece, Mr. Gedge," said Sir Arthur, who saw no need for secrecy.

The old man was very anxious indeed.

"You've heard from the Hospital, of course?"

It seemed that the old man had heard nothing; and Sir Arthur was proceeding to deplore this oversight on the part of those whom he had asked over the telephone to communicate with Number Forty-six, New Cross Street, when William, whose ear had caught the sinister word 'Hospital' could no longer restrain a painful curiosity.

The young man sprang forward with clasped hands and shining eyes. "Oh, sir, what has happened to Miss June?" he cried. "Tell me—please!"

Sir Arthur, his mission concrete in his mind, brought a steady eye to bear upon the young man before he slowly replied: "She has had a mental breakdown, and we were able to arrange for her to be taken late last night to St. Jude's Hospital." He then turned to the old man, who had either grasped the news more slowly, or was less affected by it, and said: "It's a case for careful treatment, in the opinion of the doctor who saw her soon after she arrived at my house, and upon whose advice she was sent to the Hospital. I am very sorry now that I did not communicate with you myself!"

It was the young man, however, as Sir Arthur did not fail to notice, who seemed really to be troubled by what had befallen this unfortunate girl. S. Gedge Antiques, for his part, soon shewed that his inmost thoughts were centered upon something else.

"Can you tell me, sir," he said, with an excitement he did not try to conceal, "whether the picture she took away with her is quite safe?"

Sir Arthur looked hard at the old man before he answered: "Mr. Gedge, the picture is perfectly safe."

"Thank God!" The exclamation of S. Gedge Antiques was not the less heartfelt for being involuntary.

"And Miss June?" interposed William huskily. "Is she?... Is she...?" He was too upset to frame his question.

"She is very ill indeed, I'm afraid," said Sir Arthur, in a kind tone, "but she is in the best possible hands. Anything that can be done for her will be done— I am sure you can count upon that."

"Is she going to die?"

Sir Arthur shook his head. "When I last rang up the Hospital, I asked that question, but they will not give an opinion. They prefer not to go beyond the fact that she is critically ill."

Tears gathered slowly in William's eyes. Conscience was pricking him sharply. Had he not brought this unlucky picture into the house, such a terrible thing would not have occurred.

William's brief talk with the visitor, whose unheralded appearance upon the scene was by no means welcome to S. Gedge Antiques, gave his master a much needed opportunity to decide upon the course of action. The two dealers knew now that the Van Roon was safe, but as far as William and Sir Arthur were concerned, the situation was full of complexity. Much cunning would be needed to smooth out the tangle; and to this end, as the old man promptly realized, the first thing to be done was to induce the Frenchman and his agent to quit the shop.

"You hear, Mussewer, that the picture is safe," he said to the buyer, soapily. "I will go at once and get it from this gentleman. If you will come in again to-morrow morning, it shall be ready for you."

M. Duponnet seemed inclined to await further developments, but S. Gedge Antiques had no scruples about dismissing his fellow conspirators. Without more ado, he ushered both dealers gently but firmly to the door. This new turn in the game had made them keenly curious to learn more of the affair, yet they realized that they were on thin ice themselves, and the peremptory manner of S. Gedge Antiques enforced that view. "To-morrow morning, gentlemen—come and see me then!" he said, opening the shop door determinedly, and waiting for these inconvenient visitors to pass out.

This task accomplished, the old man had to deal with one more delicate. He had to remove from the minds of William and Sir Arthur Babraham all suspicion in regard to himself. He came to them with his most sanctimonious air: "I can't tell you, sir," he assured Sir Arthur, "what a relief it is to know that my niece is in good hands. But I am afraid she is a very wicked girl." Then he turned abruptly to William, and said in a low tone that he wished to have a private conversation with Sir Arthur.

For once, however, the young man shewed less than his usual docility. He was most eager to learn all that had happened to June, and to gain a clue, if possible, to her strange conduct; besides the painful change in his master now filled him with distrust.

The shrewd judge of the world and its ways upon whom the duty had fallen of holding the balance true was quick to note the reluctance of the younger man; and even if the nature of the case would compel him in the end to take the word of the proprietor against that of the servant, he was influenced already, in spite of himself, by that open simplicity which had had such an effect upon his daughter.

"Is there anything, Mr. Gedge, we have to say to one another, which this young man may not hear?" said Sir Arthur quietly, and then, as the old dealer did not immediately reply, he added coolly, "I think not." Turning to William he said: "Please stay with us. There are one or two questions I have to put which I hope you will be good enough to answer."

This did not suit the book of S. Gedge Antiques, but he decided to play a bold game. "I'm very much obliged to you for your kindness in taking care of the picture," he said, with a smirk to his visitor. "As you know, it is a thing of great value. Had anything happened to it, the loss would have been terrible. Perhaps you will allow me to go at once and fetch it, for I don't mind telling you, sir, that until I get it back again my mind will not be easy."

Sir Arthur looked narrowly at the face of unpleasant cunning before him, and then he said very quietly: "I am sorry to have to tell you, Mr. Gedge, that your niece claims the picture as her property."

The old man was prepared for a development which he had been able to foresee. "I am afraid she is a very wicked girl," he said, in the tone of a known good man whose feelings are deeply wounded. "I ask you, sir, is it likely that a thing of such immense value would belong to her?"

Sir Arthur had to agree that it was not, yet remembering his daughter's deep conviction on the subject, he was careful to assert June's claim.

"Moonshine, I assure you, sir."

Sir Arthur, however, did not regard this as conclusive. In the light of what had happened he felt it to be his duty to seek a clear proof of the picture's ownership; therefore he now turned to William and told him that the girl in the Hospital declared that he had given her the Van Roon. A plain statement of fact was demanded, and in the face of so direct an appeal the young man did not hesitate to give one. Originally the picture was his property, but a week ago he had given it to his master's niece.

"What have you to say to that, Mr. Gedge?" asked Sir Arthur.

The heart of William seemed to miss a beat while he waited painfully for the answer to this question. To one of his primitive nature, his whole life, past, present and future seemed to turn upon the old man's next words; and a kind of slow agony overcame him, as he realized what these words were in all their cynical wickedness.

"The Van Roon is mine, sir," said S. Gedge Antiques, in a voice, strong, definite and calm. "It was bought with my money."

Sir Arthur fixed upon the stupefied William an interrogating eye. In his own mind he felt sure that this must be the fact of the matter, yet it was hard to believe that a young man who seemed to be openness itself was deliberately lying. "What do *you* say?" he asked gently.

William was too shocked to say anything. His master took a full advantage of the pause which followed. "Come, boy," he said, in a tone of kindly expostulation, "you know as well as I do that you were given the money to buy a few things down in Suffolk in the ordinary way of business on your week's holiday and that this little thing was one of your purchases."

Sadly the young man shook his head. The cold falsehood was heavier upon him than a blow from the old man's fist would have been, yet it roused him to the point of blunt denial. Quite simply he set forth the true facts.

"The master gave me twenty pounds to attend a sale by auction at Loseby Grange, Saxmundham, and I bought things to the value of twenty pounds one and ninepence."

In a voice which was a nice mingling of humour and pathos the old man interposed. "This picture, which I admit was bought for a song as the saying is, was among them."

"No, sir," said William, "I bought this picture with my own money from an old woman in a shop at Crowdham Market."

So much for the issue, which now was quite clearly defined. Sir Arthur, however, could only regret that the supremely difficult task of keeping the scales of justice true had developed upon him.

"What did you pay for the picture, may I ask?"

"Five shillings," said William, unhesitatingly.

"Five shillings!"

"It was as black as night when I bought it, sir, with a still life, which must have been at least two hundred years old daubed over it."

"Black enough, I allow," said the old man, "but it can't alter the fact that the picture's mine."

"Let me be quite clear on one point," said Sir Arthur. "You maintain, Mr. Gedge, that the picture was bought at a sale with your money, and this young man declares it was bought at a shop with his."

"That is so," said the old man.

"Do you happen to have kept a list of the things that were bought at the sale?"

"No, sir, I'm afraid I haven't one."

Here, however, the old man's memory was at fault, and this material fact William went on to prove. Under the counter was a file containing a mass of receipted bills, and from among these the young man was able to produce a document which told heavily in his favour. It was a list of his purchases at Loseby Grange, carefully written out, with the sum paid opposite each item, and at the foot of it, immediately beneath the figures "£20.1.9" was written in a rather shaky but businesslike hand, "Audited and found correct. S. Gedge."

This lucky discovery went some way towards establishing William's case. The paper contained no mention of a picture, other than a print after P. Bartolozzi, which William took at once from the shop window. Finished dissembler as he was, the old man could not conceal the fact that he was shaken, but like a desperate gambler with a fortune at stake, he hastily changed his tactics. He began now to pooh-pooh the receipt, and declared that even if his unfortunate memory had played him a trick as to where the picture had been actually bought, it did not affect the contention that it had been purchased with his money.

Sir Arthur Babraham, in his search for the truth, could not help contrasting the bearing of the claimants. Avarice was engraved deeply upon the yellow parchment countenance of S. Gedge Antiques, whereas so open was the face of William that it went against the grain to accuse its owner of baseness. In spite, of this, however, Sir Arthur could not help asking himself how it had come about that a young man so poor, who was yet clever enough to pick up such a treasure for a few shillings had parted with it so lightly.

Upon the answer to that question he felt much would depend.

"I suppose when you gave this picture away you did not realize its great value?"

"As a matter of fact, sir, I hardly thought about it at all in that way. I only saw that it was a very lovely thing, and Miss June saw that it was a very lovely thing. She admired it so much that she begged me to let her buy it."

"Did you take her money?"

"No, sir. She accepted it as a gift. I asked her not to let us think of it as money."

"Could you afford to do that?" Involuntarily the questioner looked at the young man's threadbare coat and shabby trousers, and at once decided that he, of all people, certainly could not.

William's answer, accompanied by a baffling smile, gave pause to the man of the world. "I hope, sir, I shall always afford the luxury of not setting a price on beauty."

The dark saying brought a frown to the face of Mr. Worldly Wiseman, who said in his slow voice: "But surely you would not give away a Van Roon to the first person who asks for it?"

"Why not, sir—if you happen to—to——"

"If you happen to what?"

"To like the person."

Although the young man blushed when he made this confession, such an ingenuousness did his cause no harm. Sir Arthur Babraham, all the same, was puzzled more than a little by such an attitude of mind. This indifference to money was almost uncanny; and yet as he compared the face of the assistant with that of the master, the difference was tragic. One suffused with the light that never was on sea or land, the other dark as the image of Baal whose shadow was cast half across the shop.

LIV

DOUBT was melting in the mind of Sir Arthur Babraham. He was coming now to a perception of the truth. To one who lived in the world, who saw men and things at an obtuse angle, the story as told by this young man verged upon the incredible and yet he felt sure it was true. The fellow was an Original, an unkind critic might even say that he was a trifle "cracked," but if this visionary who adored beauty for its own sake could enact such a piece of deceit it would be unwise ever to trust one's judgment again in regard to one's fellow creatures. And the reverse of the medal was shewn just as plainly in the face of the old dealer.

Man of affairs as Sir Arthur was, however, he knew better than to take a hasty decision upon what, after all, might prove to be wrong premises. It was his clear duty to see justice done in a strange matter, but he would leave to others the task of enforcing it. Thus when the old man renewed his demand to be allowed to go at once to Park Lane and get the picture, he was met by a refusal which if very polite was also final.

"Mr. Gedge, my daughter holds this picture in trust for your niece, who I am informed by the Hospital, has been most cruelly used by somebody. She accepts—we both accept—the story told by your niece as to how in the first instance she came to possess this most valuable thing, which by the way this young man has been able to confirm. If you persist in trying to establish your claim I am afraid you must apply to the law."

This speech, delivered with judicial weight, was a bomb-shell. With a gasp the old man realized that the game was up; yet as soon as the first shock had passed he could hardly mask his fury. By his own folly the chance of a lifetime had been thrown away.

As he was now to find, he was bereft of more than the Van Roon. He had lost the trust and affection of William. In the first agony of defeat, S. Gedge Antiques was far from realizing what the fact would mean, but it was brought home to him poignantly two days later.

William's first act, when Sir Arthur had left the shop, was to go to the Hospital. Here he was received by a member of its staff who told him that the patient was too ill to see anyone, and that even if she recovered, her mind might be permanently affected. The doctor who discussed the case with the young man allowed himself this frankness, because he was very anxious for light to be thrown on it. The girl had been cruelly knocked about, there were heavy bruises on her body and marks on her throat which suggested that she had had to fight for her life; and this was borne out by the delirium through which she was passing. In the main it seemed to be inspired by terror of a man whom she spoke of continually as Uncle Si.

The visitor was questioned closely as to the identity of the mysterious Uncle Si. He was pressed to say all that he knew about him, for the Hospital had to consider whether this was not a matter for the police.

William was shocked and rather terrified by the turn things had taken. The scales had been torn from his eyes with a force that left him bewildered. He had trusted his master in the way he trusted all the world, and now disillusion had come in a series of flashes which left him half blind, he felt life could never be the same. His own world of the higher reality was after all no more than the paradise of a fool. Perversely he had shut his eyes to the wickedness of men and their weak folly and in consequence he now found himself poised on the lip of a chasm.

Two days after the terrible discovery which had changed his attitude to life, he told his master that he was going to leave him. It was a heavy blow. Not for a moment had such a thing entered the old man's calculations. He had got into the habit of regarding this good simple fellow as having so little mind of his own that for all practical purposes he was now a part of himself.

So inconceivable was it to S. Gedge Antiques that one wedded to him by years of faithful service could take such a step, that it was hard to believe the young man meant what he said. He must be joking. But the wish was the anxious parent of the thought, for even if the old man's sight was failing, he was yet able to see the disdain in the eyes of William.

"I can't part with you, boy," he said bleakly.

That, indeed, was the open truth. To part with this absolutely honest and dependable fellow who had grown used to his ways, for whom no day's work was too long, for whom no task was too exacting, who was always obliging and cheerful, whose keen young sight and almost uncanny "nose" for a good thing had become quite indispensable to one who was no longer the man he had been; for S. Gedge Antiques to lose this paragon was simply not to be thought of.

"Boy don't talk foolishly. I'll raise your wages five shillings a week from the first of the New Year."

The old man could not see the look of slow horror that crept into the eyes of William; yet in spite of his other infirmity, he did not fail to catch the note of grim pain in the stifled, "I'll have to leave you, sir. I can't stay here."

Obtuse the old man was, yet he now perceived the finality of these broken words. As he realized all they meant to him, the sharp pain was like the stab of a knife. William was not merely indispensable. His master loved him. And he had killed the thing he loved.

"Boy, I can't let you go." Human weakness fell upon the old man like a shadow; this second blow was even more terrible than the loss of the Van Roon which was still a nightmare in his thoughts. "I'm old. I'm getting deaf and my eyes are going." He who had had no spark of pity for others did not scruple to ask it for himself.

William was a rock. Primitive as he was, now that he could respect his master no more, he must cease to serve him. The revelation of that master's baseness had stricken him to the heart; for the time being it had taken the savour out of life itself.

One hope, one frail hope remained to S. Gedge Antiques, even when he knew at last that his assistant was "through" with him. In times so difficult the young man might not be able to get another job; yet he had only to mention it to discover it was not a staff on which he would be able to lean.

William, it seemed, had got another job already.

"At how much a week?" Habit was so strong, there was no concealing the sneer in the tone of surprised inquiry.

Three pounds a week was to be William's salary. The old man could only gasp. It brought home to him, as perhaps nothing else could have done, the real worth of the treasure he was about to lose. It was four times the rate at which he had thought well to reward these priceless services.

"Who is being fool enough to give you that money?" he sneered, the ruling passion still strong in him.

"Mr. Hutton, sir, at the top of the street," was the mournful answer.

S. Gedge Antiques dug a savage tooth in his lower lip. Joseph Hutton was a young and "pushful" rival whom on instinct he hated. "Fellow's a fool to go spoiling the market," he snarled.

Alas, the old man knew but too well that as far as William was concerned, it was not at all a question of spoiling the market. That aspect of the matter would never arise in his mind.

LV

EVERY day for a fortnight William went to the Hospital, only to be denied a sight of the patient. June was fighting for life. And even when the crisis was passed and it began to appear that the fight would be successful, she had to face an issue just as critical and yet more terrible, for the fear remained that she would lose her reason.

In this time of darkness William was most unhappy. But as far as he was concerned, events moved quickly. He said good-bye to his master, removed his belongings from Number Forty-six, New Cross Street, and entered the employ of a neighbouring dealer, a man of far more liberal mind than S. Gedge Antiques; one who, moreover, well understood the value of such a servant.

For William, it was a terrible wrench. He was like a plant whose roots have been torn from the soil. With the ardour of a simple character he had loved his master, trusting and believing in him to an extent only possible to those endowed with rare felicity of nature. In spite of himself he was now forced to accept the hard and bitter truth that the old man upon whom he had lavished affection was not only a miser, but something worse. When the passion which ruled his life was fully roused he was tempted to anything.

Life, felt William, could never be the same again. There was still the beauty of the visible universe, the pageantry of the seasons to adore; the harmony and colour of the world's design might still entrance the senses of an artist, but not again must he surrender his being entire to the joy of abounding in these wonders. It was the duty of every man who dwelt upon the earth, however humbly, to learn something of the hearts of others. One could only live apart, it seemed, at one's peril.

While in the lower depths and beginning to despair of seeing June again, he called as usual at the Hospital one afternoon, to be greeted by the long-hoped-for news that the patient had taken a turn for the better. Moreover she had begged to be allowed to see him; and this permission was now given.

Carrying the daily bunch of flowers, by means of which June had already recognized his care for her, he was led along the ward to the bed in which she lay. The change in her appearance startled him. Little remained of the whimsical yet high-spirited and practical girl who had mocked his inefficiency in regard to the world and its ways. To see those great eyes with the horror still in them and that meagre face, dead white amid the snow of its pillows, was to feel a tragic tightening of the heart.

Tears ran down June's cheeks at the sight of the flowers. "I don't deserve your goodness," she said. "You can't guess how wicked I am."

As she extended to him her thin arms he found it hard to rein back his own tears. What suffering he had unwittingly brought upon this poor thing. But it was impossible to keep track of her mind which even now was in the thrall of an awful nightmare. God knew in what darkness it was still plunged.

Shuddering convulsively at the memories his voice and his presence brought to her, the words that came to her lips tore his heart. "Am I struck? Am I like the Hoodoo? Am I like Uncle Si?"

To him, just then, this wildness was hardly more than a symptom of a mind deranged. His great distress did not allow him to pursue its implication, nor could he understand the nadir of the soul from which it sprang. Yet many times in the days to follow he was haunted by those words. They came to him in his waking hours and often in lieu of sleep at night.

Returning from this short and unhappy interview to his new home at Number 116, New Cross Street, he found a surprise in store. A visitor had called to see him and, at the moment of his arrival, was on the point of going away.

His late master, looking very grey and frail, had come to beg him to return. He declared that he was now too old to carry on alone. Sight and hearing were growing worse. He had another quarrel with the char and had been obliged to send her permanently away, although the truth of the matter was that an oppressed female had risen at last against his tyranny and had found a better place.

S. Gedge Antiques was now a figure for pity, but William, fresh from the lacerating presence of the niece whom he had so cruelly thrown out of doors, had none to give.

The whine and snuffle of their last meeting, at whose remembrance rose the gorge of an honest man, were no more. Instead of the crocodile tricks were now the slow tears of a soul in agony. The truth was, this childless and friendless old man, who in the grip of the passion that had eaten away his life, had never been able to spare a thought for his kind, simply could not do without the one human being he had learned to love.

Their relations, as the old miser had discovered, were much closer than those of servant and master. William stood for youth, for the seeing mind, for cheerful, selfless giving, for life itself. The tones of his voice, his kindly readiness, his tolerance for an old man's megrims; even the sound of this good fellow moving furniture in the next room and the sense of him about the place had grown to mean so much that, now they were withdrawn, all other things grew null.

The old man felt now that he could not go on, and at any other moment, the force of his appeal might have touched the gentle nature to whom it was made. But the stars in their courses fought against S. Gedge Antiques. He was a figure to move the heart, as he stood in the shop of a rival dealer, the slow tears staining his thin cheeks, but William had the shadow of that other figure upon him. The wreck of youth, of reason itself, seemed infinitely more tragic than the falling of the temple upon the priest of Baal whose wickedness had brought the thing to pass.

William denied his master. And yet hearing him out to the bitter end, he was unable to withhold a little pity. All feeling for the old man was dead; the bedside from which he had just come had finally destroyed the last spark of his affection, yet being the creature he was, he could not sit in judgment.

"I'll pay you twice what you are getting now if you'll return to me," said the old man. "As I say, I can't go on." He peered into that face of ever-deepening distress. "What do you say, boy?" He took the hand of the young man in his own, as a father might take that of a beloved son. "I'll give you anything—if you'll come back. I haven't long to live. Return to-night and I'll leave you the business. Now what do you say?"

Had it been human to forgive at such a moment, S. Gedge Antiques would have been forgiven. But William could only stand dumb and unresponsive before the master he had loved.

"I'm a warm man." The voice of the old dealer who had made money his god, sank to a whisper becoming a theme so sacred. "My investments have turned out well. There's no saying what I *am* worth—but this I'll tell you in strict confidence—I own property." The hushed tone was barely audible. "In fact I own nearly half my own side of this street. Now what do you say? Promise to come back to me to-night and I'll go right now and see my lawyer."

The young man stood the image of unhappiness.

"Only speak the word and you shall inherit every stick and stone."

It was a moment to rend the heart of both, but the word was not spoken. For the second time that afternoon William was hard set to rein back his tears; but he had not the power to yield to this appeal.

Overborne by the knowledge that the hand of Fate was upon him, S. Gedge Antiques, leaning heavily on his knotted stick, moved feebly towards the dark street.

LVI

WILLIAM continued his daily visits to the Hospital, but he was not allowed to see June. Life itself was no longer in immediate danger, but she had had a relapse and the doctors were still afraid that the mental injury would be permanent. Time alone could prove if such was the case or no, but the mood induced by the interview with William, and the strange words she had used to him, which seemed to belong to some fixed and secret obsession, were not a good sign.

Following his visit there had been a rise of temperature. And this meant further weakening of a terror-haunted mind. Even if the need for anxiety was less acute, full recovery at best would be slow and more than ever doubtful.

June was still menaced by the shadow when an event occurred which intensified William's distress. One morning, about a week after he had rejected his master's last appeal, an inspector of police came to see him. Neighbours of S. Gedge Antiques had called attention to the fact that the shop had remained closed for several days, and as it was known that the old man had lately been living alone, the circumstance had given rise to a certain amount of suspicion. William's name had been mentioned as lately in his employ and he was asked to throw what light he could on the mystery.

"The neighbours think we ought to enter the shop and see if anything has happened," said the police inspector.

William thought so too. Remembering the last meeting with his master, which had left a scar he would carry to the grave, a kind of prophetic foreknowledge came to him now of a new development to this tragedy.

It was not convenient just then to leave the shop as he happened to be in sole charge of it, therefore he was unable to accompany the inspector down the street. But half an hour later, on the return of his new employer, curiosity forced him to put on his hat and go forth to see if the thing he feared had come to pass.

The police, already, had made an entry of Number Forty-six. Moreover a knot of people was assembled about the familiar door, which was half open. Its shutters were still up, but two constables were guarding the precincts. William caught the words "Murder—Suicide—Robbery" as he came up with the throng.

In a state of painful excitement, he made his way to the door.

S. Gedge Antiques, it seemed, had been found lying dead on the shop floor. The young man wished to pass in, but the police had instructions to allow no one to enter. A doctor summoned by telephone, had not yet come.

William was still discussing the matter, when the inspector whose acquaintance he had made already, hearing voices at the door, came from the shop interior to see if it was the doctor who had at last arrived. He recognized William at once and invited him in.

Outside was a murky November day, but with the windows still shuttered, it was necessary for three rather ineffectual gas-jets to be lit in the shop. The light they gave was weird and fitful, but it sufficed to enable the young man to see what had occurred.

As yet the body had not been touched. In accordance with custom in such cases, it had to lie just as it was until viewed by a doctor, for if moved by unskilful hands, some possible clue as to the cause of death might be obliterated.

The old man was lying supine, before the Hoodoo. One glance at that face, so drawn, so thwarted, and yet so pitiful in its ghastliness, was enough to convince William that death had come directly from the hand of God. With a shiver he recalled the words of a strange and terrible clairvoyance, of late so often in his ears. "Am I struck? Am I like Uncle Si? Am I like the Hoodoo?"

As the old man lay now, in all the starkness of his soul, with only the essence shewing in that tragic face, William was overcome by his likeness to the image. It was as if, at the last, his very nature had gone out to some false god who had perverted him. That splay-footed monster, so large of maw, an emblem of bestial greed, was too plainly a symbol of the mammon of unrighteousness to which the master had devoted his life.

Consumed by pity, William turned away from a sight which he was no longer able to bear.

LVII

SPRING came, and June who had had to fight for life and then for reason, won slowly to a final sense of victory. This came to her on a delicious April day, when the earth waking from its long sleep, was renewed with the joy of procreation. Her own nature, which had passed through so many months of darkness, was quickened to response in this magic hour.

The force of the emotion owed much, no doubt, to the spirit of environment. Life had begun again for June under conditions different from any she had known. Powerful friends had been gained for her by a singularly romantic story. Of certain things that had happened she could not bring herself to tell; but when as much of the truth came out as could be derived from facts precariously pieced together, she became a real heroine in the sight of Sir Arthur Babraham and his daughter.

But for her courage and keen wit a great work of art might have passed out of the country without anyone being the wiser. These staunch friends were determined that justice should be done in the matter, and kindly folk that they were, did not spare themselves in the long and difficult task of restoring her to health.

The middle of April saw her installed in the gardener's cottage at Homefield in the care of a motherly and genial housewife. Here she almost dared to be happy. The phantoms of the long night were being dispersed at last in an atmosphere of sunny and cordial well-being.

Miss Babraham, who walked across the park from the house every morning to see her, had become a sort of fairy godmother whose mission was to see that she did not worry about anything. She must give her days and nights to the duty of getting well. And she was going to be rich.

Riches, alas, for June, had the fairy godmother but known, were the fly in the ointment. They could only arise from one source, and around it must always hover the black storm clouds. She had no real right to the money which was coming to her, and although she had no means apart from it, she felt that she must never accept a single penny. It was morbidly unpractical perhaps, but there the feeling was.

When June had been at Homefield about a week, Miss Babraham found her one morning in the sunny embrasure of the pleasant little sitting room improving her mind by a happy return to her favourite "Mill on the Floss." In passing out of its mental eclipse, the angle of June's vision had shifted a little; her approach to new phases of experience was rather more sympathetic than it had been. Before "that" had happened, she had been inclined, as became a self-respecting member of the Democracy which is apt to deride what it does not comprehend, to be a little contemptuous of "Miss Blue Blood," a creature born to more than a fair share of life's good things. But now that she knew more about this happy-natured girl, she felt a tolerance of which, at first, she was just a little ashamed. Envy was giving place to something else. Her graces and her air of fine breeding, which June's own caste was inclined to resent, were not the obvious fruits of expensive clothes; in fact, they owed far less than June had supposed to the length of the purse behind them.

The kindness, the charm, the sympathy were more than skin deep. In the first place, no doubt their possessor had been born under a lucky star; much of her quality was rooted inevitably in the fact that she was her father's daughter yet the invalid could not gainsay that "Miss Blue Blood" had manners of the heart. Now that June saw her in her own setting among her own people this golden truth shone clear. And in the many talks June had with her good hostess, Mrs. Chrystal, the wife of Sir Arthur's head gardener, one radiant fact rose bright and free: there was none like Miss Babraham. Her peer was not to be found on the wide earth.

No doubt there were spots on this sun as there are spots on other suns, but June agreed that as far as Miss Babraham was concerned these blemishes were hidden from mortal eye. And each day gave cogency to such a view. This morning, for example, the distinguished visitor was brimming with kindliness. She talked simply and sincerely, without patronage or frills upon the subjects in which June was now interested. She had read *all* George Eliot and gave as the sum of her experience that the "Mill on the Floss" was the story she liked best, although her father preferred "Adam Bede" or "Silas Marner."

"Before my illness," said June, "I was getting to think that all novels were silly and a waste of time. But I see now that you can learn a lot about life from a good one."

She was in a very serious mood. Like most people who have not the gift of "taking things in their stride" new orientations were a heavy business. At school, as a little girl, she had shed many tears over her arithmetic. The process of mind improvement was not to be undertaken lightly. She could never be a Miss Babraham, but her ambition, in the words of her favourite song, was to be as like her as she was able to be.

Like true poets, however, Miss Babrahams were born. Such graces came from an inner harmony of nature. All the best fairies must have flocked to her christening. One minor gift she had which June allowed herself to covet, since it might fall within the scope of common mortals; it was the way in which her maid arranged her hair. June's own famous mane, which indirectly had brought such suffering upon her, had mercifully been spared; it had not even been "bobbed," and with careful tendence might again achieve its old magnificence. As shyly she confessed this ambition, which sprang less from vanity than simple pride in her one "asset," Miss Babraham assured her that nothing could be nicer than her own way of doing it.

From hair and the art of treating it they passed to other intimate topics; frocks and the hang of them; the knack of putting things on, in which Miss Babraham's gift of style filled June with envy since that, alas, she would never be able to copy; and above all, her friend's wonderful faculty of looking her best on all occasions.

As the good fairy, after a stay of a full hour, rose to go, she said, "If tomorrow morning is as fine as this morning, do you think you could come over to us? You know the way. It's an easy walk of less than half a mile."

June was sure she could.

"Please do, if you won't find it trying. Come about eleven. And I hope," said the good fairy, casting back her charming smile as she was about to pass out of the sitting-room door, "there may be a pleasant little surprise for you."

During the last few weeks June had known in abundance the agreeably unexpected. And though at intervals during the rest of the fair spring day, her mind toyed with this new "surprise," she was not able to guess what it was going to be.

LVIII

ELEVEN o'clock the next morning saw June, dressed very carefully indeed, before the portals of the House. She had come well. Excitement had made her feel quite strong again; moreover she had been promised a reward for the effort she was making. Apart from that besides, it was the biggest feat of her social life, so far, to press the bell of such a noble door.

The servant who answered it was not too proud to shew by his air of prompt courtesy that her coming was anticipated. She was led across a glorious hall—all black oak, family portraits, heads of deer and suits of armour, with an open gallery running round the top, like a scene on the movies—up a wide staircase, laid with a carpet thick and subtle to the tread, along a corridor into a room of great length whose glass roof gave a wonderful light. Many pictures hung upon its walls. June was thrilled at the moment she found herself in it, for this she felt sure, was the famous Long Gallery.

The thrill was not confined, however, to the room. When she entered, June thought it was empty, but a look round disclosed at the far end a tall young man in a familiar attitude of rapt absorption. Only one person since the world began could have been so lost to the present in sheer force of contemplating a mere relic of the past.

It was a rare bit of contrivance, all the same, on the part of Miss Babraham. Here, before June, was the Sawney, raised to his highest power. The fairy godmother had made a pass with her magic wand and William the amazing stood before her in the flesh.

He was too far from the door and too rapt in adoration of the masterpiece at which he was gazing, to have heard June come in. And so, before he saw her, she had time to grow nervous and this was a pity. For so effectively had the mine been sprung that she had need just now of all her courage.

A good deal of water had recently flowed under the bridge. It was as if a hundred years had passed since she had dared to label him a Sawney. He had grown up and she had grown down. So far away was the time of their equality, if such a time had ever really been, that she was just a shade in awe of him now.

Many hours had he spent by her bed. It was perhaps due to him that she had emerged at last from the chasm which so long and so grimly threatened to engulf her. His royal yet gentle nature had a true power of healing. The look in his eyes, the music of his voice, the poetry of his thoughts, the charm of his mere presence, had borne him to a plane far above that of common people like herself. If Miss Babraham was a fairy godmother, this young man was surely the true prince.

Beyond anyone she had ever known he had a perception of those large and deep things of sky and earth, which alone, as it seemed to her now, made life worth while. He was the prophet of the beautiful in deed as in word. During the long night through which she had passed, the sense of her inferiority had been not the least of her sorrows.

That sense returned upon her now as she stood timidly by the door through which she had come, watching the beams of an April sun, almost as shy as herself, weave an aureole for him. Here was the god of her dreams; she who lately had known no god and who long ago had taught herself to despise all forms of dreaming.

At last he turned and saw her.

"You!" He sprang towards her with an eager cry.

Brilliant stage management. But by fate's perversity, the players, somehow, were not quite equal to their parts. June's shy timidity communicated itself at once to this sensitive plant. There was not a ghost of a reason why he should not have taken her in his arms, for he had come to love her tenderly. The act had been devised for him, the deed expected, but this young man was less wise in some things than in others. Deep as he could look into hidden mysteries, there was certainly one mystery whose heart he could not read.

June's odd confusion summoned a mistaken chivalry. Broken in spirit, poor soul, by what she had been through, she could no longer defend herself; he must be, therefore, very gentle. It would have been easier to tackle the Miss June of New Cross Street, the rather imperious and sharp-tongued niece of his late employer, than this quivering storm-beaten flower.

With all his genius it was to be feared he would always be a Sawney.

"How are you getting on Miss June?" he said lamely. "You look very thin, but you've got quite a colour."

Something of the gawklike New Cross Street manner, which compared ill with Miss Babraham's tact and finesse was in this greeting. Phœbus Apollo took a sudden nose-dive. He came, in fact, within an ace of a crash.

June's cheeks grew flame-colour. An idiot less divine would have given her a kiss and have had done with it, but in some ways he was a shocking dunce.

"I expect you are surprised to see me here, aren't you?"

She could but stammer that she was very much surprised.

"Sir Arthur has asked me to re-hang some of these." A rather proud wave of the hand towards those august walls shewed that he was human. "And he has commissioned me"—She heard again that dying fall which always touched her ear with ecstasy—"to go over this Jan Vermeer most carefully with warm water and cotton wool."

June knitted her brow in order to accompany his finger in its mystical course.

"A Jan what?" she said, achieving a frown. Had it been possible at this early stage of convalescence to achieve a note of reproof, that authentic touch would not have been lacking.

William's the blame for a lost opportunity. But life is full of *gaffes* on the part of those who ought to know better. The ability of William was beyond dispute. Miss Babraham had acclaimed it, whereby she was no more than the mouthpiece of her father, that famous connoisseur who said openly that the discoverer of the Van Roon was a genius. To Sir Arthur it was miraculous that a tiro should expose the treasure to the view in a fashion so accomplished. It hardly seemed possible to remove the burdens of overgrowth laid by time and the vandal fingers of inferior artists upon that delicate surface without damage to the fabric. Yet experts had declared the thing to be not a penny the worse for all the processes it had been through; and on the strength of this amazing skill, the owner of Homefield had decided to entrust to those inspired hands, one of his cherished Vermeers.

LIX

TOGETHER they went round the Long Gallery, gazing at the treasure on its walls, which to him meant so much, to her so little. She tried to see it with his eyes or if this could not be, at least get some clue to the quality which made quite ordinary looking objects the things they were.

Who could have believed that an old and dirty thing which she had heard even Uncle Si describe as a daub, would turn out to be a fortune? Other fortunes were here to gaze upon, but why they were so precious would always be for June a mystery of mysteries. Even with William's help it was a subject on which she could never be really wise. She had now a great desire to reach out after Culture; the "Mill on the Floss" was most stimulating to the mind; but just now she felt, in Blackhampton phrase, that already "she had bitten off more than she could chew."

Perhaps it was the presence of William which had induced a mood of great complexity. Old unhappy things were flooding back. And as they walked slowly round the Gallery, an object at its extreme end suddenly sprang into view, which brought her up with an icy gasp. The Hoodoo was grinning at her.

In its new setting the monster was merely grotesque. Retrieved from the morose interior of Number Forty-six, New Cross Street, which it had darkened so long with its malice, it was no longer an active embodiment of evil. The force of its ugliness was less, yet for June, in a subtle way, the implication of its presence was more.

It was as if the Fates were saying to her: "We are watching you, my girl. This young man, whom now you dare to love, have you not tricked him out of his patrimony by your pretended worship of beauty? Share his ecstasy, if you please, of his Peter This and his Mathew That, but don't forget that Our eye is still upon you. What you have already received you will long remember, but you may get another dose if you are not careful."

Hearing words to this sinister effect in the secret places of her soul, June could only shiver. William, now as conscious of the invalid's frailty as of the imperious challenge of beauty, led her at once to a seat without seeking the cause of her distress.

He saw she was still very weak and hastened therefore to set her down on a chair of the Empire, heedless of the fact that she was almost cheek by jowl with the Hoodoo.

"Mustn't tire yourself," he said in a voice of rare sympathy which did but add to the feeling of misery that crept upon her. "I'm afraid you've walked a bit too far."

Again June shivered. The old unhappy things were threatening once more to submerge her. "How I wish That had not come here," she said dismally. There was no need to point at the Image; she was sure that he knew what she meant.

But amazing young man that he was, this was trying him a little too highly.

"Oh, you mean the James," he said pointing to a windmill opposite. "He isn't a Mathew, is he? I'm so glad, Miss June, you think that too, because with you to back me, I may be able to break it to Sir Arthur, that this isn't quite the place for him."

Divine humility! Mad confusion! Had she but felt a little stronger, a little less unhappy, she really could have shaken him.

"I mean the Hoodoo," she said woefully.

Her wild bird's heart went quick and high as she saw him turn casually and enfold That with a slow smile. "Right again," he said, his head a little to one side in pure connoisseurship, a trick she had learned to watch for. "I quite agree with you—the old fool swallows more than his share of this beautiful light."

June was not thinking of the beautiful light. She was trembling in spirit; but one of his nature could not be expected to know what demons from the abyss were invading her. "How I wish it was somewhere else."

His laugh of gay agreement was suddenly checked as he caught the look in her eyes and in the next instant he saw the old man lying dead at the foot of the Hoodoo.

It was like the passing of a cloud across the sun. Life for him, also, had found another notation in these terrible months. He had been through a hard school. Certain lines in his face were deeper and there were hollows under his eyes. Never again must he allow the ideal to run so far ahead of the real. Yet in this harsh moment the power of his nature kept him up.

He was able to pierce to the true reason for June's deadly pallor. It was not wholly due to the fact that she was still weak or that she had walked too far. Trolls even now were in her brain. With his instinct for healing he must do his utmost to cast them out.

"We'll try to persuade Miss Babraham to have him put in the garden."

Scarcely had he spoken the words when the fairy godmother, accompanied by Sir Arthur Babraham, entered the Long Gallery.

LX

"SO here you are!"

But the light note of Miss Babraham's greeting changed to a quick concern as a feminine eye saw at a glance that June was looking "done."

"Now don't get up, please. I am going to be quite angry with myself if your walk has made you over-tired."

June, a new shyness upon her, which the presence of Sir Arthur made much worse, found it very difficult to speak.

"I hope you are cultivating a taste for chicken and new laid eggs," said the kindly gentleman. "And for a glass of wine to your meals—which I always say is what has made Old England the country she is." Finding his jolly laugh was less effective than usual, he pointed to the Hoodoo in the tactful hope of putting an embarrassed girl at her ease. "There's an old friend I'm sure you recognize." June's distress, however, grew rapidly worse and Sir Arthur made a fresh cast. "I'm not sure all the same," he said to William in a laughing aside, "that the old fellow can be allowed to stay here. Tell me, what is your candid opinion?"

"We've been wondering, sir, if he wouldn't look better in the garden."

Miss Babraham caught gaily at the suggestion. "The very place for the jar of Knossos. And perhaps Miss June and Mr. William will plant a myrtle in it."

"A myrtle," said Sir Arthur. "In that chap—a myrtle?" He plucked at his moustache and looked at the laughing Laura. "Why—pray—a myrtle?"

"Papa, how dense you are!"

A hit clean and fair, which after a very little thought Sir Arthur was man enough to own. His one excuse, and a poor one, was that in certain things the sex to which he had the misfortune to belong, was notoriously "slow in the uptake."

It was now William's turn to acclaim the idea. Blushing deeply said that quaint and whimsical young man: "Yes, Miss Babraham, with your permission we will plant a myrtle in the jar of Knossos."

In the laugh which followed June did not share; just now her feeling was that she would never be able to laugh again.

Sir Arthur, still tactful, now conceived it to be his duty to cheer the poor girl up. "By the way," he said, "has my daughter told you what we propose to do with your Van Roon? Of course with your permission."

June simply longed for the power to say that it was not for her to give the permission as the Van Roon was not hers. But she was living just now in a kind of dream in which action and speech had no part. The only thing she could do was to listen passively to the voice of Sir Arthur, while it leisurely unfolded a tale of fairyland.

"I must tell you," he said, "subject to your approval—always, of course, subject to *that*—we have formed a sort of committee to deal with this picture of yours. It has given rise to a rather curious position. We think—three or four of us—that it ought to be acquired for the nation; but of course there's the question of price. If the work is put up at auction, it may fetch more than we should feel justified in paying. Sentiment of course; but nowadays sentiment plays a big part in these matters. On the other hand, having regard to the obscurity of its origin, it might be knocked down for considerably less than it is intrinsically worth. All the same we are quite convinced that it is a very choice example of a great master, and that the place for it is the National Gallery, where another Van Roon is badly needed. Now I hope you see the dilemma. If the nation enters the market a definite buyer, the thing may soar to a preposterous sum. At the same time, we don't want the nation to acquire it for less than its real value. So the question in a nutshell is, will you accept a private arbitration or do you prefer to run the risk of getting comparatively little in the hope of obtaining an extra ten thousand pounds or so?"

June followed the argument as closely as she could, and at the end of it burst into wild tears.

"The picture is not mine," she sobbed. "It doesn't belong to me."

It was a moment of keen embarrassment. Sir Arthur, who had doubted from the first, was hardly to be blamed for beginning to doubt again. Such an outburst was the oddest confirmation of his first suspicion, which conspiring Circumstance had enabled him perhaps too easily to forget. But Laura's faith was quite unshaken. For her the question of ownership had been settled once and for all. The poor thing was overwrought, overdriven; it was so like the tactless father of hers, to worry the girl with all kinds of tiresome details when he should have known that she was not strong enough to grapple with them.

"Come, papa," said Laura Babraham with reproof in a clear grey eye. "If we don't go at once and look at that herbaceous border we shall certainly be late for luncheon."

LXI

LEFT to themselves once more, it became William's task to comfort June's distress. Like Sir Arthur, he too, it seemed, could be tactful. Instead of discussing the question of the Van Roon's ownership or the unlucky presence of the Hoodoo, he began gently to discourse of Mathew Maris.

As far as June was concerned he might as well have discoursed of the moon. In the first place she had never heard of Mathew Maris; and in the second she was consumed by a desire to settle forever the question of the Van Roon which was now tormenting her like a fire. This was a dynamic moment, when great decisions are reached with startling abruptness and half a lifetime may be lived in half a minute.

Mathew Maris was not for June just now. Suddenly she broke again into wild sobs.

"I cheated you, I tricked you over that picture."

Again, good honest fellow, he tried to change the current of this mind distraught. But it was not to be.

"You gave it me, didn't you, because I made you think I had fallen in love with it? But I hadn't. It meant nothing to me—not in that way."

He stood an image of dismay, but he had to listen.

"Why do you suppose I did that? I'll tell you. I overheard Uncle Si talking to a dealer. You remember, don't you, the funny crooked little man in the knitted comforter and the brown billycock whom I used to call Foxy Face? One morning when you were out he offered Uncle Si five pounds for it and Uncle Si said it might be worth a good deal more. That's why I decided to get hold of it if I could, before Uncle Si got it from you. And that's why I cracked it up and made you think I could see all sorts of wonders in it, when all the time I saw no more beauty in it than there is in That." And she pointed to the Hoodoo.

William gave a little gasp. June heard the gasp. And in the mad unhappiness of that moment she determined to spare herself nothing. She would strip herself bare so that the whip might be better laid on.

"Beauty means no more to me than it does to that Thing there. All your talk about Hobbemas and Marises and Vermeers and Cromes are to me just sloppy. They bore me stiff every time. I hate the sight of all these things." The wave of a wildly tragic hand included all the masterpieces in the Long Gallery. "I hate them! I hate them! So now you know the mean and dirty liar that I am."

No longer able to bear the sound of her strange and terrible words he turned sickly away. It was almost as if they had opened a vein in his heart. He remembered again the cry that had haunted him after his seeing her first at the Hospital. "Am I struck? Am I like Uncle Si? Am I like the Hoodoo?"

Poor soul! It was not for him to judge her. He could only think of her sufferings. And it was cruel indeed to realize what they must be now.

"That's why I don't want the money. And that's why I don't mean to have it. I burn when I think of it. Now you know how low down I am. I hope you like the way I've cheated you."

He sought to take her hand, but she withdrew it fiercely. His very goodness almost made her hate him.

LXII

BY the advice of Miss Babraham they planted a myrtle in the jar of Knossos. Some days later the Hoodoo was haled into a convenient corner of the Italian garden. Here, by the marge of a tiny rock-strewn lake, the momentous rite was performed with a high solemnity. Much displacement of mould and a considerable wheelbarrowing of the same was necessary and Mr. Chrystal, the head gardener, had to advise in the use of the trowel, an art in which neither June nor William was quite so adept as they might have been. But at last, after some honest digging and shovelling on the part of William who was not afraid to take off his coat to the job, and timely help from Mr. Chrystal's George who was uncannily wise, although to be sure he had the experience of a lifetime and a fairly long one to bring to bear on such matters, the thing was done.

June and William then retired to the fragrant shade of a budding lime, feeling rather hot, yet not dissatisfied with their labours. It was a perfect morning. Larks were hovering in the bright air. Blackbirds and thrushes were trying out their grace-notes, and once June thought she heard a nightingale.

For a little they reclined in poetic comfort in two wicker chairs. Fauns in marble, and Cupid, complete with bow and arrows lurked hard by. At last June broke a delicious silence.

"You must put your coat on," she said suddenly.

"But——" said William who really had delved and shovelled to some purpose.

June was not to be Butted—not this golden day.

"If you don't you might get a bad chill," she said severely.

William rose and did her bidding. And in the midst of that simple act, a certain piece of confidential information, which Sir Arthur and Miss Laura had been kind enough to supply at frequent intervals during the last few days, recurred forcibly to his mind. It was to the effect that "Miss Gedge was so practical she would make an ideal wife for an artist."

As far as the major premise was concerned it was less irrelevant than at first it might seem, for William had recently decided that an artist was what he was going to be. In the very act of putting on his coat he now recalled the high and sacred mystery to which his life was vowed. And further he recalled that before entering the garden he had taken the precaution of slipping a neat little sketching book and pencil into his coat pocket. Thus, upon sitting down, in solemn silence he took them forth and proceeded to draw.

June it was who broke the silence, after some little while.

"If you are drawing that myrtle," she said, "it looks a bit potty to me stuck up there. There's nothing to it."

She was more her true self this happy morning than for many a tragic month.

"It'll grow," said the artist.

"Won't seem much if it doesn't in that great jar. It was Miss Babraham's idea to stick it there, so it's all right of course. She said it was an emblem of what was it?"

"Of marriage," said the artist with an air of innocent abstraction.

"Then she ought to have planted it herself—if she *is* going to be married."

"On the first of July. They've fixed the day."

"Oh," said June. "Have you seen her young man?"

"He came to lunch yesterday."

"Who is he?"

"The Honourable Barrington, a gentleman in the Blues."

June frowned portentously. "I hope he'll be good enough for her." But she didn't sound very hopeful.

"He's a very nice gentleman."

"Ought to be if he's going to marry *her*. But what I should like to know is, why was she so set on you and me planting that myrtle when she ought to have planted it herself."

"Don't know, I'm sure, Miss June," said the artist, not so much as glancing up from his work.

Once a Sawney always a Sawney. Perennially, it seemed, was she up against the relentless workings of that natural law. Marriage, money, commonsense, the really big things of life, meant so little to him compared with windmills and myrtles, and things of that kind. Like her beloved Miss Babraham, this dear and charming fellow was almost too good to be true, but day by day the conviction was growing upon her that he really did need somebody practical to look after him. And she was not alone in thinking so. Miss Babraham, who knew so much about everything, had already expressed that opinion to her quite strongly.

Here he was, in the middle of a perfect morning, with all sorts of really beautiful things about him, and larks and blackbirds quiring, and the sun on the water and the Surrey hills, wasting his time seemingly, by drawing that rather paltry looking little plant stuck up there on the top of the Hoodoo. Even if it was the emblem of marriage she could not help a subtle feeling of annoyance that he should not use his precious time a bit better.

However, the cream of the joke was to follow.

The artist it was who quaintly burst this fresh bubble of silence. "Talk as much as you like, Miss June," he said with something a little odd, a little unexpected in his manner, "but I hope you'll keep your hands in your lap just as they are now, and if you don't mind will you please bring your chin round a bit—on to a level with my finger."

"Please get on with that myrtle." Before, however, the fiat was really pronounced, she abruptly stopped. Could such a thing be? Was it possible that he was not drawing the myrtle at all?

It was more than possible.

And that was the cream of the whole matter!

LXIII

"I'M not half as good looking as that," said June.

"All depends, don't you know, on the angle at which one happens to get you," said William.

It was the tone of a gentleman in the Blues speaking to Miss Babraham. Yet it came so pat and so natural from the lips of an artist, that in spite of herself, June could not help being a little awed by it. She didn't agree, yet she didn't disagree; that is to say, as Miss Babraham would have done, she agreed to disagree without contradicting the artist flatly.

Besides it is the whole duty of an artist to know just how people look in all circumstances. Everybody looks better at some moments than at others. June had no pretensions to be considered an artist herself, but at that moment she knew just how William looked. In his new suit, neat rather than smart and smart rather than neat—all depends don't you know on the angle at which one happened to get it!—with his mop of fair hair brushed away from his fine forehead, and his yellow tie, and the curves of that sensitive mouth, and those wonderful eyes and those slim fingers, he looked fitted by nature to marry a real lady. Indeed, in the course of the last few days, a suspicion had crossed June's mind that Miss Babraham thought so too; thus the apparition of the Honourable Barrington and the definite fixing of the day had taken a load off her mind.

For all that other loads were still upon it. Since her nerve-storm in the Long Gallery a week had passed. She was feeling much better now, day by day she was growing stronger; nevertheless she was troubled about many things.

Foremost of these was the question so vital to a practical mind, of ways and means. They both had to live. And if William had really made up his mind to be an artist, he would need money and plenty of it for leisure and study and foreign travel. She was rather glad, if only for this reason, that he had been able to take such a bold decision. He would be the more likely to accept that which really belonged to him: the price of the Van Roon.

Sir Arthur had now informed her that the sum the committee proposed to offer for the Van Roon could be invested to produce a thousand a year free of tax, and he strongly urged its acceptance, as she would be relieved of all money difficulties for the rest of her life. To June it sounded fabulous. She knew in her heart, besides, that she would never be able to take this income for her own use. Every penny was William's and the task now before her was to bring home to him this fact.

It did not take long to prove to her this morning that she was attempting the impossible. The thousand a year, he declared, was hers and nothing would induce him to touch a penny. Yielding in some ways, in others as she had discovered already, for all his gentleness he was a rock.

Desperation now drove June to confess that she had never intended to take the money. Even at the moment she had filched the Van Roon from him with her wicked pretences, at the back of her mind had been the wish to save him from himself. Always she had regarded herself as the Van Roon's trustee, so that he should not be victimized by the cunning of Uncle Si, just as Sir Arthur was its trustee now, so that neither of them should be robbed by the cunning of the world.

She found all too soon, however, that it was vain to argue with him. What he had given, he had given. As far as he was concerned, that was the end of the whole matter.

"Very well then," said June vexedly, "if you won't, you won't. And I shall present that picture to the nation in your name, and then you won't have a penny to live on and you'll have to go on working in a shop all your life for a small wage to make other people rich, instead of being able to study and travel and make yourself a great artist."

She felt sure the half nelson was on him now. Even he, dreamer that he was, must really bend to the force of pure reasoning! Beyond a doubt she had got him. But he was not playing quite fair it seemed. With one of his little dancing blushes that would have been deadly in a girl, he was forced to own that he had not put all his cards on the table.

To June's sheer amazement he was keeping a little matter of twelve hundred a year or so up his sleeve.

"Didn't know you had a rich aunt," said June amazedly.

"Not my rich aunt. Your rich uncle." The odd creature grew tawnier, more girl-like than ever.

June lacking a clue as yet could only frown. "Come again. I don't get you." It was not the Miss Babraham idiom, but with her patience giving out and a new strength and sanity in her veins, she was in danger of forgetting, just for a moment, that she was an honoured guest in the most famous Italian garden in Surrey.

Nevertheless in the very height of the eclipse a light shone. One of the advantages of a mind really practical is, that when it turns to financial matters, it works automatically at very high pressure. June's brow was cleft with the harrow of thought. "Do you mean to say," she figured slowly out, "that Uncle Si has left you all his property?"

"His lawyers say so." The voice of William had a slight tremor.

"If his lawyers say so it is so," said June with imperious finality.

A pause of which a thrush, a blackbird and an entire orchestra of skylarks took great advantage, came upon these inheritors in spite of themselves; and then June pensively remarked, a little in the manner of "Mr. Leopold" asking the Head Cashier what Consols had opened at this morning, "he must have bought some property very lucky."

Quite simply William stated that such was the fact. "The lawyers say that in 1895 he bought what they call a block in New Cross Street, including Number 46, and that it's been going up and up ever since, so that now it's worth about eight times what he gave for it."

In sheer incredulity June stared at him. She must be living in fairyland. And then the sun flamed out from the merest apology for a cloud which was all the April sky could boast at that moment and there came an answering gleam from the burnished image before her eyes in which they had lately planted a myrtle.

"Much good it did him," she said with a heavy sigh.

William never told June the story of the old man lying dead before the Hoodoo, nor had he disclosed his own indirect share in that tragic end. He did not do so now, for this was not the time to enter into such an unhappy matter. Yet without coming to details, June seemed with that power of clairvoyance she had lately acquired, to divine the whole pitiful business. "Miserable old miser," she said in a voice the birds could not hear. "He must have died like a dog."

William's tragic eyes could only be interpreted by his own heart.

A look so forlorn led June to notice the new lines in his face and his smouldering depth of eye. "I believe you were the only living thing he ever cared for, and yet it used to make my blood boil the way he———" The anguish in his eyes brought her up short.

In went the sun, as quickly as it had come out. *La Signora Aprile e volubile*, in England at any rate, whatever her mood in more genial climes. June shivered slightly as if a chill breath in the gentle wind had touched her. She glanced at the new wrist watch, whose acceptance William had craved two days before she left the Hospital. Nearly one o'clock already and it would never do to shew disrespect to Mrs. Chrystal's famous chicken-broth.

They got up together, yet as they did so they felt that the best of the spring day was fled. Now that the sun had gone in, the Hoodoo yonder was monarch once more of all he looked upon.

What a thing life was! Yet by now both were wise enough not to think too much about it. God knew it could be ugly, but dwelling upon its complexities only made them seem worse.

Besides there was no time for deep thoughts. It was six minutes to one. Luncheon at the House, where William, as became a man of acknowledged genius, was an honoured guest, was sharp at the hour. The honoured guest would only just have time to wash his hands and brush his hair. And so he was not able to accompany June along the rectangular path which led from the main avenue direct to Mrs. Chrystal's.

Moreover she didn't want him to. She understood his hurry. Also he understood hers. Besides each craved a moment, after all, to consider life and just where they stood in it.

"I have to rest this afternoon," said June. "And I suppose you have to get on with the cleaning of the Mathew Thingamy. But if it's as fine to-morrow morning as it has been to-day, let us meet under this tree about eleven. And then you can put in the last touches while I read "Pride and Prejudice" by Jane Austen that Miss Babraham's lent me. Seems a bit old-fashioned, but it's classic of course. I dare say it'll improve as it gets better."

Whereon June took the bypath abruptly, and William, his six minutes reduced to four, stepped out towards the House. Life and its complexities did not get therefore, much of a show at the moment, yet both of them must have been giving these high matters some little thought, for as June reached the eucalyptus tree she halted and half-turned and looked just for one instant back. And she found that William, now on a level with the second Cupid on the main gravel, and his four minutes reduced to three and a quarter, had also halted, and half-turned to follow her example.

LXIV

JUNE always maintained that the Idea was William's. He, on the other hand, always maintained that the Idea was hers. But whatever the truth of the matter in its centrality, there was really no doubt that it was Miss Babraham who thought of the car. To her alone belonged that minor yet still substantial glory. As for the luncheon basket, although that honour was claimed for her as well, it may have owed something to Sir Arthur, for June and William were agreed that the weighty and practical genius of that man of the world was visible in this important detail.

It was just after nine on as promising a morning of early May as the much and justly derided climate of Britain was able to produce for a signal occasion, when Mr. Mitchell the chauffeur in his livery of Robin Hood green, with buff collar and cuffs, arrived at Mrs. Chrystal's door with Sir Arthur's touring car. Inside, as if to the manner born, sat William in a fleecy grey ulster which June had no idea he possessed—and for that matter it was Sir Arthur who possessed it—and almost the last word in hats, which if you happened to catch its wearer in profile, as June chanced to do at the moment the car drew up, made him look uncommonly distinguished.

But so much depends, don't you know, in these little matters upon the angle—etc.

"What time do you expect to be back, Mr. Mitchell?" asked Mrs. Chrystal from her doorstep, as that hero, a wisdom-bitten veteran of the Great War, which had ended before William began—that is to say Class 1920 was never called up—ushered June into the chariot with rare solemnity.

"Back did you say, ma'am?" said Mr. Mitchell closing the door gently upon the travellers. "There you have me. We've to go as fur as the heart o' Suffolk and back again."

Mrs. Chrystal knew that. Hence the question.

"Accordin' to this map," Mr. Mitchell pointed to the canvas back of Road Guide Number 6, Series 14, which was on the vacant seat beside his own, "Crowdham Market may take a bit o' findin'. Still if the roads are all right, I dessay we'll be home by the risin' o' the moon."

"My reason for asking is that I'm wondering about the young lady's supper. However, I'll expect you when I see you, because as you say Crowdham Market may be a funny place to get at."

In the opinion of June, who heard this conversation, Mrs. Chrystal was fully justified in thinking so. They were about to start on a journey to Cloud Cuckoo Land.

A very romantic journey it was. Up hill and down dale they went, by devious lanes and unsuspected ways across a noble sweep of country. Zephyrs played gently upon their faces; the sun shone, the birds sang; the smooth-gliding car made little dust and less noise; they sat side by side; it was a royal progress.

The Idea itself was William's, June always maintained, that they should go to Crowdham Market and find the poor old woman who kept the tumbledown shop, where perhaps as much out of pity as anything, he had given five shillings for the Van Roon. They could well afford to make her comfortable for life with an annuity, the precise amount of which Sir Arthur might be asked to fix if they could not themselves agree upon it. Indeed the whole question of the Van Roon's fabulous proceeds was still vexed. Neither would move an inch. June still vowed she would not touch the money. William vowed that he would not touch it either, but he had gone so far as to suggest that he should buy the thing back from her with a part of the property her uncle had left him. To this property he somehow felt he had no lawful claim; yet by means of it he would be able to add, free gratis and for nothing, one masterpiece the more to "his treasure house" in Trafalgar Square.

June, with the frankness for which she was famous, did not hesitate to denounce the scheme as crazy. Even the Sir Arthur Babrahams of the world, who were simply rolling in money, thought twice about giving fortunes away. What did he suppose was going to become of his career as an artist if he stripped himself of the means of pursuing it?

That, of course, was where she had him. And as they sat side by side on this golden journey to East Anglia, they divided the forenoon between admiring the scenery and discussing the problem in all its aspects.

"You talk of France and Spain and Italy." The note of scorn was mellowed considerably by the romance of the occasion. "You talk of studying the pictures in the Louvre and the Prado and the Uffizi Gallery." She had really got to grips with Culture now. With an indomitable will, an inflexible ambition and a brand new course of memory training to help her; she was not only learning to remember outlandish words, but how and when and in what order to use them. "You talk of Rembrandt and Titian and Velasky, but I'm thinking those foreign landladies'll get your size before you can say Knife. My opinion is you'll need somebody *always* with you to see that they don't take it off you."

"Take what off me, Miss June?" inquired His Innocence.

There was a question!

"Your pram, of course, your teddy bear, and your feeding bottle." She added the opprobrious term "You Gaby!" not however for the ear of this Dreamer, but for the benefit of the pleasant town of Malden, on whose outskirts they were already.

"When you get to Paris and find yourself in the Prado studying Paul Very-uneasy, you'll be lucky if you get away with as much as a bootlace. Mr. Boultby used to say French landladies were awful."

"Did he," said the Dreamer; and then with a sudden animation: "Do you see that water wagtail on the lip of that pool?"

June pointedly ignored the water wagtail.

"You ought to have somebody to look after you when you go to Paris—somebody who understands the value of money."

"The less value money has for an artist the better," said William the sententious.

"Mr. Boultby would call that poppycock," said June, equally sententious.

What William really meant to say was that the less an artist thought about money the better for his art, that an artist painted better for love than for filthy lucre and so on, that the great masters were born poor as a rule and often died poor and that nothing was so likely as money to distract the mind from the quest of beauty.

These, to be sure, were not his exact words. His thoughts were clothed more neatly in the William way. But such was the sum and substance of what they came down to, and June was so pained by his line of argument that the contents of the luncheon basket on the opposite seat were needed to sustain her.

After patiently reasoning with such wrong-headedness, she looked at her watch and found it was one o'clock. As there was never a sign at present of Crowdham Market, they decided to begin on what the gods had provided. Egg and tomato sandwiches were at the top of the basket with a layer of ham underneath, and below that a most authentic cake with almonds in it; all of which were delicious.

The meal, if anything, was even better than the conversation, though that also was on an extremely high level. They were very honourable in their dealings with the luncheon basket. Share and share alike was the order of the day, with a third share of everything religiously laid by for Mr. Mitchell whenever he might feel justified in slowing up to eat it. Even a full third of the basket's crowning glory was laid by for Mr. Mitchell—to wit, a large vacuum flask of coffee, piping hot.

It was a few minutes after two when they reached Crowdham Market and drew up at the Unicorn Inn. Here, six months ago, William had discussed the great drought with Miss Ferris, the landlady's daughter, one of those high-coloured girls who June could see at a glance was a minx.

Promising to be back in an hour, which was all that Mr. Mitchell could allow if they were to be home before the rising of the moon, June and William, feeling more romantic than ever before in their lives, set out on a pilgrimage up the High Street. It was the only street in the town which aspired to a sense of importance; the point in fact towards which all meaner streets converged. One of these it was they had now to find.

Alas, from the outset there was a grave doubt in the mind of William in the matter of his bearings. To the best of his recollection the old woman's shop was either the second or third turning up, then to the left, then across, and then to the left again into an obscure alley of which he had forgotten the name. That was like him. In June's private opinion, it was also like him, although *lèse-majesté* of course, to let him know it, to take her to look for a serendipity shop in a bottle of hay.

William knew neither the name of the old woman, nor the byway that had contained her, and in the course of half an hour's meandering it grew clear to the practical mind of June that she was in serious danger of having to go without her annuity. Having come so far it would be humiliating to return with a tale of total defeat; yet up till now these emotions had been held in check by the romance of the case.

Mr. Mitchell's hour was all but sped, when William stopped abruptly. Light had come. He had hit the trail.

At the corner of the lane into which for the third time they had penetrated, was an enticing little shop called Middleton's Dairy. The sight of it brought back to William's mind a recollection. Immediately the picture had been acquired, he went into that shop to get a bun and a glass of milk. Pausing a moment to wrestle with his sense of locality, he gazed down the street. The old woman's store would be just opposite.

Only a glance was needed to show that the old woman's store was not just opposite. The housebreakers had been recently at work and the decrepit block of which her premises formed a part was razed to the ground.

Faced by the problem of what had happened to the old woman the only thing now was to enter Middleton's Dairy and enquire. They were cordially received by a girl who in June's opinion showed too many teeth when she smiled to be really good looking; who, also, in June's opinion, wore corsets that didn't suit her figure, and whose hair would have looked better had it been bobbed.

Like Miss Ferris, the landlady's daughter, this girl seemed to remember William quite well, which was rather odd June felt, since he had only been once in the town previously and then for but a few hours. The inference to be drawn from the fact was that William was William, and that in an outlandish one-horse place like Crowdham Market, young men of his quality were necessarily at a premium.

But at the moment that was neither here nor there. And with equal truth the formula applied to the old woman. However, in regard to her it seemed, they were now in the way of getting information.

After William, with a certain particularity had described the old creature and her shop to the girl who kept on showing her teeth while he did so, he was informed that she was known among the neighbours as Mother Stark. And the poor old thing, the girl understood, had been turned out of house and home because she could no longer pay her rates and taxes.

"Half her side of the Lane's pulled down," said June, who now came into the conversation on a note of slight asperity.

"Oh, yes," said Miss Smiler, to William rather than to June, "the site has been bought by a company."

"Putting a museum on it I suppose," said June.

"No, not a museum," said Miss Smiler in a level voice ignoring June's irony either because she did not see it, or because she did, which in any case perhaps was just as well for her.

"A chicken run?" June surmised with a disdainful eye upon a nice basket of new laid eggs, five for a shilling.

No, the site had not been acquired for a chicken run. Miss Smiler understood they were going to build a picture house.

June gazed solemnly at William. And her gaze was frankly and faithfully returned. A picture house on the spot where a Van Roon had lain hidden and unknown for who knew how many years!

What a world it was! Could Mother Stark but have guessed she would not have needed a Company to take over her premises.

"What's become of her? Can you tell us?" said June.

"Had to go to the Workhouse, I believe, poor soul," said the girl, who had a good heart.

June looked at William. William looked at June.

"Is the Workhouse far from here—please can you tell us?" It was William who asked the question.

The Workhouse, it seemed, was not far. In fact it was quite near. To get there you had only to go to the end of the lane, turn to the left, cross the recreation ground and the footbridge over the canal, and keep on bearing to the left and you couldn't miss it.

"Will it take long?" The question was June's. And a glance at her wrist accompanied it.

"Not more than five minutes."

"Thank you very much indeed. We are greatly obliged to you." William it was who brought the conversation to a climax with a lift of the hat.

LXV

THERE was only one thing to be done now. Mr. Mitchell's hour was up, but there was no help for it. The Workhouse, as the girl had said—she might, in June's opinion have had a claim to good looks if she had not suffered from "a rush of teeth to the head"—was not more than five minutes away if you followed her instructions.

As June had the matter in hand, the instructions were followed to the letter and they arrived at the Workhouse without delay. But as the pile, dark and grim, came into view at the far side of the canal, an odd emotion suddenly brought them up with a round turn.

A long moment they gazed at the bleak and frowning thing before their eyes. And then June said with a laugh, "I'm thinking that's where you'll be one day, if you don't find someone who isn't a genius to look after you."

The words came from the heart, yet William did not appear to hear them. "Reminds one," he murmured half to himself, "of that little thing of Duclaux's called The Poor House."

June's puzzlement was revealed by a frown.

"There's an exhibition of his pictures just now at the Bond Street Gallery. Wonderful line. A great sense of mass effect."

"You can't tell me," said June, "there's beauty in a thing like that—in that old Workhouse?"

"Duclaux would say so, with that dark cloud cutting across the gable. And that bend of the Canal in the foreground is not without value." He smiled his rare smile which never had looked so divine. But June was a little afraid of it now. She kept her eyes the other way.

"Canal," she said with brevity. "Not without value. I should say so. As we say at Blackhampton, 'where there's muck there's money.'"

She glanced at her wrist again. Another ten minutes credited now to Mr. Mitchell's account.

"Duclaux, I suppose, would see it this way." The queer fellow stepped back two paces, put up his hand to shade his eyes and adjust his vision to look at the Workhouse.

This was Pure Pottiness, the concentrated essence in tabloid form. However, Miss Babraham had already impressed upon June the deep truth that genius must be allowed a margin.

A little faint of heart she rang the bell of the gloomy and forbidding door. The summons was heeded, tardily and with reluctance, by its janitor, a surly male.

"Can we see Mrs. Stark?" asked June.

"Eh?" said the janitor. He must have been deaf indeed not to have heard the question in its cool clarity. June repeated it; whereon the keeper of the door looked her slowly up and down, turning over the name in his mind as he did so.

"Mother Stark she was called," said June, for his further enlightenment. "She sold all kinds of old rubbish at a shop that used to be opposite Middleton's Dairy at the top of Love Lane."

"Mother Stark you say!" Light was coming to the janitor. "No, you can't see her."

"Why not? The matter's important."

"She's been in her grave this two month—that's why not," said the janitor.

"Oh," said June; and then after brief commerce with the eye of William: "Has she any relations or friends?"

The answer was no. Mother Stark had had a parish burial.

William thanked Diogenes with that courtesy which was never-failing and inimitable; and then after one more swift glance at each other, they turned away, feeling somehow, a little overcome, yet upheld by the knowledge of being through at last with the matter of the poor old thing's annuity.

Returning in their tracks across the canal footbridge, across the recreation ground, up the lane, past the site of the new picture house, past Middleton's Dairy, they entered the High Street, without haste, in spite of Mr. Mitchell, and with a gravity new and strange, as if they both felt now the hand of destiny upon them.

Heedless of all the Mr. Mitchells in the universe, they walked very slowly to draw out the last exquisite drop of a moment of bliss that, no matter what life had in store, they could never forget. And then for some mystic reason, June's brain grew incandescent. It became a thing of dew and fire. Ideas formed within it, broke from it, took shape in the ambient air. She might have been treading the upper spaces of Elysium, except that no girl's feet were ever planted more firmly or more shrewdly upon the pavement of High Street, Crowdham Market.

Four doors from the Unicorn Inn was the most fashionable jeweller's shop in the town, perhaps for the reason that there was no other; and as they came level with the window a spark flashed from its depths and met an instant answer in the eye of June. Nearly an hour behind the schedule they were now, yet they lingered one moment more, while June drew William's attention to a coincidence. The vital spark it seemed, owed its being to a gem set in a ring which was almost a replica of the one worn by Miss Babraham in honor of its giver, who of course was a gentleman in the Blues.

"It's as like Miss Babraham's engagement ring as one pea is like another pea," said June in a soft voice.

In the course of their friendship, William had been guilty of many silences of a disgraceful impersonality; and he was now guilty of one more. He glanced at the ring with a wistful eye, sighed a little, and then with slow reluctance moved on. June accompanied him to the very threshold of the Unicorn Inn. And upon its doorstep of all places, within hearing of the Office, wherein lurked Miss Ferris, the landlady's daughter, he faced about, and then by way of an after-thought, his head apparently still full of Duclaux, began to stammer.

"Miss June if I go back and get that ring will you—will you promise—to—to——?"

Miss Ferris was in the Office; the top of her coiffure was to be seen above the frosted glass. And the Office door was wide open; June, therefore, gave her answer in a very low and gentle voice.

Her answer, for all that, did not lack pith. "If only you'll cut out the Miss, I'll wear it like Miss Babraham—on my heart finger."

LXVI

BACK they went to the jeweller's four doors up. To the expert eye of William, the ring on inspection was so little like Miss Babraham's that he seemed to have a qualm about buying it. He had a fancy for moonstones and diamonds, but Crowdham Market's only jeweller did not run to these. June was firm, besides, that the ring in her hand was cheap at nine guineas, and as no one could call it vulgar, it was quite good enough.

William was sure it was nothing like good enough. "But when we get to London, you shall have moonstones and diamonds."

"That'll be lovely," said June; and a deep thrill ran in her heart as she realized that her dreams were coming true.

William took a wad of Bradburys from his breast pocket. He was now a man of property, with a rent roll of twelve hundred a year, but even a most careful counting would not let them muster more than seven. June, however, as became the lawful owner of an Old Master, whom to acquire for the nation a committee had been lately formed, was equal to the occasion. For she promptly took a wad from the vanity bag which now graced her travels instead of her mother's old purse, and made up the sum.

In the meantime, the jeweller, a man of ripe experience, had put two and two together.

"Will you wear it, madam, or will you have it packed in the box?"

An unconventional question, no doubt, but places like Crowdham Market are close to nature and get down to bedrock by short cuts.

"I'll wear it," June answered. "And I'll have the box as well. It'll do for my dressing table to keep pins in."

The jeweller, one of the old school, bowed to June as he handed her the box and also the change. And then, a jeweller with a fine technique, he smiled at William in a Masonic manner and handed him the ring.

June, as cool as if she was on parade, removed a white kid glove from her left hand. "That's the heart finger," she said.

If she blushed a little, the jeweller was too busy writing out the receipt at the other end of the shop to be aware of the fact.

LXVII

THEY decided to ask Miss Ferris, the landlady's daughter, for a cup of tea, before they set out on the journey home. June felt she could afford to take the risk, since by now the situation was well in hand. Mr. Mitchell raised no objection. Himself an ampler man for a noble lunch, he had been recounting tales of Araby and lands of fair renown in the privacy of the Office. His suit of Robin Hood green and a certain gallantry of bearing had made considerable impact in an amazingly short time, not upon Miss Ferris merely, but upon her widowed mother, the sole proprietress of the Unicorn Inn, who in the words of the local manager of the East Anglia and Overtons Bank "was the warmest woman in Crowdham Market."

While Mr. Mitchell (Sergeant, R.E., D.C.M. with clasp), and the widow were in the garden admiring the early pansies, June and William sat down to tea in the coffee room. Even there the contiguity of Miss Ferris had rather a tendency to cramp June's style. High-coloured girl, she was a little inclined to take liberties as she passed around the table. And when June, in her sweetest and best Miss Babraham manner, asked if they might have some crab apple jam, she caught the glint of the ring on June's heart finger in a way so direct that she murmured something about having to look out for her eyesight—or words equally ill-bred—and nearly dropped the tea pot.

By the time they got under way and the nose of the car was set for the pleasant land of Surrey, a doubt infected the mind of Mr. Mitchell as to whether they would make Homefield before midnight. Neither June nor William seemed to care very much whether they did or whether they didn't. The car was most comfortable, the sense of romance hot upon them still, the presence of each other vital and delicious in their consciousness. Mile passed upon mile. The endless spool of road continued to unwind itself, a little wind breathed gentle nothings, Mr. Mitchell sat four-square in front, the birds still sang, but the sun was going down.

Saying very little, they lived never-to-be-forgotten hours. Now and again William pointed to a bird or a tree, the fold of a hill, the form of a cloud, the gleam of a distant water. Yet for the most part the nearness of each other was all sufficing. June began to nestle closer; the chill of night came on. Saying less than ever now, moonstones and diamonds stole upon her thoughts. She was haunted by a lovely fear that she could not live up to them. And then softly and more soft, she began to breathe with a rhythmical rise and fall, slowly deepening to a faint crescendo that blended with the motions of the car.

East by west of nowhere came the high moment when the sun was not, and the moon not yet. Somewhere over Surrey a star was dancing. Very shyly and gently he ventured to give her a kiss. She stirred ever so little. A bird spoke from a brake, a note clear and wonderful, yet the month was young for the nightingale. But this was Cloud Cuckoo Land, a divine country in which the nightingale may be heard at odd seasons.

Psyche stirred again. With a reverence chaste and simple he gave her a second kiss, deep and slow. The solemn sacrament was fire to the soul of an artist. And then he gave a little gasp. The high gods in his brain whispered that the moon was coming.

The moon was coming.

Yes, there she was, the sovereign lady! He sat very still, praying, praying that he might surprise some holy secret, hidden even from Duclaux.

She was very wonderful to-night. Her loveliness was more than he could bear. There was a touch of intimacy in her magic; the country over which she shone was elfland. He seemed to hear a faint familiar sound of horns. Or it might have been the swift gliding of the car.

In the quietness of the spirit's ecstasy he could have wept.

Might it be given to Duclaux to see her, lovely lady, just as he could see her now!

But he mustn't dare to breathe or the vision would be forever lost.

THE END

Milton Keynes UK
Ingram Content Group UK Ltd.
UKHW042144281024
450365UK00010B/595